Wingshooter's Guide to™

WASHINGTON

Upland Birds and Waterfowl

Titles Available in This Series

Wingshooter's Guide to™

WASHINGTON

Upland Birds and Waterfowl

Dan Brandvold

Wilderness
Adventures
Press™

Belgrade, Montana

This book was made with an easy opening, lay flat binding.

Published by Wilderness Adventures Press
45 Buckskin Road
Belgrade, MT 59714
800-925-3339
Website: www.wildadv.com
email: books@wildadv.com

Printed in the United States of America

Library of Congress Cataloging-in-Publication Data

Branvold, Dan, 1960-
    Wingshooter's guide to Washington : upland birds and waterfowl / Dan Branvold.
        p. cm.
    Includes bibliographical references (p.).
    ISBN 1-885106-75-0 (alk. paper)
    1. Upland game bird shooting--Washington (State) 2. Waterfowl shooting--Washington
    (State) I. Title

SK323 .B73 2000
799.2'4'09797--dc21

00-034944

Table of Contents

HUNTING IN WASHINGTON DEPARTMENT OF FISH AND WILDLIFE REGIONS

Region 1 Eastern Washington

Region 1 Hub Cities

Region 2 North Central Washington

Acknowledgements

A book such as this is really a team effort and I owe many thanks to my "team." At the head of the list is Jesus Christ, my personal Lord and Savior - "Through Him all things are possible." Next, to my beautiful wife Dorris and my two sons and future hunting partners Jake and Zach. They have always encouraged and supported me in all my projects; they are the greatest joy in my life.

My parents, Clancy and Pat Brandvold. My dad instilled in me a love of the outdoors and hunting in particular, and mom patiently tolerated muddy boot prints, feathers, and bird cleaning sessions in her kitchen.

To Chuck Johnson - thanks for giving me the opportunity and the patient counsel with all my questions.

To all my hunting partners: Tony Pritzl, Frank Ricigliano, Rick McLean, Tom Runyan, and all the others who tolerated my camera and "...just one more picture." Some of you are still even talking to me.

To all the special outdoor writers who have entertained and inspired me: E. Don Thomas, John Holt, Michael McIntosh, Ben O. Williams, Datus Proper, Gene Hill, Stephen Bodio, Steve Smith, Dave Miesner, and many others. You allowed me the pleasure of vicariously joining you on many adventures, I enjoyed every mile, and my life is better for the experiences.

The folks at the Washington Department of Fish and Wildlife were invaluable as a source of statistics and information, thanks for the help.

My young friends, Krista and Terrie Weber, proved to be outstanding research and production assistants and definitely made my life easier during this process.

Last, but certainly not least, the dogs, currently German wirehaired pointers, Dutchess and Alex, and in the past Shadow, Lady, Penny and Inger. If not for them, bird hunting would be certainly less thrilling and my life would be less fun.

Mount Rainier and the author's dog, Dutchess, two Washington landmarks.

Introduction

When Chuck Johnson offered me the opportunity to write this installment in the very successful Wingshooter's Guide Series from Wilderness Adventure Press, I was hesitant. The project seemed overwhelming. As I gave it more consideration however, I became excited with the prospect of discovering more about the bird hunting in Washington, the state I grew up in and have hunted in since I was old enough to purchase a license.

Washington offers a huge variety of quarry for the shotgunner to pursue, with 13 species of upland birds and 19 species of waterfowl found in huntable populations within the state. Washington is one of the only places in the country that currently has a season for three of the four subspecies of wild turkey and one tag for each subspecies may be purchased each spring season.

This state is the second most densely populated of our western states following California. Fortunately, however, most of the population is located in the western part of the state in the Seattle-Tacoma metroplex.

Washington has some of the most varied topography anywhere in the country, including rain forest, high desert, alpine and sub-alpine forest. An individual with the desire, can literally hunt ducks on a Pacific Ocean estuary in the morning and chukar in the scab rock hills in the afternoon. Add to this one of the most renowned wine producing regions in the country, which is increasingly recognized internationally for its high quality vintages and you have a great mix for the road-tripping gentleman hunter.

I hope you enjoy your trip to the Evergreen state, and if in your travels you come upon a hunter with a fantastic German wirehaired pointer as his companion and a big grin on his face, I'm always pleased to shake hands with a fellow traveler in the field. Good hunting, and may God bless.

The author's oldest son, Jacob—his dog, Alex, and the dog's first chukar.

Tips On Using This Book

Washington currently has five area codes. All of eastern Washington is 509. Western Washington has area codes 425, 206, 253, and 360. Fortunately, as of this writing, the phone company has a recorded message informing you of the correct area code if you should happen to get the wrong one. In an attempt to minimize this, I have included area codes with all listed phone numbers. You must dial 1 + area code for all in-state long distance calls, even within the same area code.

For the purpose of organization, the state is broken down into the six Department of Fish and Wildlife regions. Each region is further divided by county. See map on page 6.

Although I have tried to be as accurate as possible, please note that this information is current only at the time of printing. Ownership of any business and thus quality of services provided may change.

Always check with the Department of Fish and Wildlife for current hunting regulations. Season dates, license prices, and regulations may change from year to year. Always ask permission before you hunt on private land.

All species distribution maps are approximations and may change due to weather conditions, habitat alteration, and farming practices.

Motel cost key:
    $ - less than $50.00 per night
    $$ - between $50 - 80.00 per night
    $$$ - over $80.00 per night

A father and son enjoy an afternoon's hunt.

Washington Facts

18th largest state in the union
71,303 square miles
345 miles across
235 miles north to south
29.6% of the state is Federal Land

Elevations: sea level to 14,411 feet on Mt. Rainer

Counties: 39

Population (1990 census): 4,866, 692

Nickname: The Evergreen State

State Motto: Alki - Native American word meaning "bye and bye"

Capital: Olympia

State Bird: Gold Finch

State Flower: Coast Rhododendron

State Tree: Western Hemlock

State Gemstone: Petrified Wood

State Grass: Bluebunch Wheatgrass

State Fish: Steelhead Trout

State Fruit: Apple

Primary Industries: Farming, Forestry, Aircraft/Aerospace, and Computer Technology

EASTERN / WESTERN WASHINGTON DEFINED

Eastern Washington includes all areas lying east of the Pacific Crest Trail and east of the Big White Salmon River in Klickitat and Skamania Counties. Western Washington refers to all areas west of the Pacific Crest Trail and west of (and including) the Big White Salmon River in Klickitat and Skamania counties.

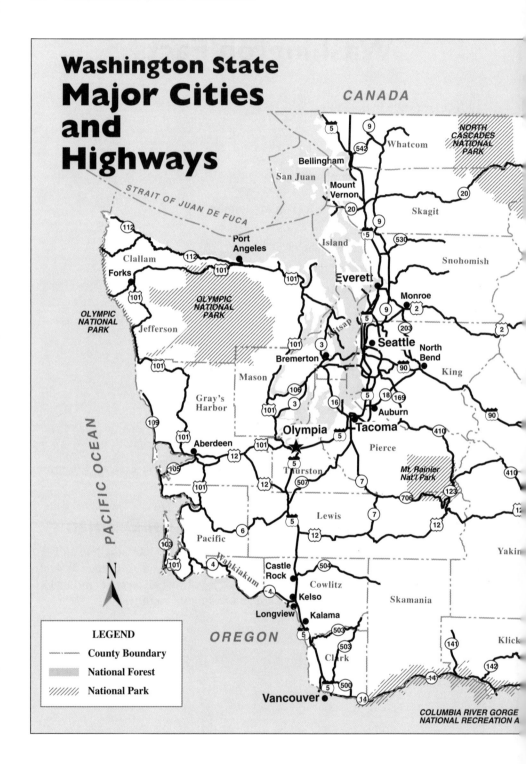

Washington State
Major Cities
and
Highways

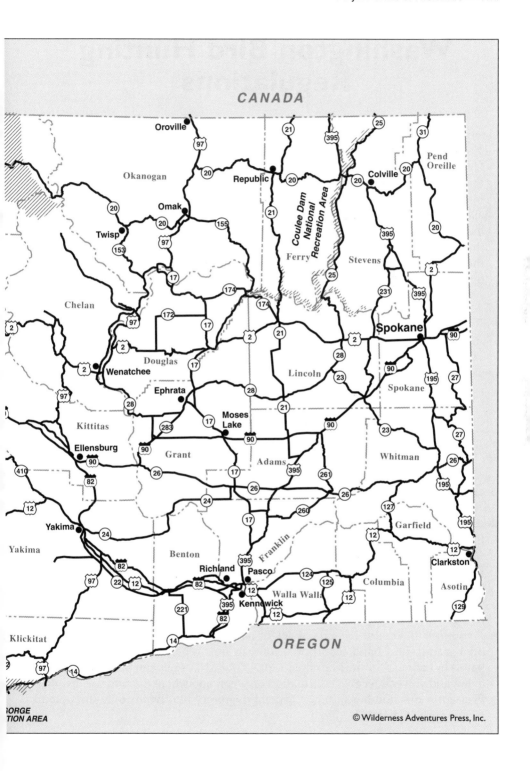

Washington Bird Hunting Regulations

Licenses

- The following licenses are available from licensing agents throughout the state. Licenses are valid April 1 through March 31. For the most up-to-date fees check the Department of Fish and Wildlife website at http://www.wa.gov/wdfw. To hunt birds in Washington state a small game license is required. The small game license allows the holder to hunt for wild animals and wild birds. The small game license includes one transportation tag for turkey and includes a prorated surcharge for the eastern Washington Pheasant Enhancement. There are additional charges for the second and third turkey tags and western Washington pheasant and migratory bird stamps.

Current 2001 fees	Resident	Nonresident
Small game license	$30.00	$150.00
Turkey tag (additional)	$18.00	$60.00
State migratory waterfowl stamp	$6.00	$ 6.00
3-day Small Game	N/A	$50.00

Upland Bird Permit (Western Washington)		
Westside full season	$36.00	$36.00
Westside 3 day option	$20.00	$20.00

Dealer fees will be charged - $1 for licenses and $0.50 for tags, stamps, and permits

State Migratory Waterfowl Stamp

- In addition to a federal migratory waterfowl stamp, a state migratory waterfowl stamp for ducks and geese is required for hunters 16 years of age and over. State stamps can be purchased at license dealers. Collector's plate block stamps can be purchased through the Department of Fish and Wildlife Headquarters Office in Olympia. Federal stamps can be purchased at post offices, National Wildlife Refuges, or by calling 1-888-534-0400.
- *Remember:* If you are 16 years of age or older you must buy a federal and state duck stamp. Bird band reporting - You can now report federal migratory bird bands by calling a toll-free number, 1-800-327-BAND. Calls can be made 24 hours a day, and you will receive information on when and where the bird was banded. Please use this number to report federal migratory bird bands only (no upland birds or private bands.)

Non-toxic Shot Requirement
• It is unlawful to possess shot (either in shotshells or as loose shot for muzzle loading) other than steel shot, or bismuth shot, or tungsten shot when hunting waterfowl, coot, or snipe.

Tribal Lands
• Check with appropriate tribal authorities before entering Indian lands. There are tribal rules pertaining to non-Indian activity upon these lands for the purpose of hunting and fishing. When hunting or fishing within the boundaries of the Colville Indian Reservation, you should contact the office of the Colville Confederated Tribes, Director of Fish and Wildlife Department, (509) 634-4711, to determine the tribal permits and regulations applicable to such activities. When hunting or fishing within the Yakima Indian Reservation you should contact the office of the Yakima Indian Nation (509) 865-5121 ext. 666.

Hunter Orange Requirements
• Anyone hunting upland birds with a modern firearm during an upland game bird season is required to wear a minimum of 400 square inches of florescent hunter orange exterior clothing. Florescent hunter orange exterior clothing must be worn above the waist and be visible from all sides.

Western Washington Goose Management
• Training materials necessary to pass the goose identification test required for Western Washington Goose Management Area 2 consists of a home study booklet and a one-hour videotape, entitled "Pacific Northwest Goose Management." The booklet is available in Olympia and at regional offices of WDFW. The videotape is available through:

Videoland Productions. Inc.
805 College Street SE
Lacey, WA 98503

The cost is $10.00, including shipping and tax.

Videoland Productions, Inc. accepts major credit cards, checks, and money orders. Their toll free number is:

1-800-861-1342
1-360-491-1332 (commercial number)
1-360-491-1333 (fax)
http://www.cco.net/~vland (website)

Goose identification testing will be conducted at designated locations throughout western Washington. All hunters will be expected to attend one of these testing sessions and pass an examination to receive their hunting authorizations.

Western Washington Goose Management Area I
- Written authorization is required to hunt snow geese. All persons hunting snow geese in this season are required to obtain a written authorization and Harvest Report from the WDFW. Applications for authorization are available at WDFW Olympia and regional offices.

Written Authorization Required for Hunting Brant
- All hunters participating in this season are required to obtain a written authorization and Harvest Report from the WHF. Applications are available at WDFW regional offices.

Additional Requirements for Upland Bird and Turkey Season
- Western Washington: A Western Washington Upland Bird Permit is required to hunt pheasant, quail, and partridge in western Washington, in addition to a current hunting license. Pheasant kills only must be recorded. Upon taking a pheasant, the holder of a Western Washington Upland Bird Permit must immediately enter on the corresponding space the date and location of kill. There are three options available for the 1997 hunting season:

  > **Full Season Option;** allows the harvest of ten (10) pheasants;
  > **Juvenile;** (14 and under) allows the harvest of six (6) pheasants;
  > **2-Day Option;** allows the harvest of four (4) pheasants during two consecutive days.

- Every person possessing a Western Washington Upland Bird Permit must return the permit to the DFW by December 31. The number of permits purchased per year is not limited. Hunters may only possess one valid permit at a time. Hunters should select one valid option at the time they purchase their Western Washington Upland Bird Permit.

Turkey Special Regulations
- Multiple turkey tags (one for each subspecies) may be purchased by April 14 of each year. Turkey season is open for shotgun and bow-and-arrow hunting only (no rifles). A turkey tag is required for hunting turkey. Each successful hunter must complete and return a game harvest report card to the DFW within ten days after taking a turkey. It is unlawful to use dogs to hunt turkeys.

Firearm Regulations
- It is unlawful to hunt game birds with a shotgun capable of holding more than three shells; game birds in a manner other than with a firearm, a bow and arrow, or by falconry; game birds with a shotgun larger than 10 gauge; wildlife with a crossbow; game birds with a rifle or pistol

Use of Firearms by a Minor
- Juveniles under 18 years of age may have a firearm in possession if they are; hunting under a valid license issued by the DFW, in attendance at a hunters safety

course or firearms safety course, target shooting at an established range, engaged in organized firearms competition, accompanied by a parent or guardian, or are at least 11 years of age, are not trespassing, have been issued a hunter safety certificate and have a firearm other than a pistol. It is also lawful to have an unloaded firearm in possession while traveling to or from any of the activities described above.

Disabled Hunters

- The citizens' Task Force for the Disabled (advisory to the WDFW) has been working cooperatively with the WDFW and various organizations and clubs since 1992 to install barrier-free wildlife viewing/hunting blinds in each WDFW region of the state. The new edition of the pocket map called "Regional Maps of Accessible Wildlife Recreation, Waterfowl Viewing and Hunting Blinds" is available from all WDFW regional offices.
- Also available at regional offices and on the Internet is a pamphlet titled "Accessible Hunting and Wildlife Viewing Opportunities" which includes more information about duck blinds, goose pits, big game hunting, and ATV access hunting areas around the state ((www.wa.gov/wdfw/viewing/wildview.htm)).For other information about hunting opportunities for persons with disabilities, call the WDFW at (360) 902-2200.

A good dog, a bird in the bag and smiles all around for this successful Washington hunter.

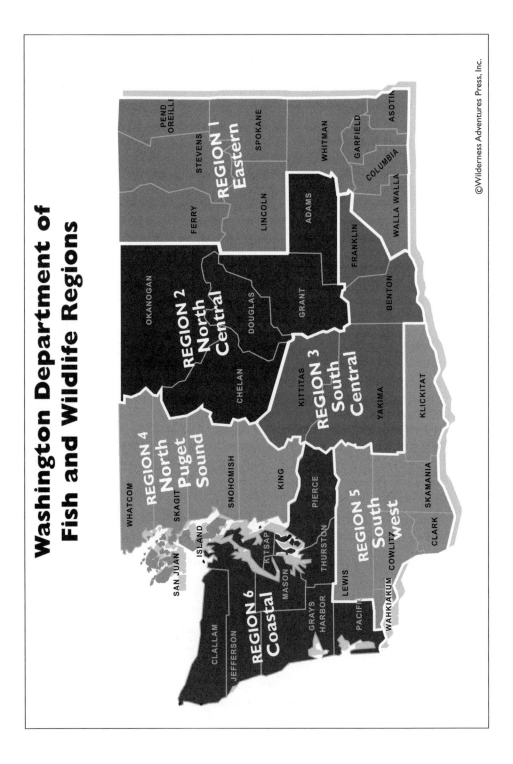

Washington Department of
Fish and Wildlife Regions

©Wilderness Adventures Press, Inc.

Summary of Seasons
UPLAND GAME BIRDS

Grouse
- Statewide is Sept. 1, through Dec. 31. Daily bag limit - 3 of any species, possession limit 9 of any species.

Pheasant
- Westside, Sept. 30, through Nov. 30. Daily bag limit 2, possession limit 15. Eastside, Oct. 7 through Dec. 31. Daily bag limit 3, possession limit 15.

Quail (valley and bobwhite)
- Westside, Oct. 7 through Nov. 30. Daily bag limit 10 valley or bobwhite, possession limit 30 valley or bobwhite. Eastside, Oct. 7 through January 15. Daily bag limit 10 valley or bobwhite, possession limit 30 valley or bobwhite.

Quail (mountain)
- Oct. 7 through November 30. Daily bag limit 2, possession limit 4. Eastside, closed season.

Partridge (chukar, Hungarian)
- Eastside, Oct. 1 through Jan. 15. Daily bag limit 6 each, possession limit 18 each. Westside, no season.

Turkey
- Statewide, April 15 through May 15. Bag limit 1 turkey of each subspecies with a total of three per year.

Mourning Dove
- Statewide, Sept. 1-15. Daily bag limit 10, possession limit 20.

WATERFOWL
(VARIES GREATLY FROM YEAR TO YEAR)

Ducks, Coots, and Snipe
- Statewide, first Saturday in October through the third Sunday in January. Daily bag limits, ducks 7, coots 25, and snipe 8, possession limits ducks 14, coots 25, snipe 16.

Geese
- Varies even more. In general, the second Saturday in October through the third Sunday in January. Daily bag limit 4, possession limit 8.

Brant
- By specific date, check current regulations. Daily bag limit 2, possession limit 4.

Washington Pheasant Release Program

The Washington Department of Fish and Wildlife provides additional pheasant hunting opportunities in both eastern and western Washington by releasing birds at designated sites with public access. This is primarily put-and-take hunting for pen-raised birds. The WDFW publishes a free pamphlet for both the Western Washington Pheasant Release Program and the Eastern Washington Pheasant Enhancement Program each year that contains information on release sites, maps, and regulations for each region of the state. Regulations within each region may vary, so check the pamphlets carefully before hunting. The release sites can become quite crowded at times, and hunters should always wear blaze orange clothing and act responsibly.

Many release sites in both eastern and western Washington require the use of nontoxic shot to protect other species in the area. The following is a list of the current sites with this requirement. Hunters should always check to be sure it is permissible before using lead shot. Refer to Region Maps for release locations.

Western Washington

Chehalis River pheasant release site, Dungeness Recreation Area, Hunter Farms pheasant release site, Lake Terrell Wildlife Area, Raymond Airport pheasant release site, Skagit Wildlife Area, and the Snoqualmie Wildlife Area.

Eastern Washington

Driscoll Island, Hegdahl, and Kline Parcel segments of the Sinlahekin Wildlife Area, Sunnyside Wildlife Area, Bridgeport Bar segments of Wells Wildlife Area, and Two Rivers and Wallula Units of McNary Wildlife Refuge.

WESTERN WASHINGTON PHEASANT RELEASE PROGRAM

Around 30,000 to 40,000 pheasants are released each year at roughly 40 release sites in WDFW Regions 4, 5, and 6. The bag limit is two pheasants of either sex per day on release sites. In addition to a small game hunting license, hunters must possess a western Washington upland bird permit to hunt pheasants in western Washington. There is no limit to the number of permits purchased per year, and short-term permits are also available at a reduced price. The bag limit is current two birds per day (either sex).

Release sites usually have established parking areas and access points. The number of pheasants released at each location is based on the estimated number of hunters using those sites. The estimate is derived from permit (punch card) returns, so it is very important to return punch cards at the end of the season to ensure future releases. Some of the most popular sites require hunters to choose only odd or even numbered weekend days to reduce crowding.

EASTERN WASHINGTON
PHEASANT ENHANCEMENT PROGRAM

Similar to the western Washington program, pheasants are released at a variety of sites in Regions 1, 2 and 3 over the first six weeks or so of the season to supplement the pheasant harvest. Releases also take place for the youth seasons on some sites in late September. Release dates are not usually published in order to reduce initial hunting pressure. The eastern Washington program also puts emphasis on enhancing pheasant habitat, the primary reason for the decline in the harvest of wild pheasants throughout Washington in recent years.

For detailed information on this program, visit the website at:

www.wa.gov/wdfw/wlm/game/water/wwapheas.htm

www.wa.gov/wdfw/wlm/game/water/ewapheas.htm

Where farmland has been put into the Conservation Reserve Program (CRP), excellent pheasant hunting can be found.

In late fall and winter, blue grouse move upslope.

Upland Wildlife Restoration Program

This program was developed to restore important upland habitats and the wildlife that utilize those habitats. To meet these goals, the WDFW:

- Acquires and restores habitat.

- Provides incentives for habitat enhancement and public access on private lands.

- Works cooperatively with federal and state agencies with compatible goals.

- Provides information and technical assistance to improve public education. Several programs and funding sources were combined to create the program in 1991. Since 1991, 16,000 acres of critical habitat have been purchased for sharp-tailed grouse, 240 acres were acquired for pygmy rabbits, and 1,143 acres of small parcels for pheasants and other farmland wildlife were purchased in the Columbia Basin. Several important upland habitat parcels have also been acquired through the Snake River Mitigation Program. All of these sites are currently being restored and enhanced by DFW staff. In addition to acquired sites, the program has added over 300 private landowners and 442,000 acres to the habitat development and public access program. When added to existing cooperators (from previous programs), there are a total of 662 landowners in 20 counties with over 1 million acres under habitat and access agreements with nearly 900,000 acres open to public use.

Evergreen State Turkey Hunting

When hunters talk of spring turkey season in this country, most thoughts turn south of the Mason-Dixon line or at least to the corn belt states of Iowa, Ohio and such. It is a surprise to many that the Evergreen State not only has wild turkeys to hunt, but has three of the five different subspecies in huntable populations within the state's borders.

Due to its highly varied climate and topography, Eastern, Rio Grande, and Merriam's turkeys have all been successfully introduced in Washington, much to the delight of longbeard hunters. The birds are doing so well that the state offers hunters the opportunity to bag one gobbler of each subspecies each spring. Washington is one of the only states in the country to offer such an opportunity.

As the turkey population has increased, so has the number of fanatical turkey hunters. In 1998, a total of 828 birds were harvested and seven different hunters collected all three subspecies during the 1998 season. One of these hunters even got his "Washington Slam" with archery tackle.

The Washington Chapter of the National Wild Turkey Federation, in cooperation with the Washington Department of Fish and Wildlife, is sponsoring brass pins in recognition of taking one of each subspecies. This achievement is verified by successful hunters returning their game harvest report cards to the Department of Fish and Wildlife and the completion of record forms available upon request from the Washington Chapter of the National Wild Turkey Federation. These forms will also be used for submission of information to establish Washington state turkey records.

Several turkey hunting guides and outfitters are listed at the back of this book.

Open meadows adjacent to forests hold opportunities for wild turkeys.

Memories

While many of God's creatures can remember, associate, and learn and some even have opposable thumbs, only man seems to have the ability to remember the past, and through those memories, create dreams for the future. Who among us, at the end of one hunting season, within weeks, isn't daydreaming of the next season? What hunter devoted to his canine companion and the process of the hunt hasn't thought, Wait 'till next year? Special memories are the trophies we bring home, regardless of the game bag's weight, that last through the years, and allow us to venture afield even when age and declining health have robbed us of our mobility.

One crisp October morning indelibly etched in my mind, occurred during the first hunting season of my German wirehaired pointer, Dutchess. At sixteen months of age she was little more than a canine child, but we had devoted considerable time and energy to her development and training during the previous twelve months. The training had paid-off when, in September, she had earned a Prize I score (highest attainable) in a North American Versatile Hunting Dog Association (NAVHDA) Natural Ability hunting test.

This particular early season day, we were hunting the edges of a harvested cornfield. I wasn't expecting much as the land was posted "Feel Free to Hunt," but it was located conveniently close to home. Dutchess was quartering nicely when she turned sharply and slowed her pace and eased into a beautiful point. At that moment I would have gladly traded my shotgun for a camera. As I walked up alongside her, cautiously reminding her to "whoa," a pheasant exploded out of the stubble from under her point, and a cockbird at that. Even more amazing is that I was able to maintain sufficient composure to mount my gun and squeeze the trigger and the bird actually fell! Dutchess had remained absolutely steady through this whole process, and at the command "fetch," made a beautiful retrieve to hand of her first wild pheasant. As near perfect a piece of dog work as I had ever been privileged to participate in, up to that point in my hunting career.

On another day the quarry was much larger. As my hunting partner and I slowly made our way through the brush he excitedly pointed and informed me it was definitely an elephant track. We pressed on, stopping frequently to slake our thirst with the lemonade our camp cook had provided us. After quite some time, my companion announced it was time to return to the vehicle. I asked him if he was disappointed, and he thoughtfully replied "No." Which is a good thing, 'cause you can go a long time through the sagebrush and cheatgrass hills of central Washington state without seeing an elephant. But when a three year old and hopefully future hunting partner says he wants to hunt elephants with dad that day, the smart man does his best to make sure the up-and-coming hunter has a good time. And a post hunt toy-with-the-meal dinner is a cheap price indeed for that first of hopefully many hunting memories with my kids.

Some memories do involve the numbers of birds bagged, like the Sunday before Thanksgiving that I went out and jump-shot two ducks, then killed a pheasant and a limit of ten valley quail all before 11:00 a.m., all with excellent dog work (got to love those continental breeds). Or the morning I bagged seven valley quail with eight shots, all over points including one Scotch double (two birds with one shot) and a true left/right double. Mostly though, the memories that last into our dotage involve the companions, good friends, good dog work, stunning sunsets and rises, or seeing a Merlin falcon take a sparrow out of the air. And if we've done enough things correctly, mentored a few youngsters along the way, when in our twilight years we begin a sentence with, "Did I ever tell you about the time . . .?", we'll be met with a smile, a willing ear, and the warm indulgence and love of good friends.

Introducing kids to the joys of upland hunting is good insurance for the future of our sport.

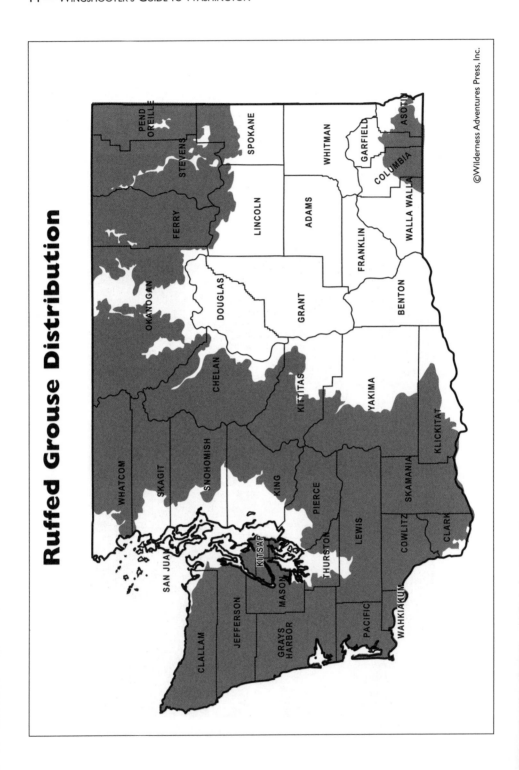

Ruffed Grouse Distribution

©Wilderness Adventures Press, Inc.

Upland Game Birds
Ruffed Grouse
Bonasa umbellus

QUICK FACTS

Local Names
Ruff or ruffs; forest grouse, ruffled grouse, fool hen

Size
Ruffed grouse range from about 1 to 2 pounds and stretch 15 to 19 inches in length.

Identification in Flight
Ruffed grouse explode suddenly, often from heavy cover, with a thunderous flapping of wings. The black-barred tail is evident in flight. They twist and turn expertly through brush and branches. Birds that have not been hunted sometimes flush to the branches of a nearby tree, where they sit nervously before rocketing out of the foliage.

- Western Washington abounds with ruffed grouse habitat, and the birds are not necessarily tied to riparian areas owing to the high moisture content in the forests and to myriad seeps and springs. Birds can range up to about 5,000 feet or more in elevation but are most common up to 3,000 feet.
- Eastern Washington ruffed grouse are tied closely to riparian areas.
- Western Washington grouse season runs from September 1 until December 31.
- The 2001 bag limit was three of any species, ruffed, blue, and spruce grouse.
- Grouse hunters are required to purchase an Upland Game Bird Validation.
- In 1999 Washington hunters harvested 73,429 ruffed grouse.

Appearance

Washington's western ruffed grouse are strikingly patterned in rich reddish-rust, brown, black, and white. Arthur Cleveland Bent called them "the darkest, most richly colored, and one of the handsomest races of the ruffed grouse" *(Life Histories of North American Gallinaceous Birds, 1932)*. Washington's eastern ruffed grouse range from the red phase to a distinctive ash-gray with black and white highlights. Along

Ruffed grouse and double guns just seem to go together.

the eastern slope of the Cascade Range, reddish or reddish-gray phase birds predominate while the gray-phase grouse occur more commonly in the mountains of northeastern Washington. The ruffed grouse derives its name from the ruff of black feathers around its neck, which is far more pronounced in adult males. Males and females sport a short crest and a squared-off tail with a black sub-terminal band. When fully fanned, the tail is a thing of beauty, and the age and sex of the bird can be determined by the tail size and pattern.

Sound and Flight Pattern

Ruffed grouse are mostly silent, but upon close approach to a family covey, the hunter might hear gentle clucks. During the breeding season, males display from a "drumming log" (or stump), fanning their tails and producing with their wings a drum-roll-type sound sometimes likened to the distant starting of a chain saw or motorcycle. Drumming generally occurs during the spring breeding season, especially at dawn and dusk, but often during late afternoon.

The thunderous whir of the ruffed grouse's short, powerful wings has startled many a hunter into missing easy shots. Often the birds hold in heavy cover, exploding from the ground at the last moment and then weaving a fast path through the lower tree limbs. Their flight speeds approach 40 miles per hour. Though ruffed grouse seldom take flight, their high-speed negotiations through thick cover often leave the hunter with nothing to shoot. This is especially true in the dense forests and bottomlands of western Washington.

Habits and Feeding

During September, brood flocks consist of a hen and two to eight young. Occasionally, abundant food sources will attract two or more broods to the same feeding location. Hunting pressure quickly breaks up the brood coveys. In areas seldom hunted, coveys of two or three birds sometimes remain together through most of the season, although singles are more typical by winter.

Early in the fall, ruffed grouse rely heavily on fruits, berries, greens, and insects; by late autumn, their diet begins to shift to the buds of alder and aspen. As snow blankets the ground, they climb trees to feed on the buds. Thick berry patches attract ruffed grouse, along with blue grouse. In western Washington, ruffed grouse seem fond of young bracken fern shoots, whose dense stands also provide excellent cover for feeding, dusting, or day-roosting coveys.

Ruffed grouse feed most actively from early to midmorning and then again during late afternoon. In between, they rest and dust. During September, when the weather remains warm, the grouse often spend midday in the shelter of heavy bracken fern or berry growth along the edges of mixed wood lots, usually near water.

Seasonal Patterns

Spring for a male ruffed grouse means daily drumming from his chosen log or stump, which will serve in that capacity for generations of grouse if the habitat remains appropriate for their existence at the site. He mates with one or more hens, and then the hens lay 9 to 12 eggs. The chicks hatch in about three weeks and can fly, weakly, at about one week after hatching.

The broods disperse in the fall, with the young males seeking their own drumming sites. Sometimes they advertise these sites with late autumn drumming. In western Washington, ruffed grouse need not live exclusively along the streams and rivers, for the water-rich Coast and Cascade ranges offer countless tiny seeps and springs, often far from the nearest creek. At the same time, heavy dew provides additional moisture. Eastern Washington grouse are closely tied to riparian zones. Unless the habitat changes, ruffed grouse utilize the same coverts for generations, so a hunter who locates birds should hunt that area in successive seasons, as the birds generally don't wander too far away.

Winter mortality is generally high for ruffed grouse, and severe winters can deplete the numbers quite rapidly. In western Washington, unusually cold, wet weather during the late spring and early summer months can decrease nesting success and increase chick mortality.

Preferred Habitat and Cover

Western Washington abounds in ideal ruffed grouse habitat. The birds thrive in moist, mixed woodlands, and in western Washington such habitat is available in extensive stands of mixed hardwoods and conifers. Douglas fir, cedar, true firs, and hemlocks are the dominant low-elevation evergreen trees in western Washington. Where these are mixed with stands of varied-age alder and maple, ruffed grouse are likely to thrive. Added to this bonanza of grouse habitat are the myriad berry species available as food and cover. These include red and blue huckleberry, salmonberry, thimbleberry, blackberry, and others. Bracken fern and sword fern provide additional cover and food.

Stands of alder and maple, mixed with a few conifers and under-storied by berries and ferns, provide perfect cover for ruffed grouse, especially when these areas border openings, including stream channels, logging roads, clear cuts, and natural meadows.

In eastern Washington, ruffed grouse depend on riparian zones for appropriate habitat, which takes the form of alder and aspen stands of varying ages mixed with young conifers. During the winter, when snow covers the ground, look for grouse feeding early and late in the leafless alders and aspens often they seek refuge from severe weather under the protective canopy of conifers. Year-round seeps and springs also hold ruffed grouse in eastern Washington. Look for moist areas in aspen groves and mixed thickets, especially in partially timbered draws and side canyons.

Hunting Methods

Ruffed grouse hold reasonably well for staunch pointing dogs and are also ideal for flushing breeds that work very close, well within average shotgun range. A good retrieving dog is critical to finding birds that fall in heavy cover.

Ruffed grouse are easiest to find during their morning and afternoon feeding times, when they frequent edges and clearings. During midday, hunt mixed timber or stands of aspen or alder. In eastern Washington, look for springs, seeps, and creeks surrounded by mixed hardwood and conifer cover. These areas serve as both feeding and day-roosting areas for ruffed grouse.

In western Washington, where dense forest often hinders access, try walking old logging road spurs, especially where they cut across low ridges or run alongside streams or seeps. Look for water along these roads and cover these areas thoroughly. Ruffed grouse often dust on logging roads and feed along the road margins, particularly if the road hangs above a creek and runs through mixed cover. Watch for dusters on the roads - grouse often leave a few feathers along with tracks.

Table Preparations

Ruffed grouse ranks among the best of upland fare, especially when young birds have fed heavily on berries. Field-dress the birds soon after harvest during warm days and store in the cooler with ice. Breasts can be prepared with a wide variety of recipes, but take care to keep them moist during the cooking process.

Shot and Choke Suggestions

All Season — No. 7½ or 8 shot

Choke — Improved and modified

Old logging roads provide great access to ruffed grouse habitat.

Spruce Grouse Distribution

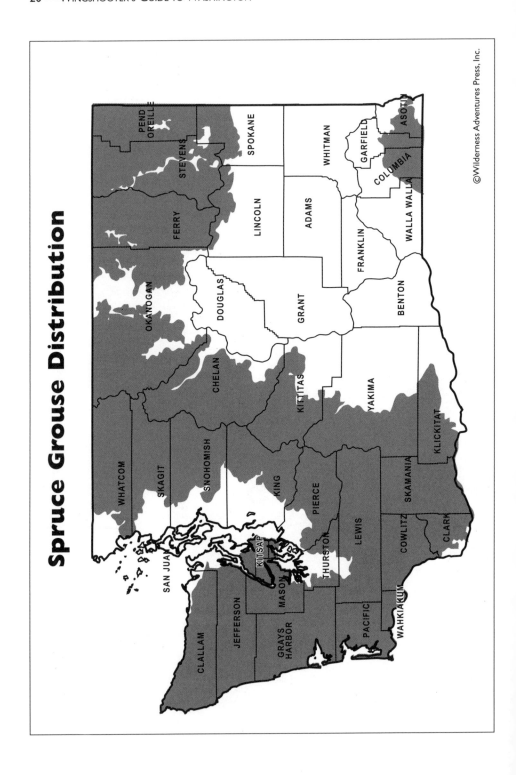

©Wilderness Adventures Press, Inc.

Spruce Grouse

Dendragapus canadensis

QUICK FACTS

Local Names
Franklin grouse, black grouse, fool hen, wood grouse, spruce partridge

Size
Adult spruce grouse typically average 15 to 17 inches long and weigh from 1 to 2 pounds.

Identification in Flight
Males and females share long brown to black tail feathers that are unbarred and tipped in white or grayish-white with bodies that appear dark in flight.

Interesting Facts
- Spruce grouse exhibit little fear of man and often stay put in trees after being located by hunters.
- Spruce grouse are native to North America.
- Spruce grouse have the darkest coloring of any mountain grouse
- Spruce grouse are found only in eastern Washington.
- Washington grouse season runs from September 1 until December 31.
- The 2001 bag limit was 3 of any species, ruffed, blue, and spruce combined.
- In 1996 Washington hunters harvested 2658 spruce grouse.

Appearance

The backs of the birds are mostly black while underparts appear whitish. Feathering extends to the base of the toes. The bare skin above the eye of the male is scarlet red and the birds are generally black and gray in body color while females are widely barred on the head and under parts with black, gray, and light brown. Spruce grouse can be easily identified as separate from ruffed grouse by their unbarred tails and a lighter, rather than darker tip to their tail feathers. Their black and white under parts help distinguish them from their other close neighbor, the blue grouse.Cocks and hens are very similar, but hens are barred with more brown on the back. The cocks of both Alberta races have red combs above the eyes that are usually hidden by feathers. The tail of the cock is black, tipped with pale brown.

Male spruce grouse

Sound and Flight Pattern

Spruce grouse flush with the same whirling of wings that all mountain grouse are noted for, although spruce grouse are just as often known to hop up into the nearest tree and sit blinking at hunters as they are to speed away in flight. Of the mountain grouse species, they are usually most deserving of the fool hen designation.

Habits and Feeding

Spruce grouse feed heavily on conifer needles such as lodgepole, jack, and white pine and on various berries and insects throughout the warmer months. Their feeding habits resemble those of all mountain grouse with feeding periods in early morning and late afternoon. As they are often consuming needles, they spend quite a bit of time in trees. Like ruffed grouse, spruce grouse rarely gather in large groups and typically the family unit breaks up into looser groups of just 1 to 3 birds in the fall.

Preferred Habitat and Cover

Spruce grouse are usually associated with thick coniferous forests, particularly as colder weather approaches. They may also be found in various types of forests and elevations in the Northwest. Edges of logging roads and skidder trails are prime areas to find spruce grouse early and late in the day. The birds will be picking up grit at these times and are easier to spot than in the thicker brush.

Hunting Methods

Spruce grouse are not usually specifically targeted by hunters as they have a reputation for not flushing when found. Usually, they are taken as found while hunting ruffed grouse and blue grouse. Look for them in darker, thicker forests with heavy growth and conifers. Pointing and flushing dogs can both be effective in finding birds, but as they are often found in trees, keeping your eyes open in prime habitat can help. When flushed, this small (38 cm, 15 in. long) grouse will often flutter into a nearby spruce tree where it will sit, and depend only on its coloration for protection. It is commonly called "fool hen" for this apparent lack of fear of people.

Table Preparation

All mountain grouse offer great eating and spruce grouse are no exception. Birds tend to taste better early in the year before their diet turns almost exclusively to coniferous needles.

Shot and Choke Suggestions

All Season — No. 7 ½ shot
Chokes — Improved and modified

Spruce grouse often reside in their namesake— the spruce tree.

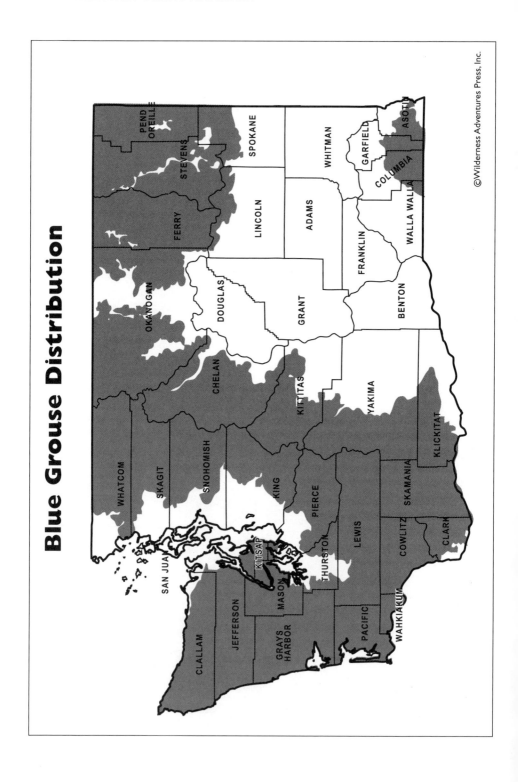

Blue Grouse Distribution

Blue Grouse

Dendragapus obscurus

QUICK FACTS

Local Names

"Blues," fool hen, pine grouse, pine hen, hooter

Size

Males, 20 to 22 inches in length; females smaller; weight, 2½ to 4 pounds; young and females noticeably larger than most ruffed grouse.

Identification in Flight

Loud, explosive flushes reveal a bird that appears uniformly dark gray. They often flush to the branches of a conifer and then either sit tight or re-flush with a very rapid downward launch. Escape flights are often low and darting through trees, typically downhill on a ridge or slope.

- Blue grouse migrate uphill during late fall.
- Blue grouse in Washington are closely tied to Douglas fir and true firs (such as, grand fir, silver fir, and sub-alpine fir).
- As the season progresses, blue grouse become increasingly arboreal; when snow falls, they spend most of their time in trees.
- Western Washington grouse season runs from September 1 until early January.
- Eastern Washington forest grouse season runs from September 1 until late November.
- The 2001 the bag limit was 3 forest grouse with a maximum of 3 each species (ruffed and blue grouse).
- Grouse hunters are required to purchase an Upland Game Bird Validation.
- In 1996, Washington hunters harvested 33,120 blue grouse.

Appearance

Male blue grouse are large, robust grayish birds. Females are somewhat lighter and more mottled but otherwise quite similar. On the ground, blue grouse look like large, dark chickens; in flight, the male's long tail is conspicuous. Adult males are generally not found with females and their brood coveys. Washington's blue grouse have a gray terminal band on the tail.

Male blue grouse displaying.

Sound and Flight Pattern

Blue grouse vocalize very little, although females and brood birds utter faint clucking notes at times. During the late spring mating season, males earn the name "hooter" by delivering, with their air sacks, a series of low-pitched hoots that might easily be mistaken for an owl. These hooting notes carry quite well through the woods, but locating a hooting bird is a difficult proposition.

On the wing, blue grouse often flush to a nearby tree, sometimes perching in plain sight to look over the threat, other times concealing themselves at the base of a densely foliated branch. If the birds then reflush from the tree, they will do so with a rocket-like downhill charge, often dodging through nearby trees and branches and usually heading down slope to the protection of a steep ridge. If caught in the open, blue grouse flush low and away and again usually make haste for a downhill retreat or the top of a distant conifer.

Habits and Feeding

Blue grouse frequent forested ridges, especially those with openings, such as natural meadows, clear cut edges, and exposed outcroppings. Any such areas that include heavy berry growth are likely to harbor blue grouse. The birds feed heavily on huckleberries, currants, gooseberries, serviceberries, thimbleberries, and others, along with a wide variety of greens and other plant matter. Blue grouse often feed along the margins of natural meadows, where they eat a variety of greens. They feed most actively from early to midmorning and again during late afternoon. In between those times, blue grouse dust, preen and roost, sometimes on the ground in protective cover, sometimes in the safety of a conifer. As winter approaches, blue grouse migrate upslope to timbered ridges and saddles where they live almost exclusively on fir needles until the following spring.

During September, expect to find brood coveys of three to eight birds. Prime feeding areas sometimes attract several broods, so large concentrations sometimes occur in forest clearings with dense berry growth. Brood coveys begin to break up as fall progresses. The large, adult males live a solitary existence, often frequenting the top and upper third of steep, timbered ridges, where safety is just a few wing beats away.

Blue grouse in a pine tree.

Seasonal Patterns

Blue grouse exhibit a unique seasonal migration pattern in that they move downhill during spring for mating and nesting and then migrate back to the ridge tops and high, timbered slopes to spend the winter. Here, they feed on fir needles and live an arboreal life. During the early part of the hunting season, they may occur on the same slopes occupied by ruffed grouse in western Washington or along the top of the highest timbered ridges. Early or late in the season, ridgelines, saddles, and forested buttes are good bets for hunters.

Preferred Habitat and Cover

Blue grouse are tied closely to coniferous forest and especially to Douglas fir. Forests in the Cascade and Coast ranges are comprised of a mix of Douglas fir, true firs, mountain and western hemlock, and cedar. Some of the best blue grouse habitat occurs in the zone where Douglas fir is mixed with hemlock and sub-alpine fir, typically at elevations of 3,000 to 7,000 feet in the Cascades. Grouse are especially drawn to timbered ridges and saddles where natural meadows and forest edges break up the timber stands. These areas often feature seeps and springs where birds take water if needed.

On the east side of the Cascades and in the mountains of eastern Washington, blue grouse are distributed throughout the Douglas fir forests and are at times found in regions of surprisingly sparse evergreen cover. Such areas include the lower edges of the forest where it reaches down into river canyons. In some parts of eastern Washington, blue grouse occupy the same slopes as chukars, with the former being found higher on the ridge. Throughout their range, blue grouse are closely tied to their preferred foods, including berries and various greens.

Hunting Methods

Blue grouse hunters can walk logging roads, spurs, and skid roads where these cut across high ridges. Often, blue grouse can be spotted from a vehicle as they dust or feed along the road edges. In many places, logging spurs lead close to the top of steep ridges. From the end of these roads, hunters can climb and then walk the ridge tops. Given a choice, choose the side where the ridge drops away suddenly and thoroughly work clearings and berry patches. Blue grouse often day-roost and feed around outcroppings of rock on steep ridges, so walk and hunt these areas carefully. Throughout their range in Washington, blue grouse tend to occupy the same places that are occupied by fire lookouts, so hunt these buttes and ridge tops as well. Blue grouse hold for staunch pointing dogs, which are especially useful when hunting large clearings and parklands. In open areas, where the birds are subject to light hunting pressure, young blue grouse are well matched to young pointing dogs, often allowing close approach by both man and dog. An effective retriever will aid in finding wounded birds, since they habitually run into dense cover.

Table Preparations

During the early part of the season, blue grouse feed heavily on berries, so their white meat offers excellent eating. During warm weather, dress them immediately and store on ice.

Shot and Choke Suggestions

Heavily timbered ridges — No. 6 to 7½ shot, improved-modified choke.
Open areas, especially late season — No. 6 shot, modified choke.

An early season blue grouse brings a smile to the author's friend and hunting partner, Tony Pritzl.

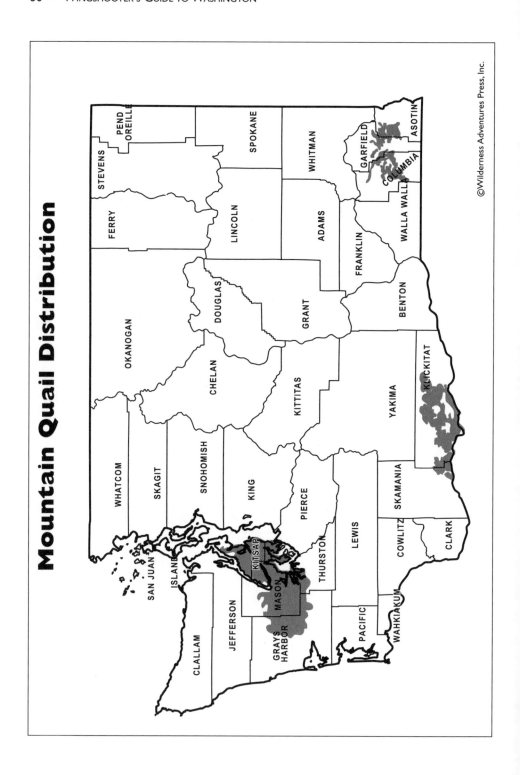

Mountain Quail Distribution

©Wilderness Adventures Press, Inc.

Mountain Quail

Oreortyx pictus

Quick Facts

Local Names
None known

Size
Largest of the quail, 10 to 12 inches in length

Identification in Flight
Mountain quail explode from the brush with a rapid whir of wings and usually with lots of excited chirping. Looping or direct flights are typical, and these birds are adept at dodging through the branches.
- Mountain quail prefer steep, brushy, rocky areas in the mountains of western Washington.
- Mountain quail exist in low densities in central Washington; no hunting season is currently in place owing to sparse populations.
- Mountain quail season runs from October 9 to November 30 in western Washington only.
- The 2001 bag limit on mountain quail was two birds.

Appearance

The adult mountain quail is an unusually handsome bird with its steel-blue/gray breast and bronze-olive-colored back. The flanks are strikingly marked with broad white and dark bands, while the chestnut-colored face is outlined in white. The mountain quail's plume is long and straight, sometimes tilting to the rear. The female is similar in overall appearance, although her plume is shorter.

Sound and Flight Pattern

Mountain quail vocalize often and readily, especially when a hunter and dog work the covey. Members of a broken covey call to each other with sharp chirps and soft clucks. The call is loud and resonant and often accompanied by a series of sharp whistles. Mountain quail fly only when necessary, but their short, powerful wings allow them to steer a rapid course through dense vegetation. Coveys tend to break up in all directions, with some birds running and others taking flight. Often, a hunter hears the bird fly away but is never afforded a shot owing to the thick brush preferred by mountain quail.

Mountain quail.

Habits and Feeding

Mountain quail feed most actively during the morning and late afternoon hours, when they frequent berry patches, road edges, clear-cut edges, and other such open areas. Their diet consists of myriad berries, seeds, greens, and some insects. Family coveys are most common, but good feeding areas may attract several such coveys, at which time all the individuals feed together in the same area. Mountain quail dust frequently, so hunters should study roads and logging landings for dusting areas and then hunt these places regularly.

In southwestern Washington, where mountain quail populations are strongest, brood coveys of 6 to 15 birds occupy the same general area throughout the season and will at times group with other coveys during winter. The result is a covey of 50 or more birds, reminiscent of a winter covey of valley quail.

Seasonal Patterns

During the fall, brood coveys of mountain quail tend to center their activities on a particular location, often near their night roosting site. These sites have been deemed "headquarters." A covey of mountain quail will use its headquarters for roosting, preening, dusting, and foraging. The birds venture out for feeding during morning and again during late afternoon or evening.

Around mid-autumn, mountain quail coveys may migrate to different elevations, and many individuals leave to mix with associated coveys nearby. At this time, hunters may find coveys missing from the areas they occupied during the early part of the season. During winter, coveys again settle into a routine.

Preferred Habitat and Cover

Mountain quail occupy some of the most difficult terrain in the forests of western Washington, due to their preference for areas of dense shrubbery located on steep hillsides at elevations up to about 6,000 feet. They are birds of the edges, so clear cuts from 5 to 15 years old often provide ideal habitat, especially if water and mixed older conifers occur nearby. Brushy, rocky slopes and outcroppings provide good cover as well. Good mountain quail habitats include dense growth of berries, seed-bearing grasses, and flowers, legumes, bracken fern, and various other greens. Dusting areas include just about any disturbed area, from clear cuts to logging roads to gopher mounds.

Hunting Methods

Consistently shooting mountain quail requires that the hunter locate several coveys and then hunt the coveys regularly. To find coveys, many hunters spend mornings and evenings driving and walking logging roads in appropriate habitat, looking for quail or quail sign (dusters and tracks) on the roads. Once birds are located, hunters can pursue the covey on foot. In future visits, hunters can park the vehicle at a distance and walk up on the covey's headquarters area unannounced.

When walking the logging roads and spurs, watch closely for dusting areas, which often contain feathers. It's likely the birds are nearby, as they tend not to wander too far from their favorite haunts. These birds often vocalize with subtle chirps and sometimes scamper nervously about in the understory. The hunter who keeps ears and eyes open will find more quail.

A good retriever is essentially mandatory for mountain quail hunting because downed birds often land in cover too dense for humans. A close-working flusher can be a big asset, and a pointing dog with good lungs and a strong uphill gait can pressure running birds into holding. In either case, flushers or pointers, the dog that hunts mountain quail on a regular basis has the opportunity to learn the peculiar habits of these running, wild-flying quail.

Table Preparations

The hunter fortunate enough to pull off a few good shots will be rewarded with exceptional white meat from mountain quail. Breasts are smaller than those of ruffed grouse but larger than valley quail. During the typically warm weather of September, dress or breast the birds soon after the kill and store on ice.

Shot and Choke Suggestions

All Seasons/locations — No. 7½ or 8 shot; improved or open bore.

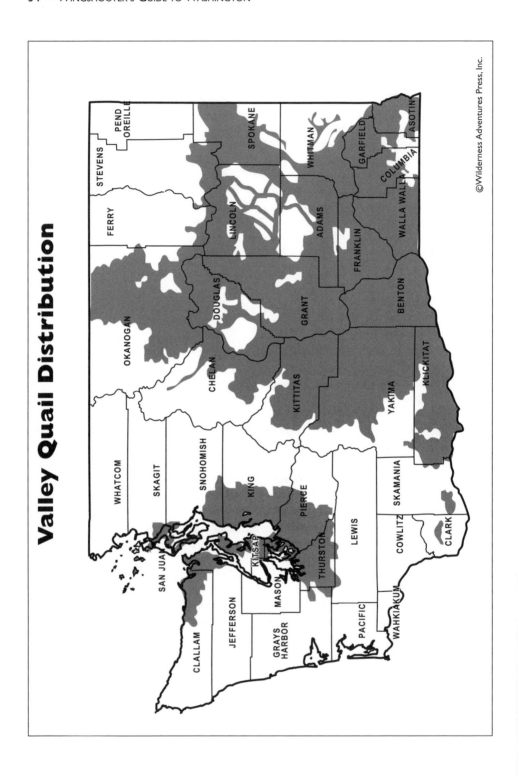

Valley Quail Distribution

Valley Quail

Callipepla californica

QUICK FACTS

Local Names
California quail, topknot quail

Size
Approximately 8 inches in length; Washington's smallest upland game bird

Identification in Flight
Valley quail explode from cover with rapid, buzzing wing beats, often chirping as they go. Only rarely does an entire covey flush in unison; instead, individuals or pairs flush one after another until all the birds have relocated.

- Valley quail are native only to the counties bordering California but were widely introduced around Washington beginning in the late 1800s and now thrive throughout most of the state.
- Valley quail are closely tied to brushy edge habitat in agricultural and suburban areas.
- In central and eastern Washington, valley quail are closely tied to water sources, including riparian areas, farms, ranches, and towns.
- In western Washington, valley quail season runs from October 7 to November 30. In eastern Washington, valley quail season extends to January 15.
- The 2001 bag limit on valley quail was 10 birds.
- In 2000, Washington hunters harvested 102,369 valley quail.

Appearance

The handsome male valley quail features a characteristic, drooping black topknot, shaped something like a question mark. His face is boldly patterned in black and white, while its head is chestnut-colored and borders a yellowish forehead. Both male and female have striped flanks and a scalloped belly. The back is deep blue-gray to olive-gray. The hen valley quail lacks the boldly patterned face and the topknot is noticeably shorter. With practice, wing-shooters can usually pick males out of the flushing coveys.

Sounds and Flight Pattern

Valley quail prefer to run, which they do remarkably well, but will flush with little provocation, as they are capable fliers. The flush depends on the cover — in western Washington, good flushing dogs can work quail out of large blackberry stands, in which case, the birds often explode out the top of the berry bushes or run through

Valley quail feeding.

and flush out the opposite side. The combination of high, arcing flights and straight-away ground-level flushes makes for interesting shooting. In sparse cover, valley quail typically flush low and somewhat straightaway, wrapping around any object that distances them from the threat. Their flushing speed is not particularly great, so shooters can pick distant birds first and work back in, creating an opportunity for easy doubles and an occasional triple.

Most characteristic of the valley quail's many vocalizations is the male's distinctive breeding call, a series of three (typically) slurred musical notes, with the middle one loudest and highest. The call is sometimes described as a question for the female quail: "where ARE you." This breeding call is typically delivered over and over from a low perch during the mid- to late spring courtship season. This same call, along with a shortened two-note version of it, is heard regularly during the summer and fall. In addition, valley quail utter a variety of chirps and chips.

Habits and Feeding

Valley quail begin feeding early in the morning, then dust, preen, and rest during midday. They forage again in the late afternoon or evening. The valley quail's diet consists of a wide variety of plant materials, including myriad seeds, buds, and greens. In agricultural areas they are drawn to waste grain. Valley quail frequent watering areas; in the arid regions of central and eastern Washington, in fact, the coveys rarely wander far from water.

Coveys of valley quail sometimes walk surprising distances to feed, picking their way through cover to a favorite foraging area and then often employing a sentinel to keep an eye out for danger. With a sentinel bird at guard, the rest of the quail pick away at their chosen food, often dusting and preening while foraging. Their distinctive bobbing walk and antics while feeding make for enjoyable observation.

Seasonal Patterns

During spring, male valley quail establish a territory for calling. They announce their presence each morning and evening with their distinctive "where-ARE-you" calls. The calling perch is usually elevated. After breeding, the female and male raise the young together. A typical spring scenario finds the male valley quail perched silently atop a lookout post while the female leads the young in search of food, generally in heavy cover where the broods of as many as 15 chicks remain protected from numerous predators. During good years, some valley quail will double clutch.

Family coveys remain together through the summer and most of the fall. In areas of prime habitat, two or more family coveys may occupy the same area. As winter approaches, family coveys converge, forming large winter coveys. In eastern Washington, during high-productivity years, winter coveys might include more than 100 individuals. Large winter coveys in western Washington typically number 20 to 50 individuals.

Cock and hen valley quail.

Valley quail.

Throughout their range in Washington, valley quail are closely tied to water. In water-rich western Washington, however, the birds have lots of cover from which to choose. In central and eastern Washington, valley quail are closely tied to riparian areas, farms, ranches, and towns. They may share habitat with chukars and pheasants in sagebrush environments and agricultural environments, respectively. In some habitats, they are the most abundant game bird.

Preferred Habitat and Cover

Valley quail can be found along river and creek bottoms, where there is good, brushy cover and adjacent open areas. Blackberry and other extensive shrubbery provides ideal cover, and birds can be found around rural, suburban, and urban areas in eastern Washington where suitable water sources are easily found.

Valley quail need edges for feeding, heavy brush stands for cover, and elevated, heavy brush cover for roosting. In many areas of Washington, they are a common urban bird and are easily attracted to backyard bird-feeding stations where appropriate escape and roosting cover are found.

Hunting Methods

Because of the brushy habitat in which valley quail thrive, a good dog should be considered mandatory. This is especially true in western Washington, where extensive blackberry growth sometimes makes downed birds impossible to find and retrieve without a dog. Valley quail are perfectly suited to pointing dogs because, after a covey is broken up, pointing breeds can locate and hold the singles and doubles. These birds do have a propensity for running, but a fleet-footed pointer can stop them, especially after the covey is scattered. Flushing breeds must work close and cover the ground thoroughly.

In agricultural areas, hunters should work fence lines, brushy edges, watering areas, and drainages. In central and eastern Washington, look for quail along brushy creeks, draws with springs or seeps, irrigation canals, and riparian margins along rivers. In prime habitat, keep an eye peeled for tracks on dusty roads. Valley quail feed actively during the early morning and late afternoon/evening, when they sometimes wander away from heavy cover. Once a covey is located, the initial flush sends birds in all directions. Hunters and dogs can then effectively work the singles and doubles.

Table Preparations

Though quite small, the plump breasts provide superb eating and can be prepared in a variety of ways. Be sure to draw the birds immediately during warm weather.

Shot and Choke Suggestions

Improved, No. 7½ or 8 shot.

A double-point on valley quail.

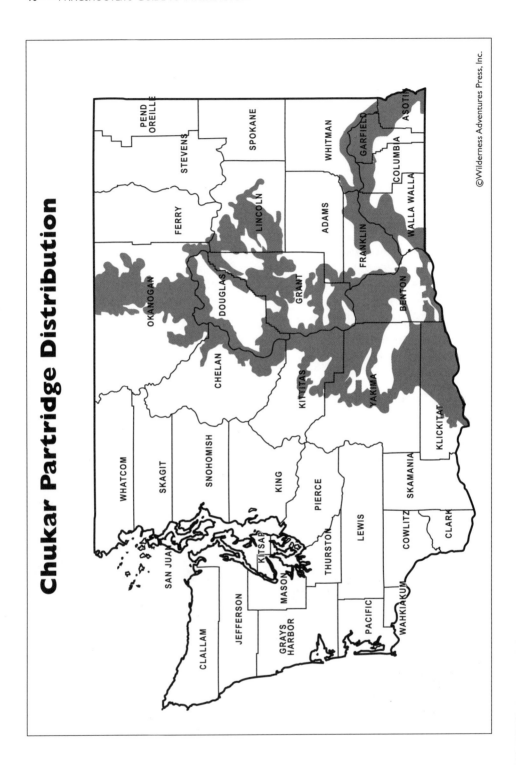

Chukar Partridge Distribution

©Wilderness Adventures Press, Inc.

Chukar Partridge

Alectoris chukar

QUICK FACTS

Local Names
Chukar

Size
Both sexes range from 13 to 15 inches in length; adult males average 19.6 ounces in weight, while adult females average 15.7 ounces.

Appearance in Flight
Chukars are quick flyers that prefer to flush and fly downhill. On the wing, they exhibit fast wing beats like that of a quail, and their handsome face pattern and striped flanks are often clearly discernible. Being covey birds, chukars often flush in unison. They are superb athletes on the ground, able to run uphill and climb rim rocks and talus slides like mountain goats.

- Chukar are non-indigenous partridge native to central Europe but widely introduced in western North America, especially in Washington, Oregon, Idaho, and Nevada.
- Chukar populations fluctuate rather widely from year to year and are largely determined by spring nesting and rearing conditions as well as by winter weather.
- Chukar are closely tied to water in their arid habitat and will make daily or twice daily trips to water sources until autumn weather brings moisture to the high rims and slopes.
- Southeastern Washington offers an abundance of public land that allows wing-shooters expansive opportunity to hunt on many thousands of acres of prime chukar habitat.
- Chukar hunters and their dogs must be in good physical condition to hunt the steep, arid country these birds inhabit.
- Pointing dogs are especially well suited to hunting chukars; flushing dogs need to work fairly close.
- The 2001 daily bag limit on chukar was 6 birds.
- In 2000, Washington hunters harvested 25,807 chukars.

Appearance

The chukar partridge, a most handsome game bird, is elegantly adorned with black and white bars on its taupe flanks, a soft gray mantle and a striking black-and-white face pattern. The chukar's bright red legs and bill further enhance this beautiful plumage.

Chukar country.

Sound and Flight Pattern

Chukars are readily identified by their call, from which their name derives: "chuka, chuka, chuka." The call often rings from high above, near the rimrocks, and is especially pronounced early in the season before the birds have learned the virtues of silence. Often, the call of the chukar simultaneously tells the hunter that birds are present and that he or she has a lot of climbing to do before reaching said birds. Once a covey is broken, members call to announce their location. Chukars flush with a whir of short, powerful wings, and fly low and away down slope, often wrapping around a ridge or spine before landing again. Chukars flush in coveys, although often a few stragglers are late in exiting.

Habits and Feeding

Cheatgrass forms an important ingredient in the chukar's diet. When available, chukars feed readily and heavily on waste grain, namely in areas where wheat fields sit atop canyon slopes occupied by chukar populations. Prior to the arrival of autumn or winter moisture, chukars generally make their way to water in the morning and then feed their way upslope. In the late afternoon, after feeding, preening, and loafing on the slopes, the birds again move down to water prior to roosting in the rimrocks, talus, or other cover. Clutch birds feed heavily on insects.

After the first rain or snow, chukar need no longer make regular trips to open water. Instead, they disperse to higher slopes and obtain water from pools in the rocks or moisture on the vegetation. Cool winter weather further reduces their need for water.

Seasonal Patterns

Family clutches remain separated until fall, when they begin joining to form larger winter coveys. During good years, areas of ideal habitat may produce winter coveys of more than 100 birds. Coveys remain closely associated with available water sources until rains arrive in mid- to late autumn. Substantial moisture during the late fall allows chukar coveys to disperse to higher and more remote slopes. During winter, the birds prefer south-exposure slopes, which offer warmer temperatures due to direct sunlight.

Preferred Habitat and Cover

Chukars are most at home in arid, steep, rugged canyons where streams or rivers provide a water supply. They roost in rimrocks, talus slides, brushy draws, and other such covers. Perfect habitat combines steep slopes with abundant cheatgrass, myriad talus slides, and cover in the form of rabbitbrush, sage, and bunchgrass. If the same slope has wheat fields on flatlands above and a year-round stream below, all the elements for ideal habitat are in place for these hardy partridge. During winter,

Chukar partridge.

chukar seek areas devoid of snow and are most comfortable on southern exposures where they gather what little warmth is offered by the sun.

Hunting Methods

Success in chukar hunting requires that hunters always seek ground at or above the level at which the birds will be found. Such position can be accomplished in one of three ways: Early in the season, you can ambush the birds as they seek water at the canyon bottoms, typically at midmorning and again during late afternoon. Otherwise, you have to get to their level by either walking up or hunting an area where you can drive to the top. Topography maps produced by the Bureau of Land Management and United States Geological Survey show roads that provide access to the top of many canyons. Otherwise, you're stuck with the option of hiking up the steep slopes inhabited by chukar, which is one reason for the old adage that the first time you hunt chukars you do so for the enjoyment of it, and every time thereafter you are motivated solely by revenge. That adage also derives from the chukar's maddening tendency to run rapidly uphill, never flushing unless approached from above or pinned down by a dog.

Once you reach appropriate altitude, start walking the contour and give up elevation only begrudgingly. Even walking a contour can be exhausting, especially on steep, rocky, unstable ground where one leg remains forever higher than the other.

A good dog (or dogs) helps immensely in finding chukars, especially later in the season when the birds appreciate the value of stealth and silence. Pointing breeds are especially well-suited to chukar hunting: the birds usually hold well for a dog, and pointers can cover lots of ground while the hunter continues along on the same contour, only walking up or downhill to flush birds in front of the dog. Also, speedy pointing breeds have the ability to catch up with birds running uphill, hopefully pinning them down until the gunner can get there.

Often chukars reside atop the canyons, where flat or rolling country makes for much easier walking. These birds always remain but a short flight or run from the safety of the canyon edge, where they can disappear with a burst of speed. Thus, in many areas, a viable tactic involves getting to the top and then hunting along at the edge of the slope or just down from the edge. In some places, the breaks of the Snake River for example, wheat stubble attracts birds to the top of the slopes.

Table Preparations

The white-meat chukar ranks amongst the best of gamebirds with a mild, tender flavor. Birds should be drawn soon after the kill, especially in warm weather. They lend themselves to numerous preparations.

Shot and Choke Suggestions

Early season with pointing dogs — No. 5, 6, or 7½ shot, modified chokes.
Late season with pointing dogs — No. 5 to 6 shot, modified and full chokes.
Any season with flushing dogs — No. 5 to 6 shot, modified and full chokes.

Wheat country—where chukar and Huns can usually be found.

Hungarian (Gray) Partridge Distribution

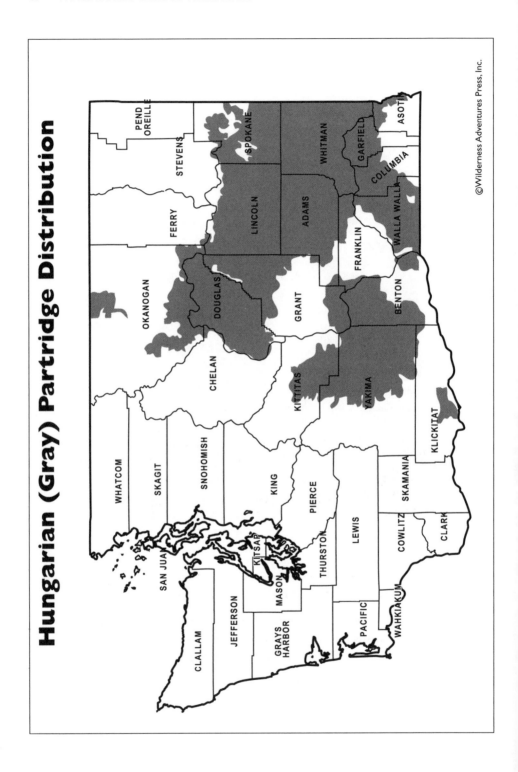

©Wilderness Adventures Press, Inc.

Hungarian Partridge

Perdix perdix

QUICK FACTS

Local Names
Hun, gray partridge

Size
Gray partridge range from 12 to 13 inches in length with a wingspan of 15 to 17 inches and weighing up to a pound.

Appearance in Flight
Hungarian partridge are strong, quick flyers with rapid wing beats not unlike a quail. They are capable of quick twists and turns and often wrap around a ridge or hill before landing again. They typically flush as a covey, sometimes with a few stragglers.

- The Hungarian partridge is a non-native game bird introduced widely in North America. They are indigenous to central Europe. The first stocks in Washington occurred in the early 1900s.
- The Columbia Basin offers Washington's best Hun populations with fairly strong populations in the Snake River Basin counties.
- Huns are typically hunted incidentally to pheasant and chukar.
- The 2001 daily bag limit on Hungarian partridge was 6 birds.
- In 2000, Washington hunters harvested 15,338 Huns.

Appearance

The Hungarian partridge is a handsome bird characterized by a grayish plumage throughout, a chestnut-colored belly, cinnamon-colored head and a rust-colored tail, this latter feature usually visible in flight. Generally, Huns are easily told from chukar and valley quail, the only other upland birds with which they might be confused. They sometimes occupy wheat stubble alongside chukar and pheasant, and their habitat overlaps that of the valley quail near ranch and farm buildings and around brushy draws on grasslands and grain fields.

Sound and Flight Pattern

Upon flushing, Huns usually utter a series of fairly loud squealing calls. Their initial burst of rapid, explosive wing beats soon gives way to an alternating series of flaps and glides. The covey tends to depart in tight formation. If a covey is broken, individuals will call to one another and reassemble.

Habits and Feeding

Generally, Huns are early risers and begin their quest for food by daybreak or before. After a morning feeding, the coveys water, loaf, dust, and preen before an afternoon feeding. Huns feed on a wide variety of seeds and grains, especially waste grains in wheat fields. They also consume some insects and green vegetative matter. Much of their water intake comes from morning dew and from irrigation, but when available, they drink from streams, seeps, and ditches. During winter, snow provides a source for water. Like other game birds, Huns gather grit from the edges of roads, especially those running alongside good feeding areas, such as wheat fields and prairies.

Seasonal Patterns

Huns are strictly covey birds. These social flocks define their entire life history. During late spring, the hen lays 12 to 17 eggs, so ideal nesting and rearing conditions can produce large family coveys. Hens and cocks rear the young together. The hot summer months are spent in the coolest, most comfortable part of their range, especially if water becomes a commodity not easily gathered. By fall, family broods assemble into larger coveys where they remain throughout the winter and early spring. Severe winter weather drives the coveys to areas offering the best combination of cover and available feed. In the absence of large accumulations of snow, the birds often reside in sheltered, brushy draws. If snow fills such places, they may feed on windswept knolls and windward slopes where grain and seed is most easily gathered.

Preferred Habitat and Cover

Hungarian partridge are most abundant in the grain country of eastern Washington, especially where grasslands border wheat and other grain tracts. The best Hun country features geography characterized by rolling hills, draws, grassy slopes, and high, shortgrass knolls. Large tracts featuring a mix of native grasses and brushes offer ideal cover for Huns, especially when bordered by large grain fields. Early in the season, when eastern Washington is hot and dry, coveys often occupy irrigated lands or moist draws, especially those with water.

Hunting Methods

Consistent success hunting Hungarian partridge generally means covering lots of ground with the aid of good pointing dogs. Huns can range widely across expansive tracts of good habitat, but productive areas tend to remain that way over time. Birds are most active during morning and late afternoon when they forage for food; otherwise they tend to collect grit, loaf, preen, and dust on exposed rises, and slopes; or, in cold or hot weather, under heavier cover. Once a covey is found and flushed, hunters can follow along for subsequent flushes until the covey is broken. Then, with the aid of dogs, hunters can work the singles as they call to regroup. Unless the covey is pursued rather ardently, it will rarely break. Huns begin moving about very early in the day and are quite wary. Nonetheless, hunters who begin the pursuit at daybreak are rewarded by perfect scenting conditions for the dogs and it is the bird dog that really defines a successful hunt for gray partridge. Without dogs, consistent success on Huns is highly improbable.

Table Preparations

The Hungarian partridge offers darker meat than that of the chukar partridge. In fact, Hungarian partridge compares favorably to valley or mountain quail. During hot weather, birds should be drawn immediately and cooled as soon as possible. When so treated, the breasts offer fine eating and lend themselves to a variety of preparations.

Shot and Choke Suggestions

Chokes — Modified chokes for singles barrels; for doubles, improved/modified early in the season with pointing dogs; improved/full late season or with flushing dogs.

Shot — No. 7½ or 6 (with single guns, try two 7½s followed by a load of 5s or 6s).

Hungarian partridge.

Ring-necked Pheasant Distribution

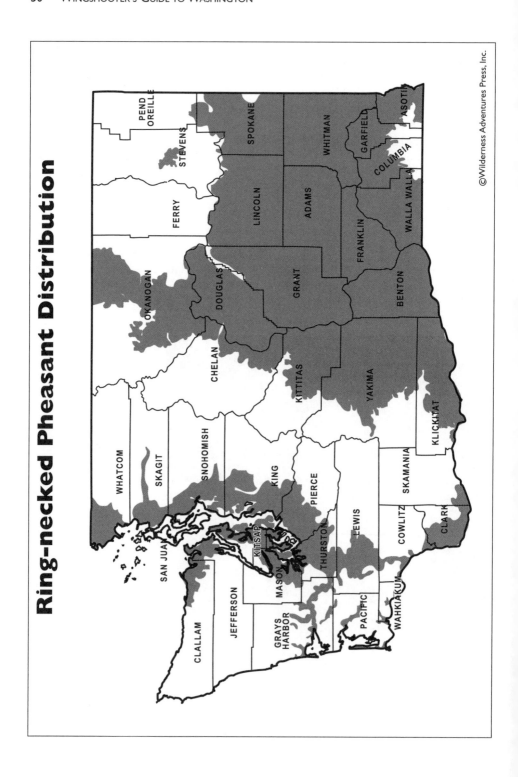

©Wilderness Adventures Press, Inc.

Ring-necked Pheasant

Phasianus colchicus

QUICK FACTS

Local Names
Pheasant, ring-neck, rooster, cockbird

Size
Roosters up to 3 feet long, including tail; weight from 2 to 3½ pounds with a wingspan of 32 to 34 inches. Hens, which are fully protected, range from 20 to 25 inches.

Appearance in Flight
Male pheasants appear much darker in flight than the brownish hens. In good light, the rooster's resplendent plumage is quite obvious and it frequently cackles loudly upon being flushed.
- Ring-necked pheasants are the most sought-after upland game bird in Washington.
- The 2001 daily bag limit on pheasants was three roosters in eastern Washington and 2 birds of either sex in western washington.
- In 2000, Washington hunters harvested 127,738 pheasants.

Appearance

The rooster ring-necked pheasant ranks as the most stunning and colorful of North America's upland game birds. Their glossy, deep green head terminates at a gleaming white neckband and is highlighted further by a bright red cheek and ear patches. The body plumage is a mix of orange, brown, gray, black, iridescent purple, and bronze. The long, brownish tail is heavily banded with black. The hen is mottled brown and tan throughout.

Sound and Flight Pattern

The loud, raspy display call of the male pheasant is a familiar and pleasing sound throughout much of Washington's agricultural area. Otherwise, the hunter is most likely to hear the excited cackling of a flushed and rapidly departing rooster. Pheasants flush explosively and unpredictably. Their flight is strong and rapid for short distances. Once on the wing and headed hard away, they flap and glide alternately, then hit the ground at a full run, especially when cover is sparse. Their escape flight may cover half a mile or more.

Habits and Feeding

Pheasants rise early to begin feeding around daybreak, especially early in the season when warm weather dominates the afternoon. As the season progresses, shorter, colder days, prompt the pheasants to remain active longer and later in the day. In western Washington, the birds must cope with extensive rainy spells, during which pheasants seek deep, protective cover from which they emerge only long enough to feed. Any sun break brings birds out to sun themselves and preen lazily, especially during midmorning.

Seasonal Patterns

The springtime rooster courting behavior begins early each day and consists of strutting about and calling from a favorite ground perch. His red wattle becomes bright and swollen, the ear tufts erect, and tail fanned. Each raspy call is delivered with plenty of body English. The hens seek protective cover for their ground nests and lay 8 to 12 eggs. Like most upland game birds, chicks are capable of short flights at about one week of age. While pheasants don't really form coveys, good years sometimes lead to flocks of 20 or more birds concentrated around ideal food sources. Otherwise, they spend fall and winter as singles, doubles, or small flocks. Winterkill can take a heavy toll on pheasants, especially when heavy snow occurs with or prior to bitter cold.

Preferred Habitat and Cover

Pheasants are closely tied to agriculture and fare best when grain production is inefficient, meaning that lots of native cover remains in the form of rows and coverts and that lots of waste grain remains after harvest. In western Washington, such habitat is increasingly scarce as clean farming - most noticeably by the grass-seed industry - leaves little in the way of cover and food for pheasants.

The best pheasant cover exists where more varied terrain includes smaller agricultural plots planted with a greater variety of crops and interrupted more frequently by rows and islands of wild vegetation, including native and introduced grasses and shrubs. When seeking pheasant cover in western Washington, look for tracts of fallow land featuring a mix of tallgrass cover, blackberry patches, vegetated fence- and ditch-rows, scotch-broom groves, and scattered mixed stands of cottonwood, ash, Douglas fir, and oak. This kind of habitat is most abundant on small plots of land where hunters might be well served to gain permission from several landowners with abutting properties. With permission to cross fences and hunt several side-by-side parcels of land, pheasant hunters increase their odds of covering enough suitable habitat.

In eastern Washington, pheasants have fared better owing to more extensive habitat. They occupy agricultural lands along with riparian areas, always using the most diverse cover available to them. Throughout most of eastern Washington, pheasants are closely tied to available water. They thrive in agricultural areas where grain fields mix with large plots of fallow or native grass and shrub cover; add a permanent stream, river, canal, or ditch system, and you have ideal habitat. Hunting

A successful pheasant hunter.

Cock pheasant.

pressure exerts a profound effect on pheasants, which explains why roosters surviving on public hunting areas soon head for the heaviest, most impenetrable cover. Where it exists, roosters are especially fond of heavy cattail cover.

Hunting Methods

Throughout Washington, a pheasant hunter's success is largely determined by his or her dog and by his or her choice of locations. Long before the season begins, pheasant hunters should seek permission to hunt private lands as these areas habitually offer the best prospects on a season-long basis. Hunters should also familiarize themselves with the daily routine of the birds on the land they intend to hunt.

The hunt itself can take many forms. Working in pairs or groups, hunters can force running roosters into the edges of cover, where the birds often stop and hold for pointing dogs. The solo hunter - and I often fit this category - should hunt the cover thoroughly behind a good dog. Try walking in a ditch, row, or draw through good cover, forcing birds to run ahead or to run into side coverts where they can then be pursued systematically.

A flushing dog, trained to work well within gun range, makes an excellent pheasant breed because he or she can follow and often outmaneuver a running, zigzagging rooster. In many cases, of course, it is left to the hunter to keep up with both dog and pheasant. Flushing dogs also shine when hunting heavy cover, such as cattail stands, where the staunch point of a pointing breed goes completely unseen by the hunter. With a flusher fighting through heavy cover, hunters can walk the edges and wait for birds to fly out.

Pointing dogs make fine pheasant hunters assuming they learn how to cope with running birds, which for many dogs is simply a matter of experience.

Table Preparations

Among the best of wild game, pheasants lend themselves well to roasting, baking, and many other preparations. The birds should be drawn immediately, especially in hot weather. A good marinade helps prevent over-drying of the white-meat breasts and dark thighs. Because of their tendency to dry during cooking, pheasants are ideally suited to recipes that take advantage of baking bags or crock-pots.

Shot and Choke Suggestions

Choke — Modified for singles; improved/modified for doubles or modified/full for late season in sparse cover.

Shot — Strong field loads of No. 6 or No. 5; even magnum No. 4 for long shots late in the season; or on sparse cover.

Alfalfa fields are always a good bet to find pheasants.

Springer spaniel after a successful hunt.

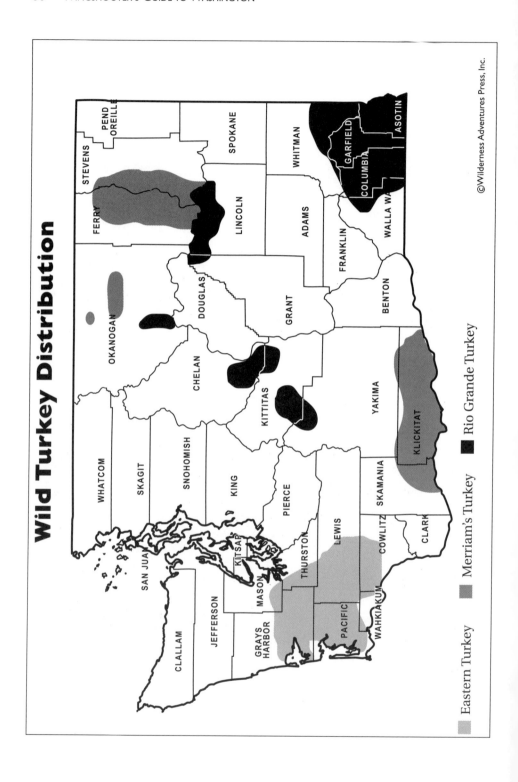

Wild Turkey Distribution

©Wilderness Adventures Press, Inc.

Eastern Turkey

Merriam's Turkey

Rio Grande Turkey

Wild Turkey

Meleagris gallopavo

QUICK FACTS

Local Names
Tom, turkey, gobbler

Size
Males can weigh 25 pounds, but 15- to 20-pound toms are more typical. Females weigh 8 to 12 pounds. The male is 3 to 4 feet long with a wingspan of 4 to 5 feet.

Identification in Flight
Wild turkeys prefer to run and are exceptionally good at doing so, reaching top speeds upward of 20 miles per hour. They are strong flyers as well, though, and can use their long powerful wings to disappear quickly. In flight they can hardly be confused with any other fowl.
- Wild turkeys are not native to Washington and were first introduced by biologists in 1960.
- Washington has three subspecies of wild turkey: Merriam's, Rio Grande, and Eastern.
- Please see the section on Evergreen State Turkey Hunting later in the book for sub-species distribution and hunting information.

Appearance

The wild turkey, North America's largest upland game bird, is a striking bird, with the hen being adorned in rich tones of brown, chestnut, tan, and black. A glossy iridescent cast highlights the male's black and dark brown plumage. Long, mottled tail feathers, each tipped with a black sub-terminal band and a tan or buff-colored terminal band, form a broad fan that the male raises and spreads during the courtship dance. The turkey's head is devoid of feathers, and the tom sports a bright red wattle. Tom turkeys also grow a long beard on their breast, which, on an old bird, might be 10 to 12 inches long. The wing quills are alternately barred with black and white.

Sound and Flight Pattern

Turkeys use myriad sounds in many varieties. The most familiar of the turkey's sounds, of course, is the male's spring gobbling, which sometimes occurs during the fall and winter as well. Hunters learn to mimic several of the turkey's calls. A turkey's flight can be both surprisingly agile and humorously labored. When leaving a high night-roost at dawn, turkeys essentially launch themselves and then flap and glide seemingly in an effort to land on the ground with some degree of dignity. Once a turkey gains a head of steam, however, its flight is powerful and direct. Most often, turkeys remain on the ground, where they use their strong legs to distance themselves from predators.

Habits and Feeding

Turkeys consume a wide range of foods, with the extensive list including many fruits, seeds, nuts, and legumes. In western Washington and in the Columbia Gorge, where oak stands abound, acorns are one of many favorite foods. Turkeys feed actively during the morning, then preen, dust, and loaf during midday, often feeding at the same time. During late afternoon, turkeys again move about in search of food prior to roosting.

Eastern wild turkey.

Seasonal Patterns

Early spring marks the beginning of turkey courtship activities. Toms disperse from the winter flocks and begin fighting for dominance and then gobbling and strutting for hens. Toms mate with as many hens as possible. Hens build simple ground nests and lay from 6 to 15 eggs. During the 28-day incubation period for the eggs, toms continue to gobble and strut in an attempt to attract unmated hens or hens whose first clutch failed. Research shows that about 50 percent of nests are lost to weather, predation, or abandonment. Half the successful broods are subsequently lost to weather and predation.

After the chicks hatch, the hen remains with the brood throughout the summer and fall. Sometimes several broods join together forming large droves. During the late fall, young toms (jakes) may separate from the brood, forming flocks of their own. In regions where snow accumulates, turkeys move down slope to areas where food is more easily gathered.

Preferred Habitat and Cover

In Washington, wild turkeys utilize a variety of habitats. In western Washington, turkeys prefer hardwood cover, especially oak, but often range into mixed coniferous forest, brushy edges, and farmlands. The Columbia Gorge offers substantial oak and mixed oak/conifer woodlots that are preferred by turkeys. In central and eastern Washington, turkeys prefer riparian areas, along with open stands of ponderosa pines.

Hunting Methods

Turkey hunting is a game of ambush, wherein a well-concealed hunter, by imitating the sounds made by a hen, calls a gobbler into firing range. Successful hunters almost always scout out locations well ahead of the season, learning as much as possible about the movements and daily patterns of local birds. In scouting for turkeys, look carefully for sign, including tracks and droppings. Turkey tracks are unmistakable, since no other upland bird leaves such a sizeable impression. Male turkeys leave large, elongated j-shaped droppings. Also look for feathers, dusting areas, and large scratches where turkeys tear through leaf cover in search of food. Dusting and preening stations typically include lots of feathers and droppings.

Once you find a turkey population, start searching for a place from which to call. Calling areas should be in fairly open terrain, not only because turkeys avoid dense brush but also to allow you unrestricted visibility. The calling station should also be at least 150 yards from a roosting site if one is known. Select a tree at least as wide as your shoulders and taller than your head, thereby breaking up your profile while also protecting yourself from careless hunters who might stalk your decoys or your calls. (Turkey hunting has rapidly become the most dangerous variety of upland game bird hunting, primarily because people fail to take simple precautions). Wild turkeys can easily detect motion and sound, so hunters must remain motionless and well camouflaged.

Rio Grande turkey.

Arrive at your calling location before dawn, then begin listening for turkeys. If you have scouted and then set up in the vicinity of a known roost, listen for wing rustling and soft calls. When you begin calling, do so softly and infrequently at first. Aggressive calling can spook experienced toms, but only experience in turkey calling and turkey hunting can help hunters determine how and when to call.

Table Preparations

As one might expect, wild turkey makes exceptional table fare. The birds should be drawn as soon as possible.

Shot and Choke Suggestions

In Washington, only shotguns and bows may be used to hunt turkeys. Shotgun gauges must be 10, 12, 16 or 20. Recurve, long, and compound bows are legal. Generally, the specific size shot depends on the area being hunted, but loads of No. 2 and 4 assure clean kills assuming hunters lure the turkey into optimum range of 25 yards or less. Full chokes help center the shot charge on the turkey's head.

Migratory Game Birds
Mourning Dove

Mourning doves live throughout most of Washington where suitable habitat exists. Local populations and migrating flocks generally depart with the first cold weather in September or October, especially in central and eastern Washington. Some of the state's best dove shooting occurs in the grain-agriculture belt of the Columbia Basin. The tender breast meat of these small game birds lends itself well to many different preparations.

Habits

Doves flock daily to feeding areas, especially those with an abundance of waste grain. During the afternoon (and often during the morning) they fly to favorite water-holes. They collect grit at favorite gravel sites. Deciphering the daily habits of doves can be as easy as watching for and observing concentrations of birds prior to and during the season.

Hunting Methods

Doves are best ambushed at either the feeding or watering locations, where hunters can set up in good cover and await the daily or twice-daily flights. Mourning doves are notoriously fast flyers and have caused the demise of many a box of shotgun shells. No. 7½ and 8 shot is best combined with a modified choke.

Washington Harvest

In 2000, 65,450 doves were harvested in the state of Washington.

Mourning dove.

Pheasant With A Stick

For most upland bird hunters, shotgun gauges, chokes, shot patterns, and size are nearly as important as the type of dog they will hunt over. Arguments rage over stock shape, modified versus improved cylinder, and 20-gauge versus 12. But for a small, but growing number of us, all of these factors have become less important. It is not because we have given up shooting birds just to watch our dogs work, rather we have chosen a weapon that for whatever reason has more appeal to us, at least on some occasions. That weapon is the bow and arrow.

I first started shooting birds with a bow, as an incidental bonus to my deer and elk archery hunts. Grouse were abundant in the wilderness areas where I pursued big game. Admittedly, I never tried to shoot a grouse on the wing, the birds I did get were ground sluiced. But one year after the early archery seasons for big game was over and I was preparing for the opening day of pheasant season, I discovered that somehow the firing pin on my trusty pump gun was broken. The local gunsmith said I was looking at three to four weeks before I would get the gun back (he was headed to the Midwest for two weeks of pheasant hunting himself).

I discussed this situation with my favorite bird hunting partner, who made it clear that missing opening weekend was not an option (German wirehaired pointers are notoriously stubborn about these things). I then discussed the possibility of purchasing a new over/under gun I had my eye on for some time with the other female in my life. Her look was nearly as venomous as the dog's! Since the only other shooting weapon I owned was my trusty longbow, my remaining options were limited.

I knew there were special arrows that I could make called flu flu's that the Seminole Indians of the Okeefenokee, and Everglades regions had used to wing shoot birds in centuries gone by. These arrows have oversized feathers on them, which severely restrict the distance the arrow will travel. This is very important as an arrow with normal feathers, shot from a hunting draw weight bow at an angle of 45 degrees, can easily travel 100-150 yards! These flu flu arrows typically will not fly beyond 30 or 40 yards, so I reasoned they could probably be located rather easily after the shot and re-used many times.

After making up four of these arrows I needed to determine the best type of tip to use. Knowing that pheasants can be tough birds to kill cleanly, I initially considered using a razor sharp big game hunting "broad head." I quickly rejected this idea as the mental image of my wirehair retrieving a bird with something so deadly sticking out of it, made me shudder. The safety of my companion is too important to me. I next considered a common target or field tip - not nearly as dangerous to my dog, but would most certainly kill a solidly hit bird. Again though, the mental image of my four-legged friend impaled on a sharp object made me reject that option.

Finally I came across a tip designed specifically for bird hunting. The head, called a Snarro, is a blunt tip that has heavy gauge spring wire looped through it so it resembles a four-leaf clover. The shape of the head had several advantages. Foremost was the safety factor, it would be very difficult for Dutchess to hurt herself on a retrieve, also the shape gave me a six to eight inch "pattern," to use in trying to hit one of the fast flying ringnecks.

On opening day I showed up at a local farm where I had hunted for many years, and met a few bird-hunting buddies. As I pulled out my bow and arrows, I heard snickering, guffawing, and plain old-fashioned belly laughs. My buddies were sure I had finally lost what had remained of my sanity. They kindly reminded me I could barely hit anything with my scattergun, let alone a stick and a string. With my rapier-like wit I retorted that I didn't need to stand for that type of abuse, I had walked away from my wife that very morning when she made similar remarks, and I could certainly walk away from them.

As this first hunt was an experiment, we did decide it might be best if I hunted by myself. I had made up my mind that to avoid excessive frustration, I would limit myself to taking only shots at tight sitting roosters that flushed no more than five yards in front of me. By hunting on my own I would not have to ask my friends to hold their fire until after I had shot. At high noon, opening time on opening day in our state, we started out, Dutchess and I working fence rows and field edges.

Our first bird contact came within fifteen minutes of starting out. Dutchess slammed on a solid point with her nose close to the ground and her tail and rump high in the air. As I approached her, gently reminding her about whoa, a large mature cock flushed while I was still about fifteen yards away - no shot. Oh well, I thought, I didn't expect this to be easy. The next half hour brought several hens, and I was having a great time watching my dog work. She was having a great day! Suddenly she went on point again, I eased up to her and this time the bird was holding tight and didn't take flight until I was about six feet away, well within my self imposed five yard limit. I quickly drew, swung and released my arrow at the disappearing bird. The arrow rapidly caught up to and then passed by the bird with the feathers of the arrow just brushing the young rooster's wing - so close!

I had several more shots that day but no hits. Still the day's events had left me excited. Not only was I convinced that eventually I would be able to hit a ringneck, actually being able to see how close the arrow came to hitting the bird was thrilling. At times the miss was by mere inches, then again sometimes the misses were measured in feet. Nevertheless, I was sure it was just a matter of time before we scored on a pheasant.

I didn't have long to wait. The next day, on the second bird I shot at, the arrow connected solidly with the bird's right wing, and down came my quarry. As the bird was struggling to get its feet under it, I sent Dutchess for the retrieve. When she brought the still very much alive bird to hand, I took note of the bird's badly broken wing and quickly finished the job that the arrow had started. The rest of that particular hunt remains a blur, other than how good the weight felt in my game bag, and the feeling of accomplishment I carried for several days afterward.

Since that first season, I have learned many things that make this type of hunting more enjoyable, which is my sole purpose in hunting in the first place. First, if your objective is to kill your limit each time out, forget it. If on the other hand you enjoy walking the fields, and love watching your dog work, it has some real potential to enhance your hunting experience. Second, I would strongly recommend hunting over a pointing dog. In my experience spaniels and other flushing breeds too often flush out of effective bow range. Pointing breeds on the other hand, with cooperative birds, will let the hunting archer get in position for a shot that has a reasonable chance of connecting. Also essential is the ability of your dog to track down and retrieve cripples, like my first wing shot bird. Third, equipment - any hunting draw weight bow will work well for birds, however, "stick" bows - recurves and longbows - are best suited for the fast swing, draw, point, and release of bird shooting. Forget about trying to use any type of sighting system, you just won't have the time. Arrows as described above work very well. What I have found is that a solid body hit will usually kill a bird instantly, as will one of the wire loops striking the bird in the neck. The wire loops will also break wings very easily, and a good dog can recover a wing-crippled bird. In the last seven years I have never lost a solidly arrow-hit bird.

On the average over the last several years, I have hit and killed about one bird out of every ten to twelve at which I have taken shots. I get to shoot at about one in five birds that my dog actually works. As any experienced upland hunter will attest, that is a lot of birds to move. To help increase the number of bird contacts in any given year, I occasionally go to a local pheasant shooting preserve where I am allowed to shoot hens as well as roosters. This simply increases the odds of bagging a bird on any given day.

Waterfowl

DUCKS

Between 1992 and 1996, an average of 417,033 ducks were harvested annually with 482,575 harvested in 2000. Mallards comprised nearly 47 percent of the annual harvest, followed by American widgeon (14 percent) and green-winged teal (12 percent).

Dabbling Ducks

Dabbling ducks, often called puddle ducks, are so named because they frequent shallow water, where they feed by tipping and reaching underwater with their heads and necks. Dabblers jump straight off the water with powerful wings. In Washington, a variety of dabbling ducks occur on virtually all water types, including slow-moving rivers, small ponds and lakes, marshes, large sump lakes, and estuaries. Dabblers, especially mallards, widgeon, pintail, and gadwall, often feed in grain stubble. With the exception of the rare Eurasian widgeon, all of the dabblers that occur in Washington also nest within the state, but northern migrants comprise a majority of most species by late autumn. Color, wing pattern, and flight characteristics are major aids in identifying the different species.

Bob Ferris' Pudelpointer enjoys a successful retrieve.

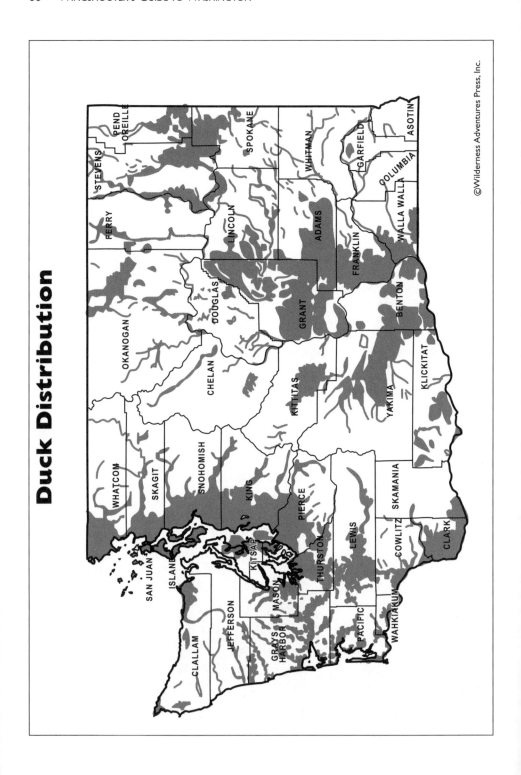

Duck Distribution

©Wilderness Adventures Press, Inc.

Hunting Methods

Due to their widespread distribution and the variety of wetland habitats available to them in Washington, dabbling ducks present myriad opportunities for all kinds of hunting. Most dabblers respond to decoy spreads and calling, and these classic methods remain the foundation of duck hunting on most water types. In some places (sheltered ponds, creeks, canals), jump shooters can find excellent sport. Even pass-shooting can be productive.

Regardless of method, duck hunting peaks at dawn and dusk when dabblers are on the move between feeding and roosting areas. Inclement weather only improves hunting because wind and rain causes ducks to stir and move more frequently. All-day hunting often accompanies storm fronts. Understanding the schedule and flight routes used by ducks in a particular place allows hunters to set up in the right places at the appropriate times.

Many dabbling ducks circle above to survey decoy spreads before pouring in to the landing zone. Mallards, pintail, and widgeon frequently approach in this manner. Teal and shoveler often buzz decoy spreads, flying directly in or over — wood ducks are apt to do this as well. Early in the season, when locally produced birds comprise the bulk of the duck population, hunters often find that most species respond readily to calling and decoying. Later, after birds have been shot at quite a bit and when the northern migrants arrive, they are more wary.

The mix of dabbler species in Washington varies somewhat from region to region. Mallards, pintail, and widgeon abound everywhere. Northern shovelers are widely dispersed across the state. In eastern Washington, cinnamon teal and gadwall are quite abundant, whereas locally produced blue-winged teal, though common in eastern Washington, tend to depart early in the fall. In western Washington, green-winged teal are prevalent, but there are also tremendous flocks of widgeon, especially along the coast, and along the lower Columbia. The largest and most spectacular flocks of mallards assemble during late fall in the Columbia Basin of southeastern Washington, where tens of thousands of birds form massive flocks that descend on large fields of grain stubble.

Gun and Shot Suggestions

Gauge — 10 and 12; 16 and 20 for close range decoy shooting or teal hunting.

Choke — Modified or modified/improved for double guns.

Shot — Only federally approved, nontoxic shot may be used for waterfowl hunting. No. 4, 2, or BB size shot is ideal, and light "scatter" loads of No. 6 are ideal for dispatching cripples.

Pintail.

Species and Identification

MALLARD — *Anas platyrhynchos*

Length	20 to 28 inches.
Male	Bright green head and dark, chestnut-colored breasts; white belly and white under wing linings; black rump; yellow bill; and bright orange feet.
Female	Mottled brown orange bill with black spotting.
Wing	Dark gray above with purple speculum bordered on both sides by white bands.
Identification in Flight	Large size; powerful and direct flight; dark head, neck, and breast (male).
Common Range	Found throughout the state.

NORTHERN PINTAIL — *Anas acuta*

Length	20 to 30 inches.
Male	Large, streamlined duck with long, pointed tail; gray mantle highlighted with black and white; white throat and breast; brown head with white streak extending up along sides; blue bill with black streak on top.

Eurasian widgeon.

Female	Mottled brown but paler than female mallard bill similar to males.
Wing	Long and sleek with copper-colored speculum bordered on the trailing edge by white.
Identification in Flight	Long neck and streamlined appearance evident; graceful and fast.
Common Range	Found throughout the state.

AMERICAN WIDGEON — *Anas americana*

Length	18 to 23 inches.
Male	Rust-colored breast and flanks; white belly; large, iridescent green eye streak that covers a full third or more of the face and back of the neck; white cap and forehead; black-and-white speckled cheeks and throat; blue bill with black base and tip.
Female	Rust-colored flanks; mottled brown above; bill same as in male; juvenile males similar but often showing some green in the head.
Wing	Entire shoulder covered by white patch that is quite evident in flight; white shoulder most evident in males; green speculum.
Identification in Flight	Combination of white shoulder and characteristic wavering; flight whistle identifies this medium-sized duck; flight is usually rapid and often erratic; compact flocks.
Common Range	Found throughout the state.

Gadwall.

EURASIAN WIDGEON — *Anas penelope*

Length	16 to 20 inches.
Male	Eurasian widgeon are grayer overall than American widgeon rust-colored head with cream-colored crown and forehead large white wing patch.
Female	Eurasian females are similar to the female American widgeon.
Wing	Same as American widgeon.
Identification in Flight	This regular visitor along the Pacific coast is most often seen as a single specimen among a flock of American widgeon or some times with flocks of mallards or pintail.
Common Range	Found only occasionally along the coast.

GADWALL — *Anas strepera*

Length	18 to 23 inches.
Male	Grayish overall with distinctive black rump; white belly; unique head profile (sharply sloping, high forehead) black bill.
Female	Gray brown overall; white belly; orange bill with black spots.
Wing	White patch in speculum bordered above in the male by a rust-colored band.
Identification in Flight	Medium-sized; streamlined; white belly and wing linings sharply bordered by darker feathers; fast, somewhat erratic.
Common Range	Abundant numbers in eastern Washington; numbers are increasing in western Washington.

NORTHERN SHOVELER — *Anas clypeata*

Length	18 to 20 inches.
Male	Have a huge bill; green head; white breast; rust-colored flanks and belly.
Female	Huge bill; mottled brown overall.
Wing	Entire shoulder is light blue gray; green speculum.
Identification in Flight	Large bill; blocky appearance; contrast between dark head, white breast, dark belly (male); small flocks.
Common Range	Found throughout Washington.

GREEN-WINGED TEAL — *Anas crecca*

Length	12 to 16 inches (smallest dabbler).
Male	Striking coloration includes tan breast spotted with black, silvery gray flanks, yellow under-tail coverts, and cinnamon-colored head with green eye stripe.
Female	Mottled brown and tan overall.
Wing	Green speculum long and narrow.
Identification in Flight	Quick, twisting and turning flight; swift wing beats; tightly formed flocks that dive, twist, and turn in unison; green speculum.
Common Range	Found throughout Washington, especially abundant in western Washington.

CINNAMON TEAL — *Anas cyanoptera*

Length	14 to 17 inches.
Male	Rich cinnamon red overall with blue-gray wing coverts visible in flight.
Female	Mottled brown overall (essentially indistinguishable from female cinnamon teal).
Wing	Blue gray coverts (shoulders) and green speculum.
Identification in Flight	Small flocks, fast, erratic flight.
Common Range	Most common in eastern Washington but occurs throughout the state.

Cinnamon teal.

Blue-winged teal.

BLUE-WINGED TEAL — *Anas discors*

Length	14 to 16.5 inches.
Male	Striking slate gray head with white crescent in front of eye; tan flanks and breast spotted with black.
Female	Mottled brown and tan overall, (essentially indistinguishable from female cinnamon teal).
Wing	Blue gray coverts (shoulders) and green speculum.
Identification in Flight	Fast and erratic; twisting and turning in small, compact flocks.
Common Range	Primarily found in eastern Washington; migrates south early.

WOOD DUCK — *Aix sponsa*

Length	15 to 21 inches.
Male	The most colorful of North American waterfowl; unmistakable in its stunning array of color and pattern.
Female	Grayish overall with soft crest and white eye patch and speckled breast.
Wing	Purple speculum.
Identification in Flight	Erratic flight often accompanied by distinctive call; distinctive long tail.
Common Range	Found throughout the state but most common in western Washington

Wood duck drake.

Diving Ducks

Washington offers extensive habitat for diving ducks. Coastal bays and estuaries provide expansive migrating and winter range for divers of many species. Washington's large rivers also host good numbers of diving ducks. Huge rafts of scaup, for example, assemble on the Columbia River. Some diving ducks — the ring-neck being the most obvious — are closely tied to freshwater while others (at least during the winter) rarely venture away from the saltwater environs. Among the species found predominantly along the coast are the harlequin duck and red-breasted merganser. Among waterfowlers, the most sought-after divers include canvasback, redhead, and scaup. Others — especially mergansers and buffleheads — are of little interest to most duck hunters. Many diving ducks respond to decoy spreads, but hunters who specialize in pursuing canvasback, redhead, and scaup employ special tactics. These ducks often occur in large rafts on big, open waters, where large, species-specific decoy spreads and sink-boats produce the best results.

Hunting Methods

Most diving duck hunting occurs incidentally to hunting for dabblers. Some species of divers — buffleheads, goldeneyes, ring-necked ducks, and hooded mergansers, for example — respond readily to spreads of decoys intended for dabblers. Often, divers swim into the decoy spreads. Less desirable targets, such as buffleheads, make great natural decoys when allowed to swim along and feed among the hunter's decoys.

Purposeful hunting for divers generally centers on the most desirable species: canvasback, scaup, and redheads. On some of Washington's bays and estuaries, sink-boat hunters can work over large rafts of decoys. Without the benefit of a sink-boat, which are rarely seen these days, set up large species-specific decoy spreads along likely flight paths. Often a point of land jutting well into the bay or estuary provides the best opportunity for decoying divers, which head straight into the decoys without circling like the dabblers.

On estuaries, cover is at a premium, especially out on points and exposed shorelines. Use natural materials to construct a blind against an old root-wad or tree trunk or use stakes and camo netting to arrange a ground blind on open shores.

Often a mixed spread of dabbler and diver decoys produces excellent results, especially in areas where both types of ducks abound. Use one type or the other as the main spread, then arrange the others some distance away. A large raft of diver decoys, arranged in lines, can be bolstered with the addition of a dozen mallard decoys set closer in or grouped inside and to one side. Similarly, a dozen or so bluebill or canvasback decoys might be clustered outside a main spread of dabbler decoys.

Gun and Shot Suggestions

Gauge — 10 or 12.

Choke — Modified for open water; modified/improved for smaller waters.

Shot — Only federally approved nontoxic shot may be used for waterfowl hunting. Number 2, BB, or BBB for large open-water divers; Number 4, 2, or BB for ring-necked ducks and other small divers.

Species and Identification

CANVASBACK — *Aythya valisineria*

Local Names	"Cans"
Length	19 to 22 inches.
Male	Gleaming white back and flanks contrasting vividly with black breast; chestnut red head; distinctive slope to the forehead and bill.
Female	Grayish back, sandy brown head, distinctive slope to forehead and bill.
Wing	White and light gray.
Identification in Flight	Distinctive black-white-black pattern of male's body; flickering of white in the wings; rapid wing beat and fast, direct flight; wedge-shaped flocks.
Common Range	Found throughout the state.

Canvasbacks.

REDHEAD — *Aythya americana*

Length	18 to 22 inches.
Male	Black breast and rump contrasting with white belly and gray back; bright red head; blue bill tipped in black.
Female	Dark rusty brown overall with blue bill tipped in black.
Wing	Pale gray secondaries contrast with darker shoulders.
Identification in Flight	Male's black-white-black body pattern; pale gray secondaries; low, direct flight in compact, wedge-shaped flocks.
Common Range	Found throughout the state, but most common in eastern Washington.

RING-NECKED DUCK — *Aythya collaris*

Local Names	Bluebill, ring-billed duck.
Length	14 to 18 inches.
Male	Small, dark duck with gleaming white flanks; white vertical stripe on sides below neck; dark gray bill with a white ring at the base and near the tip and with a black tip; peaked crown.
	Dark gray brown overall faint white eye ring, bill like males but less striking.
Wing	Black with gray stripe along trailing edge.
Identification in Flight	Fast, agile flight; twisting and turning; generally in small flocks but may raft in large concentrations.
Common Range	Mostly in western Washington, but some found throughout.

LESSER SCAUP — *Aythya affinis*

Local Names	Bluebill.
Length	15 to 18 inches.
Male	Glossy purple head, which often appears black; black breast; white belly, flanks and mantle; at close range and in hand, duck's mantle is heavily vermiculated with black; blue bill; head pointed toward the rear.
Female	Head shape same as male; brown head and breast; gray brown flanks and mantle; white patch surrounds base of bill.
Wing	Distinctive, black leading edge contrasts vividly with broad white stripe extending through secondaries, then bordered on the trailing edge by a narrow dark stripe.
Identification in Flight	Wing pattern is distinctive and also aids in separating the lesser scaup from the similar greater scaup. Flight typically low, direct, and fast.
Common Range	Found throughout, but most numerous in eastern Washington's large marshes and along the Columbia River.

Canvasbacks.

GREATER SCAUP — *Aythya marila*

Local Names	Bluebill.
Length	15 to 20 inches.
Male	Glossy greenish head that typically appears black; black breast and rump; white belly, flanks and mantle; mantle vermiculated with black but not so heavily as in lesser scaup. Head shape rounded instead of peaked; pale blue bill.
Female	Brown overall, flanks lighter, back gray brown, trace of white at base of pale blue bill.
Wing	Distinctive; white stripe extends through secondaries and well into primaries and is bordered in front by black shoulders and at the rear by a narrow black lining.
Identification in Flight	Distinctive wing pattern; low, fast, direct flight.
Common Range	Mostly found in western Washington, specifically along the coast and lower Columbia River.

Common goldeneye.

COMMON GOLDENEYE — *Bucephala clangula*

Local Names	Whistler.
Length	16 to 20 inches.
Male	Large, plump black-and-white duck; head is rounded and glossy dark green, often appearing black with round white spot in front of yellow eye; neck, breast, belly and flanks bright white; mantle and rump black; black bill.
Female	Gray body and large, rounded brown head.
Wing	Black with broad, square white patch extending most of the way across inner half of wing.
Identification in Flight	Distinctive white wing patch; wings whistle loudly; fast, direct flight, typically in small flocks, often flying high.
Common Range	Found throughout the state.

BARROW'S GOLDENEYE — *Bucephala islandica*

Local Names	Whistler.
Length	16 to 20 inches.
Male	Generally similar to common goldeneye, but head glossy purple with crescent-shaped white patch in front of eye; more extensive black on back.
Female	Brown head and gray brown body yellowish bill.
Wing	Similar to common goldeneye but with narrow black stripe extending across white patch.
Identification in Flight	Distinctive white wing patch; wings whistle loudly; fast, direct flight, typically in small flocks, often high.
Common Range	Found throughout, but mostly in western Washington.

RUDDY DUCK — *Oxyura jamaicensis*

Local Names	Stiff-tailed duck.
Length	15 to 16 inches.
	During fall and winter, male is grayish overall with lighter checks contrasting with brown cap; long, stiff tail; broad flat bill; (breeding season male is rusty throughout with a black head, large white cheek patch, and bright blue bill).
Female	Similar to winter male but with dark line across light check.
Wing	Gray.
Identification in Flight	Rapid wing beats, low, direct flight long tail.
Common Range	Found throughout the state.

BUFFLEHEAD — Bucephala albeola

Common Names	Butterball.
Length	13 to 15 inches.
Male	Tiny in size but plump; brilliant pattern of black and white; glossy black head with large white patch extending over back half of crown; large white wing patches with black stripes at base of wings and down center of back; gleaming white flanks and breast.
Female	Also tiny but plump brownish overall with small white patch behind eye.
Wing	Male's wing black at tip, white through center and black at base; female has gray wings with a small white patch on the inner secondaries.
Identification	Low to water, fast and direct, sometimes twisting and turning as they follow narrow watercourses.
Common Range	Found throughout the state.

HOODED MERGANSER — *Lophodytes cucullatus*

Local Names	Hoody.
Length	16 to 19 inches.
Male	Spectacular black head with fanlike white crest outlined in black; black back; white breast with a vertical white stripe dividing two black stripes at the front of rust-colored flanks; long, white-edged tertials; small, thin black bill.
Female	Soft gray overall with cinnamon brown, fanlike crest.
Wing	Both sexes have small white speculum; males have gray patch along leading edge of shoulder.
Identification in Flight	Fast and streamlined in flight; note male's wing pattern.
Common Range	Found in western Washington.

COMMON MERGANSER — *Mergus merganser*

Local Name	Fish duck.
Length	22 to 27 inches.
Male	Very large with bright white breast, belly, and flanks; black back; green head; long, narrow, bright red bill.
Female	Gray with white belly and breast; brown, crested head; long, thin red bill.
Wing	Male has extensive white speculum and shoulder patch; female has gray shoulders and small white speculum.

Identification in Flight	Low, fast flight; very large size.
Common Range	Found throughout the state.

RED-BREASTED MERGANSER — *Mergus serrator*

Length	19 to 26 inches.
Male	Very large; green head with shaggy crest; white collar; bright red bill; tan, spotted breast; black mantle with black extending down sides in front of shoulders; gray flanks.
Female	Brownish gray, lighter below but with no distinct border between lighter under-parts and darker upper parts as in common merganser; thin red bill; cinnamon-colored head with shaggy crest; red eye.
Wing	Males with white inner wing divided by two thin black bars; females have small white speculum.
Identification in Flight	Fast, low and direct males with much less white on body than common merganser.
Common Range	Coastal.

Harlequin ducks.

Sea Ducks

Sea ducks are rarely targeted by waterfowlers, but are sometimes killed incidentally on the coastal estuaries and lakes. Two scoters — the white-winged and the surf scoter — are common all along the Washington coast. Black scoters are less abundant. Scoters are large, black, heavy-bodied ducks and are common inside bays and harbors, especially during stormy weather. The beautiful oldsquaw is an uncommon visitor to the Washington coast, but hunters take a few each year. The Harlequin — one of the world's most beautiful and striking ducks — winters along the coast in good numbers but is seldom available to hunters because of its preference for rocky surf zones and jetties. Harlequins nest along rushing mountain streams, then descend to the coast for the winter.

Hunting Methods

In Washington, hunters targeting dabblers and divers on coastal bays and estuaries typically harvest sea ducks incidentally. See hunting methods for divers.

HARLEQUIN DUCK — *Histrionicus histrionicus*

Local Names	"Lords and Ladies."
Size	14 to 19 inches.
Male	Spectacular and unmistakable pattern of white slashes and spots against a rich gray plumage with ruddy flanks; white teardrop-shaped crescent in front of eye.
Female	Grayish overall with dark gray head marked with white spots behind the eye and at the base of the bill.
Wings	Dark wings, male having small, inconspicuous white spots on inner half.
Identification in Flight	Male's gray white pattern is evident, including white stripes extending down the length of the back; smallish and plump with long tail; flight usually fast and direct; small flocks.
Common Range	Winters along the coast; breeds along mountain streams.

WHITE-WINGED SCOTER — *Melanitta fusca*

Length	19 to 24 inches.
Male	Black with small white eye patch; red-orange bill with black knob.
Female	Dark brown with pale spots on sides of head
Wing	Dark with white speculum.
Identification in Flight	Low and direct flight, typically in lines white speculum.
Common Range	Coastal but occasionally found on large bodies of fresh water (especially after severe coastal storms).

BLACK SCOTER — *Melanitta nigra*

Local Names	Butterbill, common scoter.
Length	17 to 21 inches.
Male	Large and all black; males have orange knob at base of bill.
Female	Dark gray brown with pale cheek patch.
Wing	All dark, but silvery under-wing linings contrast with darker leading edge.
Identification in Flight	Silvery wing linings; flight is fast and direct.
Common Range	Coastal.

SURF SCOTER — *Mellanita perspicillata*

Local Names	Skunkhead, goggle goose.
Length	17 to 21 inches.
Male	All-black body; black head with bright white patch on forehead and back of neck; large multicolored bill.
Female	Dark brown overall with pale spots on cheeks.
Wing	All dark with no white.
Identification in Flight	Strong, direct flight, often in lines low over the water; lands on water with wings extended up over the back.
Common Range	Coastal.

OLDSQUAW — *Clangula hyemalis*

Length	16 to 21 inches.
Male	In winter, white head with darker marks; black-and-white back pattern; long, black, pointed tail; black wings.
Female	White head with darker patches; dark back; short, stubby bill.
Wing	All dark.
Identification in Flight	Quick and direct; all dark wings; male's long tail.
Common Range	Rare winter visitor to coastal waters.

Surf scoter.

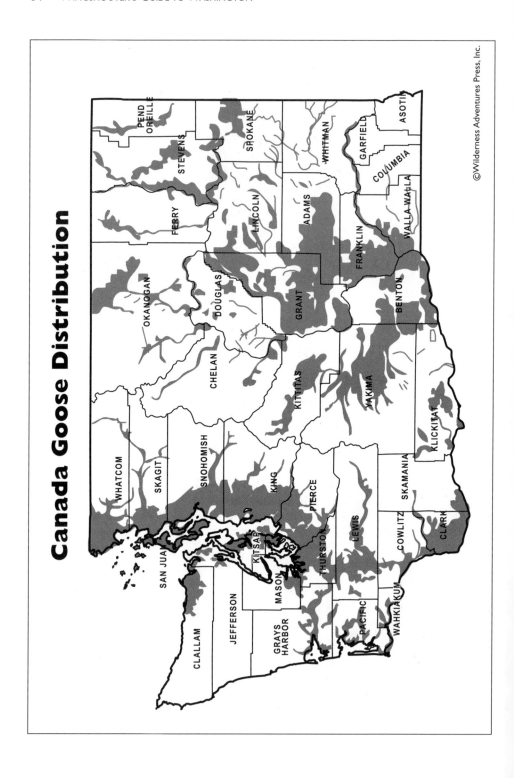

Canada Goose Distribution

Sleeping Canada goose and chicks.

Geese

Of the 11 recognized subspecies of Canada goose, Washington is home to seven, including wintering populations of the threatened dusky and Aleutian races. Others include the lesser, cackling, Western, Vancouver, and Taverner's Canada geese. The existence of dusky and Aleutian geese in western Washington has a profound impact on the management of hunting seasons for the other, far more numerous subspecies.

Washington's second most numerous goose is the snow goose, which is most abundant in eastern Washington, where Summer Lake and Malheur Lake attract huge migrating flocks of these beautiful, white geese. Geese stage on these areas and each day, during their travels from feeding to staging and roosting locations, the massive flocks present one of nature's most stunning spectacles in the form of huge, undulating waves of elegant and noisy white geese. Mixed among the snow geese in eastern Washington are a few very similar but noticeably smaller Ross' geese, a few of which are harvested each year by hunters.

The white-fronted goose occurs throughout much of the state in small, migrating flocks. They are more common east of the Cascades. White-fronted geese, often called "specklebellies," migrate through Washington early, so the best hunting opportunity occurs during the first half of October (be sure to check opening dates). White-fronted geese sometimes mix with flocks of Canada geese, so be sure of your target.

Black brant, medium-sized geese that are closely tied to estuarine environments, winter in small numbers at various locations along the Washington coast. Brant hunters are afforded a short November season and should scout flocks ahead of time to determine the birds' movements in relation to tide levels.

Hunting Methods

Goose hunting in Washington takes many forms, but gunners who use decoys and calls experience the most consistent success, especially on snow geese, but also on Canada geese and other species. In agricultural areas, hunters can set up large spreads to attract birds. Snow goose specialists use large numbers of decoys — often nothing more than "rag" decoys — to lure birds into range. Washington hunters harvest about 56,000 geese annually.

Gun and Shot Suggestions

Gauge — 10 or 12.

Choke — Modified or improved/modified for doubles.

Shot — Only federally approved nontoxic shot may be used for waterfowl. Use heavy loads: No. 1, BB, BBB, T or F.

Species and Identification

CANADA GOOSE — Branta canadensis

Identification   All subspecies share a black neck and head with full or partial white chinstrap; body deep rusty brown to light tan, depending on subspecies. Range from very large (westerns) too slightly larger than a mallard (cackling). Large western Canada geese weigh up to 12 pounds. Distinct honking call, but the pitch varies among species.

LESSER SNOW GOOSE — *Chen caerulescens*

Identification   Adults are pure white with black wing tips; highly vocal — call is a high-pitched, raspy "uk-uk." Weighs from 6 to 8 pounds.

ROSS' GOOSE — *Chen rossii*

Identification   Almost identical to the larger snow goose, but its bill is shorter and stubbier, lacking the black "lips" characteristic of the snow goose. Neck relatively shorter than that of the snow goose. Call similar to that of snow goose, but higher and less melodious. Weighs 4 to 6 pounds.

WHITE-FRONTED GOOSE ("Specklebelly") — *Anser albifrons*

Identification	An attractive brown goose with a white lower belly and dark blotches and bars on the upper belly and breast. Large pink bill outlined in white at its base. Adults have orange legs while juveniles have yellow legs. Average weight is about 6 pounds. The distinctive call is a melodious laugh-like series of three or four high-pitched "kow-kow-kow-kows."

BLACK BRANT — *Branta bernicla*

Identification	This medium-sized dark goose features a black breast, head, and neck. The neck is ringed with a broken white collar, and the flanks are streaked with white and brown. The under-tail coverts are white; bill and legs are black. Range is limited to coastal bays and estuaries during winter.

Identifying Waterfowl

The identification of ducks and geese is critically important to any hunter pursuing these species. While Washington state does not have a point system in determining bag limits, some species do have more stringent restrictions than others. For example only one Canvasback duck may be taken per day, and no more than two hen mallards per day. In addition, that big white bird coming toward your blind, may be a legal snow goose or an illegal swan.

It is not in the scope of this book to attempt teaching waterfowl identification. There are many good books and videotapes on this topic that cover color, size, shape, flight patterns, sound, etc. The best field guide for waterfowl (and upland birds for that matter) is Chris Smith's *Field Guide to Upland Birds and Waterfowl*, available from Wilderness Adventures, Inc. by calling 1-800-925-3339 (see page 73).

Additionally, Washington state has a specific Western Washington Goose Management Area, which requires the hunter to pass a goose identification test. As of 1998, the available training materials consisted of a home study booklet and a one-hour videotape entitled "Pacific Northwest Goose Management." The booklet is available at the Olympia and regional offices of the Washington Department of Fish and Wildlife. The videotape is available through Videoland Productions , Inc., 805 College Street SE, Lacey, WA 98503, at a charge of $10.00, including shipping and tax. Videoland Productions, Inc. accepts major credit cards, checks, and money orders. Their toll free number is 1-800-861-1342, the commercial number is 1-360-491-1332.

Testing schedules and locations information may be obtained from the Olympia office of the WDFW.

REGION I

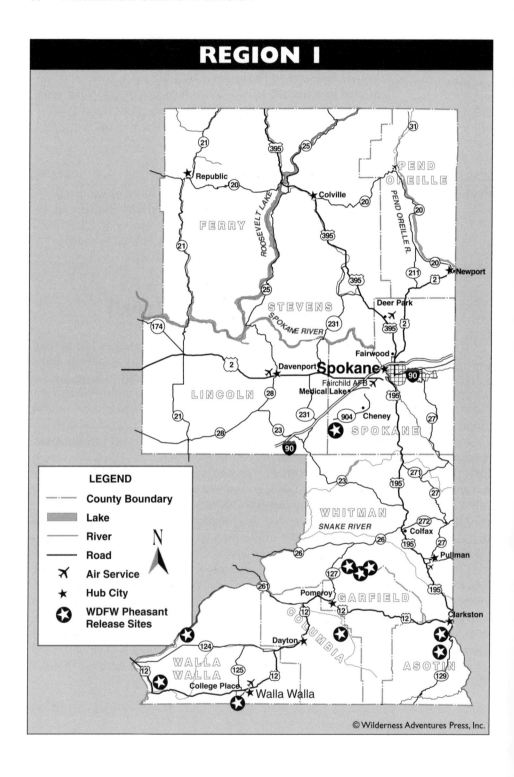

LEGEND

- County Boundary
- Lake
- River
- Road
- ✈ Air Service
- ★ Hub City
- ✪ WDFW Pheasant Release Sites

N

© Wilderness Adventures Press, Inc.

REGION I

Eastern Washington

This region includes Washington's ten easternmost counties from Canada to Oregon and from Idaho to the Columbia Basin. It is well known for its agriculture with a fairly equal mixture of timber, dryland and irrigated farming.

Alpine forests of the Selkirk Mountains in the north are home to endangered caribou and grizzly bears. Hungarian partridge and valley quail live in the central shrub steppe; elk, bighorn sheep, cougar, and black bear on the high plateaus and ridges of the Blue Mountains. Streamside and wetland habitats host a myriad of reptiles and amphibians, small mammals, songbirds, and waterbirds, like tundra swans and sandhill cranes. The northern timbered portion of Region 1 provides the best grouse hunting in the state, and pheasant hunting can be excellent in the central and southern areas of this region.

Four Washington Department of Wildlife Areas provide wildlife viewing and hunting opportunities. The region also includes two national wildlife refuges and two national forests. The Colville Forest includes two wildlife viewing sites cooperatively managed by the Department: Sullivan Lake Bighorn Sheep Winter Feeding Station and Flume Creek Mountain Goat Viewing Area.

The Blue Mountains of southeastern Washington are steep, hot and dry in the early season.

REGION I
Ring-necked Pheasant Distribution

© Wilderness Adventures Press, Inc.

1999-2000 Pheasant Harvest Information

County	Harvest	Hunters	Days	Hrv/Day
ASOTIN	2,005	887	2,718	0.74
COLUMBIA	6,703	1,600	6,916	0.97
FERRY	445	324	753	0.59
GARFIELD	7,483	2,045	7,394	1.01
LINCOLN	3,732	1,785	5,071	0.74
PEND OREILLE	185	14	6,445	0.42
SPOKANE	5,997	2,200	10,564	0.57
STEVENS	1,894	454	2,107	0.9
WHITMAN	14,056	4,336	20,601	0.68
REGION 1 TOTAL	**49,054**	**13,078**	**67,031**	**0.73**

Hunting in Conservation Reserve Program (CRP) lands.

REGION I
Valley Quail Distribution

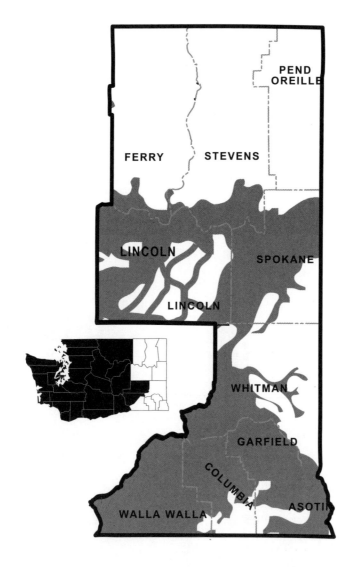

PEND OREILLE

FERRY

STEVENS

LINCOLN

SPOKANE

LINCOLN

WHITMAN

GARFIELD

COLUMBIA

WALLA WALLA

ASOTIN

© Wilderness Adventures Press, Inc.

1999-2000 Valley Quail Harvest Information

County	Harvest	Hunters	Days	Hrv/Day
ASOTIN	2,309	555	1,097	2.1
COLUMBIA	3,686	677	3,005	1.23
FERRY	446	178	1,288	0.35
GARFIELD	2,716	776	3,042	0.89
LINCOLN	4,579	773	2,330	1.97
PEND OREILLE	0	0	0	0
SPOKANE	5,161	1,113	4,639	1.11
STEVENS	291	179	302	0.96
WALLA WALLA	3,337	679	2,952	1.13
WHITMAN	5,336	1,386	5,802	0.92
REGION 1 TOTAL	**27,861**	**5,020**	**24,457**	**1.14**

Valley quail can often be found near grape vineyards.

REGION I
Chukar Partridge Distribution

PEND OREILLE

FERRY

STEVENS

SPOKANE

LINCOLN

WHITMAN

GARFIELD

COLUMBIA

WALLA WALLA

ASOTIN

© Wilderness Adventures Press, Inc.

1999-2000 Chukar Harvest Information

County	Harvest	Hunters	Days	Hrv/Day
ASOTIN	3,547	901	2,548	1.39
COLUMBIA	111	218	730	0.15
FERRY	0	0	0	0
GARFIELD	1,337	609	1,973	0.68
LINCOLN	148	198	394	0.38
PEND OREILLE	0	0	0	0
SPOKANE	55	145	193	0.28
STEVENS	0	0	0	0
WALLA WALLA	0	156	176	0
WHITMAN	1,875	748	2,385	0.79
REGION 1 TOTAL	**7,073**	**2,307**	**8,399**	**0.84**

Eastern Washington's high desert with broken coulees and cliffs provide excellent chukar habitat.

REGION I
Hungarian (Gray) Partridge
Distribution

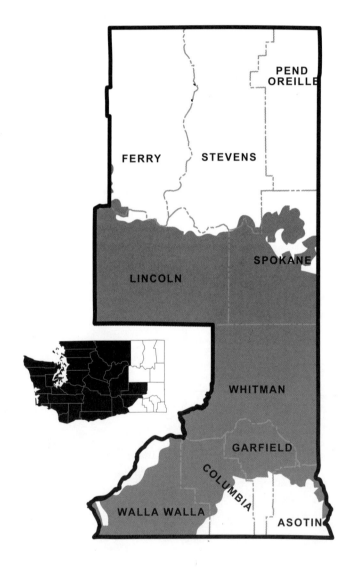

© Wilderness Adventures Press, Inc.

1999-2000 Gray (Hungarian) Partridge Harvest Information

County	Harvest	Hunters	Days	Hrv/Day
ASOTIN	1,651	563 1	609	1.03
COLUMBIA	352	293	1231	0
FERRY	0	0	0	0
GARFIELD	1,335	541	2,206	0.61
LINCOLN	1,187	733	1,998	0.59
PEND OREILLE	0	0	0	0
SPOKANE	1,224	625	3,484	0.35
STEVENS	0	0	0	0
WALLA WALLA	37	194	210	0.18
WHITMAN	2,875	1,248	5,226	0.55
REGION 1 TOTAL	**8,661**	**3,171**	**15,964**	**0.54**

Where wheat stubble and native grasses meet, Huns can usually be found.

REGION I
Forest Grouse Distribution

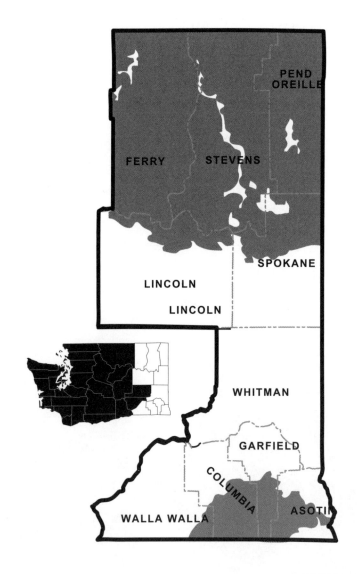

PEND
OREILLE

FERRY   STEVENS

SPOKANE

LINCOLN

LINCOLN

WHITMAN

GARFIELD

COLUMBIA

WALLA WALLA   ASOTIN

© Wilderness Adventures Press, Inc.

1999-2000 Forest Grouse Harvest Information

County	Harvest	Hunters	Days	Hrv/Day
ASOTIN	693	346	602	1.15
COLUMBIA	1,317	636	3,148	0.42
FERRY	5,153	1948	9,258	0.56
GARFIELD	277	437	1,498	0.18
LINCOLN	739	394	2,448	0.3
PEND OREILLE	60,08 1	683	8,750	0.69
SPOKANE	2,449	1,312	6,328	0.39
STEVENS	17,332	4,187	31,258	0.55
WALLA WALLA	1,594	406	1,986	0.8
WHITMAN	23	243	1,662	0.01
REGION 1 TOTAL	**35,585**	**8,954**	**66,938**	**0.53**

Mixed hardwood and conifer forests are excellent grouse habitat, typical of northeastern Washington.

REGION 1
Duck Distribution

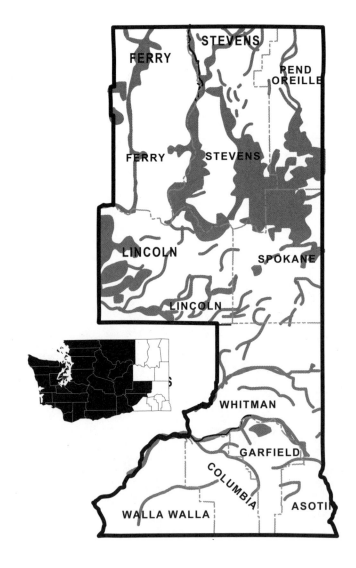

© Wilderness Adventures Press, Inc.

1999-2000 Duck Harvest Information

County	Harvest	Hunters	Days	Hrv/Day
ASOTIN	1,369	197	685	2
COLUMBIA	869	194	550	1.58
FERRY	1,924	221	2,231	0.86
GARFIELD	1,295	226	733	1.77
LINCOLN	16,190	1,622	7,141	2.27
PEND OREILLE	6,753	579	2,960	2.28
SPOKANE	11,490	1,309	6,516	1.76
STEVENS	2,794	544	2,081	1.34
WALLA WALLA	18,355	1,174	6,612	2.78
WHITMAN	5,643	746	4,179	1.35
REGION 1 TOTAL	**66,682**	**5,707**	**33,688**	**1.98**

A variety of duck species are available to waterfowlers in eastern Washington.

REGION 1
Canada Goose Distribution

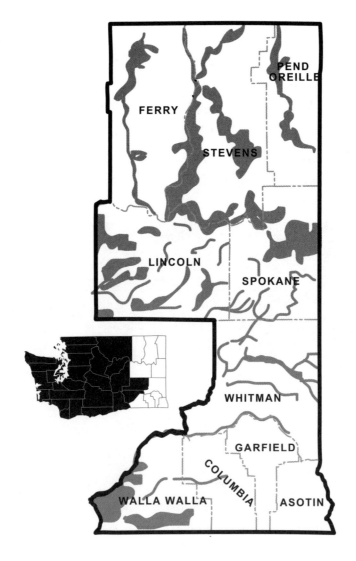

PEND OREILLE

FERRY

STEVENS

LINCOLN

SPOKANE

WHITMAN

GARFIELD

COLUMBIA

WALLA WALLA

ASOTIN

© Wilderness Adventures Press, Inc.

1999-2000 Goose Harvest Information

County	Harvest	Hunters	Days	Hrv/Day
ASOTIN	192	170	403	0.48
COLUMBIA	460	192	424	1.08
FERRY	921	235	1,224	0.75
GARFIELD	115	132	273	0.42
LINCOLN	4,397	1,214	4,490	0.98
PEND OREILLE	864	532	2,281	0.38
SPOKANE	3187	1,143	4,719	0.68
STEVENS	768	389	1,077	0.71
WALLA WALLA	2,861	586	1,704	1.68
WHITMAN	1,344	466	2,339	0.57
REGION 1 TOTAL	**15,109**	**3,685**	**18,934**	**0.8**

Canada geese take flight over an eastern Washington stubblefield.

Clarkston
and Asotin County

City Population - 6,750	County Population - 21,200
County Area - 1,900 sq. miles	October Average Temperature - 51.75°
Annual Precipitation - 12.9"	Acres in CRP - 21,397

Clarkston is the largest community in Asotin County and is the most southeasterly county in the state of Washington. The topography of Asotin County varies from rolling wheat fields to the foothills of the Blue Mountains. Clarkston, and its sister city, Lewiston, Idaho, are the gateway to Hell's Canyon on the mighty Snake River.

UPLAND BIRDS
Chukar, Quail, Pheasant, Hungarian Partridge, Ruffed Grouse, Dove, Blue Grouse

The rolling hills and Snake River Breaks provide many cliffs and edge habitat for upland game. Asotin is the number one chukar-producing county in the state due primarily to this rugged terrain. Wheat field edges and brushy draws provide cover for quail, pheasant and Huns. While most of the county is private land, there is good public access along the Grand Ronde River on Department of Wildlife lands and the western portion of the county contains part of the Umatilla National Forest.

WATERFOWL
Ducks, and Geese

The Snake and Grand Ronde rivers as well as Asotin and George Creeks provide decent waterfowling.

ACCOMMODATIONS
Astor Motel, 1201 Bridge St. / (509) 758-2509 / 8 rooms / Dining on site and nearby / Dogs allowed / $
Golden Key Motel, 1376 Bridge St. / (509) 758-5566 / 6 rooms / Dining on site & nearby, non-smoking rooms available / Dogs allowed / $
Hacienda Lodge Motel, 812 Bridge St. / (888) 567-2287
30 rooms / Dining on site & nearby, non-smoking rooms available / Dogs allowed / $-$$
Motel 6 - Clarkston, 222 Bridge St. / (509) 758-1631 / 85 rooms / Dining on site & nearby / Dogs allowed / non-smoking rooms available / $

CAMPGROUNDS AND RV PARKS
Golden Acres RV Park, 1430 Chestnut St. / (509) 758-9345 / 10 units / Full RV hookups.
Rainbows End Estates, 1325 Libby #13 / (509) 758-9586 / 18 units / Full RV hookups.

RESTAURANTS

Four-Ten Drive-In, 1296 Bridge St. / (509) 758-4908 / Open at 5:30 a.m., take out orders for breakfast, lunch and dinner.

Tomato Brothers, 200 Bridge St. / (509) 758-7902 / Pizza and pasta, casual Italian dining.

Station 23 Restaurant & Lounge / (509) 758-3288 /Gourmet sandwiches, burgers, steak, prime rib, and seafood. Open 9:00 a.m. to midnight 6 days a week.

Paraiso Vallart Mexican Restaurant, 518 Bridge St. / (509) 751-9077 / Family style lunch and dinner.

VETERINARIANS

Clarkston Veterinary Clinic, 1409 Peaslee Ave. / (509) 758-9669

SPORTING GOODS

Schurman's True Value Hardware, 801 6th St. / (509) 758-6411

Ron's Gun's, 510 3rd St/ (509) 758-0160

Tri-State, 120 Thain Road, Lewiston, ID / (877) 878-2835 / www.t-state.com

AUTO REPAIR

Brook's Auto Service, 1427 15th St. / (509) 758-7411

Earl's Shop, 1104 Boston St. (509)758-6594

Advance Radiator & Automotive, (509) 758-8867

AIR SERVICE

Lewiston-Nez Perce County Regional Airport, (208) 746-7962 / Horizon and United Express via air partnerships with Alaska, Northwest and United Airlines.

MEDICAL

Tri-State Memorial Hospital Inc., 1221 Highland Ave. / (509) 758-5511

BANKS WITH ATMS

Seafirst Bank, 748 6th St. / (509) 758-5544

US Bank, 615 6th St. / (509) 758-2584

FOR MORE INFORMATION

Clarkston Chamber of Commerce
502 Bridge St
Clarkston, WA 99403
(800) 933-2128

DAYTON
and Columbia County

Dayton Population - 2,558	County Population - 4,200
County Area - 553,000 sq. miles	October Temperature - 51.4°
Annual Precipitation - 18.5"	Acres in CRP - 26,134

Dayton, the county seat of Columbia County, is rich in history. The area was originally explored by Lewis and Clark on their return from the Pacific Ocean in 1806. The terrain is almost equally divided into rolling grain fields and the forested foothills of the Blue Mountains.

UPLAND BIRDS
Pheasant, Quail, Ruffed Grouse, Turkeys, Dove, Hungarian Partridge, Chukar, Blue and Spruce Grouse

Grain field edges, brushy draws, and creek bottoms provide excellent pheasant and quail cover, most of which is on private farm land, while the timbered hills and canyons hold good grouse numbers. For grouse and turkey hunters especially, the Umatilla National Forest provides plenty of public access to good hunting for those willing to burn some shoe leather.

WATERFOWL
Ducks and Geese

The Snake, Tucannon, and Touchet rivers provide the best opportunities for waterfowl hunters although occasionally some small farm ponds can hold a few birds.

ACCOMMODATIONS
Weinhard Hotel, 235 E. Main St. / (509) 382-4032 / 15 rooms / Dining on site & nearby, continental breakfast, non-smoking rooms, and dogs allowed, senior discounts / $$-$$$

Blue Mountain Motel, 414 W. Main St. / (509) 382-304 / 23 rooms / Dining on site & nearby, non-smoking rooms, and dogs allowed / $-$$

CAMPGROUNDS AND RV PARKS
Lyons Ferry Marina, P.O. Box 187 / (509) 399-2001 / 60 units / Dining on site & nearby, full breakfast / Dogs allowed, tent sites, boat launch, full RV hookups, showers / $

RESTAURANTS
Cracker B's Pub, 214 E. Main St. / (509) 382-2775 / Fine beers and good food, for lunch and dinner.

Gasoline Alley, 134 E. Main St. / (509) 382-2775 / Old fashioned burgers, fries and shakes.

Panhandlers Restaurant, 404 W. Main St. / (509) 382-4160 / Open 7 days a week, serving breakfast, lunch and dinner.

Woodshed Bar & Grill, 250 E. Main St. / (509) 382-2004 / Fine foods, spirits, beer, and wine, along with pool and darts 10:00 a.m. to 2:00 p.m. Monday through Saturday, and families are welcome.

Patit Creek Restaurant, 725 E. Dayton Ave. / (509) 382-2625 / The only four star restaurant in eastern Washington, reservations recommended.

VETERINARIANS

Dayton Vet Clinic, 127 W. Main St. / (509) 382-2661

SPORTING GOODS

Dingle's True Value of Dayton, 179 E. Main St. / (509) 382-2581

AUTO REPAIR

Bill's Auto Service, 218 W. Main St. / (509) 382-2162
Ricks Auto Repair, 109 S. Cottonwood St. / (509) 382-2154
Walker's Auto Repair, 326 W. Main St. / (509) 382-2341

AIR SERVICE

Walla Walla Regional Airport, Nearest to Dayton / Route 4, Box 177 H / Walla Walla, WA 99362 / (509) 525-2070
Served by Horizon Air (800) 547-9308

MEDICAL

Dayton General Hospital, 1012 S. Third St. / (509 382-2531

BANKS WITH ATMS

Seattle First National Bank, 306 E. Main St. / (509) 382-4771

FOR MORE INFORMATION

Dayton Chamber of Commerce,
(800) 882-6299

Republic
and Ferry County

Republic Population - 940	County Population - 6,295
County Area - 2,202 sq. miles	October Temperature - 42.6°
Annual Precipitation - 19.05"	Acres in CRP - 1,057

The town of Republic, seat of Ferry County, is located at the junction of State Routes 20 and 21. It is 130 miles northwest of Spokane and 35 miles south of Grand Forks, British Columbia, Canada. Republic is situated in the San Poil River Valley surrounded by the Colville National Forest.

UPLAND BIRDS
Ruffed, Blue, and Spruce Grouse, Turkey, Quail, Dove, and Pheasant

The timbered hills of this area provide good grouse and wild turkey hunting, with the forest grouse being the most popular game bird pursued here. The riverside habitat and farmland produce some pheasant, dove, and quail. Good public access is available as the county is approximately half Colville National Forest and half Colville Indian Reservation.

WATERFOWL
Ducks and Geese

Curlew, Swan, Ferry, and Fish lakes provide the waterfowler some decoy and blind hunting opportunities, while the San Poil River may be floated or jump-shot.

ACCOMMODATIONS
Frontier Inn Motel, 979 S. Clark Ave. / (509) 775-3361 / 30 rooms / Dogs allowed, dining on site or nearby, non-smoking rooms available, continental breakfast / $

K-Diamond-K Guest Ranch, 404 Hwy. 21 S. / (509) 775-3536 / 4 units/ Dogs allowed, dining and full breakfast on site or nearby, non-smoking rooms available / $$$

Klondike Motel, 150 N. Clark Ave. / (509) 775-3555
20 rooms / Dogs allowed / Dining on site or nearby, non-smoking rooms available / $

Northern Inn, 852 S. Clark Ave. / (509) 775-3371
25 rooms / Dogs allowed / Non-smoking rooms available / $

The clouds lie low and heavy over a Ferry County forest.

The body language of Dutchess says, "There's a bird right here!"

CAMPGROUNDS AND RV PARKS

Fishermans Cove Resort, 1157 Fishermans Cove Rd. / (888) 775-3641 / Dogs allowed, dining on site or nearby / $$

Tiffany's Resort, 1026 Tiffany Rd. / (509) 775-3152 / Dogs allowed, tent spaces, boat launch, full hookups, and showers / $-$$$

*In addition: Curlew Lake State Park, 974 Curlew Lake State Park Road, Republic, WA 99166. There are also US Forest Service campgrounds at Swan Lake, Ferry Lake and Fish Lake, all located up the Scatter Creek Road, and 10 campgrounds on the San Poil River.

RESTAURANTS

Eich's Mercantile, 21 N. Clark Ave / (509) 775-2846 / Luncheon specials.

San Poil Saloon / (509) 775-2139 / Lunch and after-hunt libations.

Hitch-in-Post/Back Alley Pizza / (509) 775-2221 / Pizza and sandwiches.

Hometown Pizza, 680 S. Keller / (509) 775-2557 / Pizza, sub sandwiches, salad bar

VETERINARIANS

All Creatures Veterinary Services, 1447 S. Clark Ave. / (509) 775-3544

K Diamond K Veterinary Clinic / (509) 775-3536

SPORTING GOODS

Republic Appliance, 15 N. Clark Ave. / (509) 775-3222

Harding Hardware, 85 N Clark / (509) 775-3368

Republic Sports Shop, 8 Creamery Rd. / (509) 775-3040

AUTO REPAIR

Smith & Sons Repair, 665 S. Newton St. / (509) 775-3941

AIR SERVICE

County Airport, 3,500 feet - Paved and lighted, six miles N.E. of Republic.

MEDICAL

Ferry County Memorial Hospital, 36 Klondike Rd. / (509) 775-3333

BANKS WITH ATMS

Bank Of America National Trust, 702 S. Clark St. / (509) 775-3315

FOR MORE INFORMATION

Visitor Information Center
P.O. Box 1024
Republic, WA 99166
(509) 775-3387

POMEROY
and Garfield County

Pomeroy Population - 1,400	County Population - 2,300
County Area - 710.5 sq. miles	October Temperature - 51.9°
Annual Precipitation - 17.37"	Acres in CRP- 25,066

Pomeroy is a small, rural farming community located near the Blue Mountains and the Snake River. Dryland wheat is the primary crop, but there is some irrigated alfalfa in the rolling Palouse country hills.

UPLAND BIRDS
Pheasant, Quail, Chukar, Hungarian Partridge, Turkeys, Dove, Ruffed and Blue Grouse

Farming edges, Snake River draws, and brushy draws hold good numbers of upland birds (good pheasant and quail hunting) while the timbered foothills and the Umatilla National Forest will prove fruitful for turkeys and grouse. Good public access is available in the southern portion of the county, in the Umatilla National Forest, and while the central and northern part of the county is mostly private, a polite request has a good chance of gaining access to a farmer's land.

WATERFOWL
Ducks and Geese

The Snake River is the primary waterfowl magnet in this area although jump shooting small creeks or ponds can sometimes be productive.

ACCOMMODATIONS

Pioneer Motel, 1201 Main St. / (509) 843-1559 / 11 rooms / Dining on site & nearby, non-smoking rooms / Dogs allowed, senior discounts / $-$$

CAMPGROUNDS AND RV PARKS

Central Ferry State Park, 10152 SR 127 / (509) 549-3551 / 68 sites / Dogs allowed, tent sites, boat launch, full RV hookups and dump, showers / $

RESTAURANTS

Donna's Drive-in, 1412 Main St. / (509) 843-1510 / Old fashioned diner type food- breakfast, lunch, and dinner, 6:00 a.m. to 9:00 p.m., seven days a week.

Pioneer Eatery, 1794 Main St. / (509) 843-1990 / Home style meals - breakfast, lunch and dinner served 8:00 a.m. to 10:00 p.m. Monday through Saturday, and 7:00 a.m. to 7:00 p.m. on Sundays with a brunch buffet available.

Up & Up Tavern, 870 W. Main St. / (509) 843-1165 / Open for lunch and dinner with a separate dining area available, or have dinner with adult libations. Hours are 10:00 a.m. to 9:00 p.m. Sunday through Thursday, Friday and Saturday 10:00 a.m. with the bar open until the patrons are gone or 2:00 a.m., which ever occurs first!

VETERINARIANS
Pomeroy Veterinary Clinic, 34 W. Main St. / (509) 843-1671

SPORTING GOODS
Meyers Hardware, 796 Main St. / (509) 843-3721

AUTO REPAIR
Fischer's Auto Repair, 996 Main St. / (509) 843-1911
Ken's Auto Repair, 747 Columbia St. / (509) 843-1615

AIR SERVICE
For nearest air service please see Clarkston and Asotin County.

MEDICAL
Garfield County Memorial Hospital, 66 N. 6th St. / (509) 843-1591

FOR MORE INFORMATION
Chamber of Commerce
80 7th St.
Pomeroy, WA 99367
(509) 843-1601

Southeastern Washington—where rolling hills and wheat fields merge with the foothills of the Blue Mountains.

DAVENPORT
and Lincoln County

Population - 1,730	County Population - 8,814
County Area - 2,187.5 sq. miles	October Temperature - 46.1°
Annual Precipitation - 13.2"	Acres in CRP - 66,525

The city of Davenport, county seat and largest town in Lincoln County, is a small rural community whose lifeblood is dryland wheat farming. Rolling hills, broken by rugged coulees and draws, make up the countryside. Lake Roosevelt, only 25 miles north, offers recreational opportunities, including good upland hunting along the lake edges, as well as waterfowl hunting on the lakes and its many coves. Davenport is located on Highway 2.

UPLAND BIRDS
Pheasant, Quail, Dove, Turkeys, Huns, Ruffed and Blue Grouse, and Chukar

Lincoln County is primarily "flatland" wheat farming country with coulee breaks. The field edges, brushy draws, breaks, and pond or creek edges provide the best habitat structure for upland hunting, with pheasant and quail being the primary quarry. The county is virtually all private land, with a few sections of BLM land thrown in. Knocking on doors and polite requests can gain you access on occasion.

WATERFOWL
Ducks and Geese

Small lakes, ponds and creeks, as well as the Spokane and Columbia rivers, provide a lot of potential for waterfowlers whether they are jump shooting, drifting, or setting up with decoys.

ACCOMMODATIONS
Black Bear Motel & RV Park, Hwy. 25 and US 2. / (509) 725-7700 / 11 units / Dining on site & nearby, non-smoking rooms available / Dogs allowed, full RV hookups and dumpsite / $
Davenport Motel, 1205 Morgan St. / (509) 725-7071 / 9 rooms / Dining on site & nearby, non-smoking rooms available / $

CAMPGROUNDS AND RV PARKS
Seven Bays, Rt..1 Box 624 / (509) 725-1676 / 38 units / Dining on site & nearby / Dogs allowed, full RV hookups, showers / $
In addition, Lake Roosevelt National Recreation Area, administered by the National Park Service, has campgrounds situated throughout. The campgrounds range from small boat-in campgrounds to vehicle campgrounds with boat launch facilities, flush toilets and dump stations. For more information call (509) 725-2715.

RESTAURANTS

Cottonwood Inn Restaurant & Lounge, 303 6th St. / (509) 725-2222 / Open for breakfast, lunch and dinner seven days a week, with an ever changing Sunday buffet.

Ellie's Great Food, 1325 Morgan St. / (509) 725-3354 / Open seven days a week at 6:00 a.m. for breakfast, lunch & dinner, with daily specials

The Hangar #1 Restaurant & Lounge, 499 Morgan St. / (509) 725-6630 / Relaxed family atmosphere, open Monday through Saturday, breakfast is seasonal, and they specialize in lunch and dinner.

VETERINARIANS

The nearest vet is in Reardan:

County Animal Care, 500 W. Broadway / (509) 796-7030

SPORTING GOODS

Davenport Building Supply, 801 Morgan St. / (509) 725-7131 / The only place in town for licenses and hunting supplies.

AUTO REPAIR

Elliott Motors, 735 Morgan St. / (800) 487-4379

AIR SERVICE

Nearest air service is Spokane International Airport 35 miles to the east. Served by commercial carriers - United, Delta, Alaska, Horizon, Northwest, Continental, and Southwest.

MEDICAL

Lincoln Hospital, 10 Nichols St. / (509) 725-7101

BANKS WITH ATMS

US Bank, 626 Morgan St. / (509) 725-5011
United Security Bank, 639 Morgan St. / (509) 455-5847

FOR MORE INFORMATION

Davenport Chamber of Commerce
P.O. Box 869
Davenport, WA 99122
(509) 725-6711

Lincoln County is characterized by broken wheat fields mixed with native grasses.

SPOKANE
and Spokane County

Population - 188,300	County Population - 409,900
County Area - 1,758 sq. miles	October Temperature - 46.0°
Annual Precipitation - 16.10"	Acres in CRP - 24,895

The city of Spokane is located along the eastern border of Washington state, and is the county seat for Spokane County. It is the largest city between Seattle and Minneapolis. Spokane is 18 miles west of the Idaho border and 110 miles south of the Canadian border. A major metropolitan area, Spokane is the hub of activity in eastern Washington. The terrain of Spokane County varies from rolling wheat fields to snow-capped mountains, and from lush forests to deserts.

UPLAND BIRDS
Pheasant, Quail, Ruffed Grouse, Dove, Hungarian Partridge, Blue Grouse, Chukar, and Spruce Grouse

Farm edges, brushy draws, and creek and river bottoms are the ticket here for pheasant and quail hunters with good numbers of both these birds and fair public access on Department of Wildlife and Federal Fish and Wildlife Service lands. Decent ruffed grouse hunting is found in the timbered foothills in the eastern portion of the county.

WATERFOWL
Ducks and Geese

Spokane County has many small creeks, ponds, and lakes, as well as the Spokane River, which bring waterfowl into the area, and will hold some birds until complete ice-over.

ACCOMMODATIONS
Angelica's B & B, 1321 W. Ninth Ave / (509) 624-5598 / The elegance of a fine European Manor with the charm of a cozy inn.

Ramada Inn - Spokane Airport, Spokane International airport. / (509) 838-5211 / 165 rooms / Dining on site & nearby, continental breakfast, non-smoking rooms available / Dogs allowed / Senior discounts / $$

Bel-Air Motel 7, E. 1303 Sprague St. / (509) 535-1677 / 17 rooms / Dining on site & nearby, non-smoking rooms available / Dogs allowed / $

Best Western Northpointe, 9601N. Newport Hwy. / (800) 888-6630 / 76 rooms. / Dining on site & nearby, continental breakfast, non-smoking rooms available / Dogs allowed / Senior discounts / $$

Cavanaugh's Inn at the Park, W. 303 N. River Dr. / (509) 326-8000 402 rooms / Dining on site & nearby, full breakfast / Non-smoking rooms available / Dogs allowed / Senior discounts / $$$

River Bluff Log House, 117 Covada Rd, Inchelium, WA / (509) 722-3784 / Secluded cabin in the woods with spectacular views of the river.

Dutchess quartering a field in northern Spokane County.

Two Spokane County hunters heading out for a day in the grouse woods.

CAMPGROUNDS AND RV PARKS

Klink's Williams Lake Resort, 18617 W. Williams Lake Rd., Cheney / (509) 235 2391

Mallard Bay Resort, S. 14601 Salnave Rd. / (509) 299-3830 / 50 units / Dogs allowed / Tent spaces, boat launch, full RV hookups and dump station, showers / $

Rainbow Cove RV & Fishing Resort, 12514 S. Clear Lake Rd. / (509) 299-3717 / 20 units / Dining on site & nearby, full breakfast / Dogs allowed, tent sites, boat launch, full RV hookups, showers / $

RESTAURANTS

Azteca, 200 W. Spokane Falls Blvd. / (509) 456-0350 / Award-winning Mexican food and Amigo style hospitality

The Bayou Brewing Company, 1003 E. Trent, (509) 484-4818 / Micro brewery, featuring Cajun cuisine / Live music / On the banks of the Spokane River

The Calgary Steak House, 3040 E. Sprague Ave. / (509) 535-7502 / Spokane's best steaks, serving lunch and dinner.

Ichi Shogun Restaurant, 821 E. 3rd Ave. (509) 534-777 / Asian cuisine, cooks a steak right before your eyes

Patsy Clark's Mansion, 2208 W. 2nd Ave. (509) 838-8300 / Award-winning continental cuisine in an unforgettable turn-of-the century mansion / Live pianist nightly / Open for lunch, dinner and Sunday brunch

Perkins Family Restaurant, 5903 N. Division St. / (509) 489-2160 / Open seven days a week for breakfast, lunch, and dinner. Open 24 hours on Friday and Saturday.

Mustard Seed, 245 W. Spokane Falls Blvd. /n(509) 747-2989 / Contemporary Asian restaurant with emphasis on fresh vegetable, leans meats and light sauces. Cocktails. Open for lunch and dinner.

Waffles N' More, 5312 N. Division St. / (509) 484-4049 / Breakfast served all day long.

RAM Family Restaurant/Big Horn Brewery, 988 N. Howard St. (509) 326-3745 / Good food and local microbrews.

Longhorn Barbecue, 2315 N. Argonne Rd. / (509) 924-9600 / For the hearty barbecue lover.

Milfords, 719 N. Monroe St. / (509) 326-7251 / Excellent seafood, dinner only.

The Old Spaghetti Factory, 152 S. Monroe St. / (509) 624-8916 / Very good pasta, open for lunch and dinner.

Casa de Oro, 4111 N. Division St. / (509) 489-3630 / Mexican favorites for lunch and dinner seven days a week.

VETERINARIANS

Spokane Valley Animal Hospital, 14219 E. Sprague Ave. / (509) 926-1062

AAA Evening Pet Clinic, 933 N. Washington St. / (509) 327-9354

SPORTING GOODS

All American Arms, 3601 East Boone Ave / (509) 536-3834
Big 5 Sporting Goods, 7501 N. Division St. / (509) 467-6970
Big 5 Sporting Goods, 5725 E. Sprague Ave. / (509) 533-9811
Brocks Gunsmithing, Inc. 2104 N. Division Street / (509) 328-9788
Creative Arms, 1200 N Freya Way / (509) 533-9801
General Store Ace Hardware, 2424 N Division St / (509) 444-8000
White's Outdoor, 4002 E Ferry Ave (509) 555-1875
Classic Guns of Spokane, 9119 E. Boone Ave. / (509) 926-4867
Ed's Gunatorim, 5323 N. Argonne Rd. / (509) 924-3030
Gart Sports, 15118 E. Indiana Ave. / (509) 891-1500 / (509) 446-2100
Outdoor Sportsman, 1602 N. Division St. / (509) 328-1556
White Elephant, 1730 N. Division St. / (328) 3100
White Elephant, 12614 E. Sprague Ave. (509) 924-3006

AUTO RENTAL AND REPAIR

Advanced Auto Technicians, 34 E. Trent Ave. / (509) 624-7793
Bateman Towing & Repair, 2406 E. Trent Ave. / (509) 534-0387
Alamo Rent A Car, (800) 327-9633
Thrifty Auto Rental, 5830 N. Division St. / (509) 483-7716

AIR SERVICE

Spokane International Airport, 9000 W. Airport Dr. / (509) 455-6455 / Commercial
carriers: Central Mountain Air/Air Canada, Alaska, America West, Delta,
Horizon, Northwest, Southwest, United.

MEDICAL

Deaconess Medical Center, 800 W. 5th Ave. / (509) 458-5800
Sacred Heart Medical Center, 101 W. 8th Ave. / (509) 455-3131

BANKS WITH ATMS

Virtually every downtown bank, the shopping malls, and the airport have ATMs
available.

FOR MORE INFORMATION

Spokane Area Convention and Visitors Bureau
801 W. Riverside Ave. Suite 301
Spokane, WA 99201
(509) 624-1341

COLVILLE
and Stevens County

Population - 4,700	County Population - 36,600
County Area - 2,500 Sq. miles	October Temperature - 47.8°
Annual Precipitation - 17"	Acres in CRP - 3,752

Colville is located in the forested mountains of northeastern Washington. The city of Colville is the business, educational, and population center of Stevens County. It is also the center of medical, cultural, timber, and manufacturing activities. The area's economy is based on timber, agriculture, mining, recreation, and tourism.

UPLAND BIRDS
Ruffed and Blue Grouse, Turkeys, Valley Quail, Pheasant, Spruce Grouse, and Dove

The Colville National Forest and the Little Pend Oreille Wildlife Area provide excellent habitat and hunting for grouse and turkeys. Stevens County has the highest ruffed grouse harvest in the state. The many rivers and agricultural lands that provide edge habitat are prime spots for quail and pheasant, although privately owned, a polite request can sometimes gain you permission to hunt.

WATERFOWL
Ducks and Geese

Deer and Loon lakes, as well as the many rivers and streams in this county provide good waterfowl hunting.

ACCOMMODATIONS
Lazy Bee Bed & Breakfast, 3651 Deeplake/Boundry Rd / (509)534-1426
4 rooms / Dogs allowed, dining on site & nearby, full breakfast, non-smoking rooms available.-$$

Maple at Sixth Bed & Breakfast, 407 E. 6th / (800) 446-2750 / 2 rooms / Dogs allowed / Dining on site & nearby, continental breakfast, non-smoking rooms available / $$

My Parents' Estate Bed & Breakfast, 719 Hwy. 395 / (509) 738-6220 / 5 rooms / No dogs / Full breakfast, non-smoking rooms available / $$

Beaver Lodge Resort and Campground, 2430 Hwy. 20 E. / (509) 684-5657
40 units plus full RV hookups / Dogs allowed / Dining on site & nearby, continental breakfast / $

Benny's Colville Inn, 915 S. Main St. / (509) 684-2517 / 106 rooms / Dogs allowed / Dining on site & nearby, non-smoking rooms available, senior discount / $-$$$

The Downtown Motel, 369 S. Main St. / (509) 684-2565 / 18 rooms / No dogs / Dining on site & nearby, non-smoking rooms available / $

CAMPGROUNDS AND RV PARKS
The Homeland RV Park & Campground, 4706 North Point Waneba Rd. / (509) 732-2565 / 30 units / Dogs allowed / Dining on site & nearby, senior discounts / $

Beaver Lodge - See above
In addition: Colville National Forest has 23 campgrounds for tents and RVs.

RESTAURANTS
Angler's Grill and Trophy Room, 995 S. Main St. / (509) 685-1308
Cookie Cafe, 157 N. Oak St. / (509) 684-8660
Ronnie D's Drive In, 505 N. Lincoln St. / (509) 684-2642 / Old fashioned burgers,
shakes, and fries.
Whistle Stop Diner, 695 N. Hwy. 395 / (509) 684-3424 Open 7:00 a.m. to 3:00 p.m.
Monday through Saturday, breakfast served till 11:00 a.m.
Woody's of Colville, 986 S. Main St. / (509) 684-4458 / Family style dining with
adult libations available. Open 7:00 a.m. to 9:00 p.m., Sunday through
Thursday, 7:00 a.m. to 10:00 p.m. weekends.

VETERINARIANS
Colville Animal Hospital, 572 S. Main St. / (509) 684-2102

SPORTING GOODS
Clark's All-Sports, 557 S. Main St. / (509) 684-5069
Wal-Mart, 810 N. Hwy. 395 / (509) 684-3209

AUTO REPAIRS
A. Automotive, 361 W. 5th St. / (509) 684-6945
Performance Motors, 240 Williams Lake Rd. / (509) 684-5767

AIR SERVICE
Ione Municipal Airport, Hwy 31, & Greenhouse Rd. / 18.5 miles from Colville

MEDICAL
Mount Carmel Hospital, 928 E. Columbia Ave. / (509) 684-2561

BANKS WITH ATMS
Key Bank, 211 S. Main St. / (590) 684-4591
Seafirst Bank, 225 E. 1st Ave. / (509) 684-2551
United Security Bank, 621 S. Main St. / (509) 684-5017
Washington Mutual, 298 S. Main St. #100 / (509) 684-528

FOR MORE INFORMATION
Colville Chamber of Commerce
P.O. Box 267
Colville, WA 99114
(509) 684-5973

WALLA WALLA
and Walla Walla County

Population - 28,930	County Population - 53,400
County Area - 1,261 sq. miles	October Average Temperature - 50.7°
Annual Precipitation - 14.42"	Acres in CRP - 93,887

Walla Walla is nestled in a valley at the foot of the Blue Mountains, a town rich in history and diverse in activity. Agriculture is a major industry; Walla Walla sweet onions are grown exclusively in this area, although wheat is the number one crop. The topography consists of rolling hills and the forested foothills of the Blue Mountains.

UPLAND BIRDS
Pheasant, Quail, Dove, Turkeys, Ruffed Grouse, Chukar, Hungarian Partridge, Blue, and Spruce Grouse

Varied agriculture, creek bottoms, and brushy draws provide the habitat that draws and holds most of the upland birds. Pheasant and quail are the most abundant species. The Blue Mountain foothills hold turkey and grouse. Public land is very limited in this county, so your best bet is to try and find a friendly local farmer.

WATERFOWL
Ducks and Geese

The Snake, Walla Walla, and Touchet rivers all hold good numbers of both local and migratory waterfowl. The McNary National Wildlife Refuge is also an excellent high demand public waterfowling area.

ACCOMMODATIONS

A & H Motel, 2599 Isaacs / (509) 529-0560 / 9 rooms / Dining on site & nearby / Dogs allowed / $

City Center Motel, 627 W. Main St. / (509) 529-2660 / 17 rooms / Dining on site & nearby, non-smoking rooms / Dogs allowed, senior discounts / $-$$

Capri Motel, 2003 Melrose St. / (800) 451-1139 / 40 rooms. Non-smoking rooms / Dogs allowed / Senior discounts / $$

Comfort Inn - Walla Walla, 520 N. 2nd / (509) 525-2522 / 61 rooms / Dining on site & nearby, continental breakfast, non-smoking rooms / Dogs allowed / Senior discounts / $$

Best Western Walla Walla Suites Inn, 7th E. Oak / (509) 525-4700 / 78 rooms / Dining on site & nearby, continental breakfast, non-smoking rooms / Dogs allowed / Senior discounts / $$-$$$

Howard Johnson Express Inn, 325 E. Main St. / (509) 529-4360 / 85 rooms / Continental breakfast / Dogs allowed / Senior discounts / $$$

CAMPGROUNDS AND **RV PARKS**
Country Estates, 938 Scenic View Dr, College Place / (509) 5442
Golden West Estates, 1424 Jasper St. / (509) 529-4890 6 units / Full RV hookups.
RV Resort Four Seasons, 1440 Dallas Military Rd. / (509) 529-6072
89 units / Dogs allowed / Full RV hookups, showers / $

RESTAURANTS
Red Apple Restaurant & Lounge, 57 E. Main St. / (509) 525-5113 / Open 24 hours
seven days per week with daily specials, moderate price
Cactus Grill, 320 S. 9th St. / (509) 525-5468 / Open daily at 11:00 a.m. serving
Mexican favorites for lunch and dinner.
Jacob's Cafe, 416 N. 2nd St. / (509) 525-2677 / Open for lunch and dinner seven
days per week with steak, seafood, ribs, pasta, microbrews and fine wines.
Moderately priced.
Golden Horse, 628 W. Main St. / (509) 525-7008 / Cantonese and Mandarin
favorites for lunch and dinner / Good prices.
Clarette's Restaurant, 15 S. Touchet / (509) 529-3430 / Family prices, breakfast
served all day.

Walla Walla is in the heart of Washington's agricultural country.

Veterinarians
Animal Clinic of Walla Walla, 2089 Taumarson Rd. / (509) 525-6111
Associated Veterinary Clinic, 208 Wildwood / (509) 525-2502

Sporting Goods
Bi-Mart, 1649 Plaza Way / (509) 529-8840

Auto Rental & Repair
Budget Rent-A-Car, Walla Walla Regional Airport / (509) 525-8811
Enterprise Rent-A-Car, 491 N. Wilbur / (509) 529-1988
Abajian Motor Sales, Inc., 606 N. Wilbur / (509) 525-1920
Teague Motor Co., 11 N. Colville / (509) 525-1520

Air Service
Walla Walla Regional Airport, Route 4, Box 177 H / (509) 525-2070
Horizon Air.

Medical
Walla Walla General Hospital, 1025 S. 2nd / (509) 525-0480

For More Information
Walla Walla Valley Chamber of Commerce
P.O. Box 644
Walla Walla, WA 99362
(509) 525-0850

Heading out for a Pend Oreille County grouse hunt.

PULLMAN
and Whitman County

Population - 25,562	County Population - 33,673
County Area - 2,159 sq. mi.	October Average Temperature - 48.3°
Annual Precipitation - 19.45"	Acres in CRP - 58,856

Pullman is nestled in eastern Washington's rolling hills and surrounded by farm-land, primarily wheat. Washington State University is found in Pullman and is responsible for nearly two-thirds of the city's population. The Palouse area is a photographer's dream, with rolling foothills, grain fields, and brushy creek bottoms. A National Geographic cover story called it, "A Paradise Called the Palouse."

UPLAND BIRDS
Pheasant, Quail, Hungarian Partridge, Chukar, Turkeys, Dove, Ruffed, Blue, and Spruce Grouse

Rolling wheat field edges, coulees, brushy draws and creek bottoms provide the edge cover most favored by upland game in this area. It is the top producer of both pheasant and Hun in the state. Most of the county is private land, so door knocking, smiling, and polite asking are valuable skills to bring with you.

WATERFOWL
Ducks and Geese

The Snake and Palouse rivers, Rock Lake, plus numerous small creeks and ponds hold good numbers of waterfowl during the season.

ACCOMMODATIONS

American Travel Inn, S. 515 Grand Ave. / (509) 334-3500 / 35 rooms / Dining on site & nearby, non-smoking rooms / Dogs allowed / Senior discounts / $

Best Western Heritage Inn, 928 N.W. Olsen St. / (509) 332-0928 / 59 rooms / Dining on site & nearby, continental breakfast, non-smoking rooms dogs allowed / Senior discounts / $$

Holiday Inn Express - Pullman, S.E. 1190 Bishop Blvd. / (509) 334-4437 / 130 rooms / Dining on site & nearby, continental breakfast, non-smoking rooms / Dogs allowed / Senior discounts / $$

Manor Lodge Motel, 455 S.E. Paradise / (509) 334-2511 / 31 rooms / Dining on site & nearby, non-smoking rooms / Dogs allowed / Senior discounts / $$

Nendels Motor Inn - Pullman, 915 S.E. Main St. / (509) 332-2646 / 60 rooms / Dining on site & nearby, non-smoking rooms / Dogs allowed / Senior discounts / $

Eastern Washington pine forests are excellent for mountain grouse hunting.

Campgrounds and RV Parks

Pullman Parks & Recreation Department, S.E. 325 Paradise / (509) 334-4555 / 24 RV sites with full hook-ups, plus tent sites, no showers / $

Restaurants

Cougar Country Drive-In, N. 760 Grand Ave. / (509) 332-7829 / Basic drive-in fare for lunch and dinner.

Nuovo Vallarta, 1110 N. Grand / (509) 334-4689 / "The Best Mexican Restaurant on the Palouse" - good south of the border food for lunch and dinner seven days per week.

Denny's Restaurant, S.E. 1170 Bishop Blvd. / (509) 334-5339 / Predictable food served 24 hours, seven days per week.

The Lotus Restaurant, 1005 E. Main St. / (509) 332-8270 / Chinese favorites for lunch and dinner seven days per week.

Hilltop Restaurant, Davis Way & Wawawai Rd. / (509) 332-8270 / Fine dining, also serving lunch, reservations required.

Veterinarians

Washington State University Veterinary Hospital, Pullman / (509) 335-0711 24-hour emergency care available from the top veterinary school in the West.

Sporting Goods

Rite Aid Pharmacy, 1630 S. Grand Ave. / (509) 334-1521

Tri-State, 1104 Pullman Rd, Moscow ID / (208) 882-4555

AUTO RENTAL AND REPAIR

U Save Auto Rental, 1115 S. Grand Ave. / (509) 334-5195
Budget Rent-A-Car, 3200 airport Complex N. / (509) 332-3511
Bauer Auto Repair, 640 S. Grand / (509) 334-5117
Jeff's Welding & Auto Repair, 2791 Albion Rd. / (509) 332-3629

AIR SERVICE

Pullman/Moscow Regional Airport, 3200 Airport Complex N. / (509) 334-4555
Horizon Air

MEDICAL

Pullman Memorial Hospital, 1125 N.E. Washington St. / (509) 332-2541

FOR MORE INFORMATION

Pullman Chamber of Commerce
415 N. Grand Ave.
Pullman, WA 99163
(800) 365-6948

*Rolling hills of the
Palouse wheat
country.*

NEWPORT
and Pend Oreille County

Population - 1,910	County Population - 11,500
County Area - 1,400.5 sq. miles	October Temperature - 45.1°
Annual Precipitation - 19.33"	Acres in CRP - 0

Newport is located in southeast Pend Oreille County and is the County Seat. It is at the end of the Pend Oreille River valley on the south bank of the Pend Oreille River, adjacent to the Idaho-Washington border at the intersection of U.S. Highways 2 and 195, State Highway 20 and Idaho State Highway 41. Forested hillsides and mountains ranging from 1,900 feet to 4,500 feet surround Newport.

UPLAND BIRDS
Ruffed, Blue, and Spruce Grouse, Pheasant, Quail, Turkey and Dove

The mountains and timber provide excellent habitat and hunting for forest grouse, the most popular species hunted here, and wild turkeys. Transition zones between agricultural areas and riverbanks, and forested land provide pheasant, quail, and dove hunting. The vast majority of the county is contained within the Colville and Kaniksu National Forests, so public access is excellent.

WATERFOWL
Ducks and Geese

The Pend Oreille River and its riparian zones provide miles of duck and goose hunting opportunities, by floating, decoying, or jump shooting. The river passes through the Colville and Kaniksu National Forests for the majority of its length, so there is plenty of access.

ACCOMMODATIONS
Golden Spur Motor Inn, 924 W. Hwy. 2 / (509) 447-3823 / 24 rooms / Dogs allowed / Dining on site & nearby, non-smoking rooms available, senior discounts.-$$
Newport City Inn, 220 N. Washington Ave. / (509) 447-3463 / 13 rooms / Dogs allowed / Dining on site & nearby, non-smoking rooms available, senior discounts / $

CAMPGROUNDS AND RV PARKS
Audrey's RV Park, 332391 N. Hwy. 2 / (509) 447-3220 / 18 units / Dogs allowed, tent spaces, senior discounts / $
Marshall Lake Resort, 1301 Marshall Lake Rd. / (509) 447-4158 / 42 units / Dogs allowed, tent spaces, full hookups / $

RESTAURANTS

Big Wheel Pizza, 201 N. Washington Ave. / (509) 447-5531
Golden China, 924 W. State Route 2 / (509) 447-2753 / Sunday through Thursday 11:30 a.m. to 9:00 p.m., Friday and Saturday 11:30 a.m. to 10:00 p.m.

VETERINARIANS

Panhandle Animal Clinic, 217 N. State Ave. / (509) 447-5158
Pend Oreille Veterinary Clinic, Kootenai Cutoff Rd. / (208) 263-2145

SPORTING GOODS

Pend Oreille Valley Sportsman, 307 N. State Route 2 / (208) 437-3636

AUTO REPAIR

Clifner's Auto Electric/Repair, 325214 N. State Route 2 / (509) 447-3689
Jerry's Auto Clinic, 121 Pine St. (509) 447-2050

AIR SERVICE

Ione Airport, (52 miles north) Private aircraft with 4,300 feet blacktop runway.
Spokane International Airport, (50 miles south) Commercial carriers - United, Delta, Alaska, Horizon, Northwest, Continental, Southwest.

MEDICAL

Newport Community Hospital, 714 W. Pine St. (509) 447-2441

BANKS WITH ATMS

Pend Oreille Bank, 330 N. Washington Ave. (509) 447-5641

FOR MORE INFORMATION

Newport-Oldtown Chamber of Commerce
325 W. 4th St.
Newport, WA 99156
(509) 447-5812

REGION 2

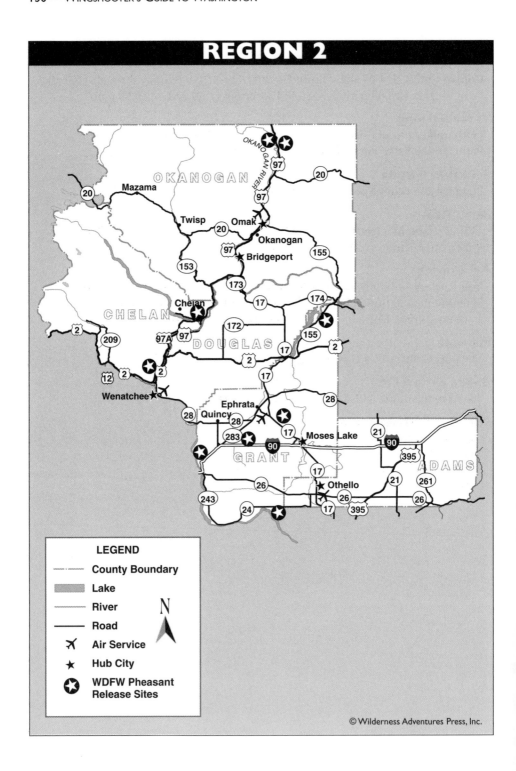

LEGEND

- - - - County Boundary

▬ Lake

— River

— Road

✈ Air Service

★ Hub City

✪ WDFW Pheasant
Release Sites

N

© Wilderness Adventures Press, Inc.

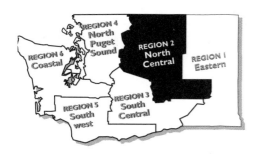

REGION 2
North Central Washington

Adams, Chelan, Douglas, Grant, and Okanogan counties are in this region. From the boreal forests of the North Cascades to the irrigated farm lands of the Columbia Basin Project, diverse landscapes provide habitat for wolverine, grizzly bear, lynx, mule deer, sage and sharptail grouse, huns, pheasant and valley quail. This important waterfowl area provides habitat for wintering, migrating and breeding ducks and geese migrating from Western Canada and Alaska to warmer climates.

The Department of Fish and Wildlife owns more than 300,000 acres which have been set aside for wildlife and public recreation. Most areas are open to hunting, fishing, camping, and a variety of other outdoor experiences. The agency also maintains 200 water and wildlife access areas adjacent to public lands, lakes, and streams.

Another highly rural area, there are excellent hunting opportunities for upland birds and waterfowl harvest.

Farmhouses can be few and far between in dryland wheat country.

REGION 2
Ring-necked Pheasant Distribution

OKANOGAN

CHELAN

DOUGLAS

GRANT

ADAMS

©Wilderness Adventures Press, Inc.

1999-2000 Pheasant Harvest

County	Harvest	Hunters	Days	Hrv/Days
ADAMS	6,462	2,262	10,888	0.59
CHELAN	817	686	1,709	0.48
DOUGLAS	1,689	1,048	3,145	0.54
GRANT	17,083	6,748	36,856	0.46
OKANOGAN	2,339	756	3,290	0.71
REGION 2 TOTAL	**28,390**	**10,184**	**55,888**	**0.51**

A Brittany retrieving a pheasant for its owner.

REGION 2
Valley Quail Distribution

OKANOGAN

CHELAN

DOUGLAS

GRANT

ADAMS

1999-2000 Quail Harvest

County	Harvest	Hunters	Days	Hrv/Days
ADAMS	2,542	665	1,604	1.58
CHELAN	12,632	1,152	5,185	2.44
DOUGLAS	5,685	1,092	2,582	2.2
GRANT	6,190	1,568	8,707	0.71
OKANOGAN	8,538	781	4,226	2.02
REGION 2 TOTAL	**35,587**	**4,454**	**22,304**	1.6

If you look closely, you can see a double top-knot on this valley quail.

REGION 2
Chukar Partridge Distribution

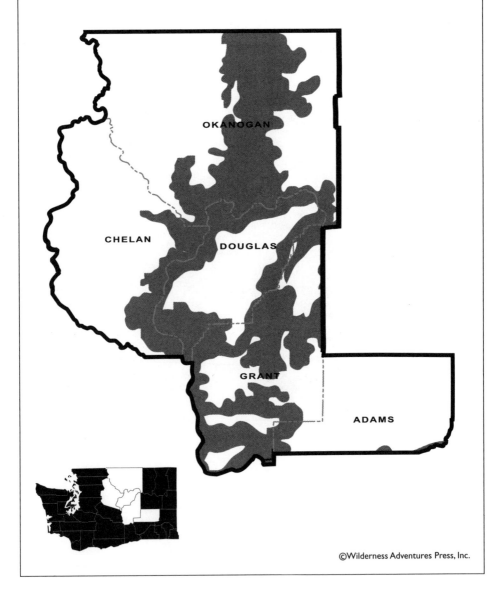

OKANOGAN

CHELAN

DOUGLAS

GRANT

ADAMS

©Wilderness Adventures Press, Inc.

1999-2000 Chukar Harvest

County	Harvest	Hunters	Days	Hrv/Days
ADAMS	111	241	408	0.27
CHELAN	5,553	1,098	4,730	1.1
DOUGLAS	1,188	797	1,683	0.7
GRANT	3,138	1,113	3,767	0.83
OKANOGAN	1,355	264	1,588	0.85
REGION 2 TOTAL	11,345	2,840	12,176	0.93

Typical chukar country in Region 2.

REGION 2
Hungarian (Gray) Partridge
Distribution

OKANOGAN

CHELAN

DOUGLAS

GRANT

ADAMS

©Wilderness Adventures Press, Inc.

1999-2000 Hungarian Partridge Harvest

County	Harvest	Hunters	Days	Hrv/Days
ADAMS	408	359	943	0.43
CHELAN	538	464	1,420	0.38
DOUGLAS	797	440	670	1.19
GRANT	1,317	808	2,355	0.56
OKANOGAN	872	232	1,357	0.64
REGION 2 TOTAL	**3,932**	**1,825**	745	**0.58**

Rolling wheat stubblefields are prime locations for Huns.

REGION 2
Forest Grouse Distribution

OKANOGAN

CHELAN

DOUGLAS

GRANT

ADAMS

1999-2000 Forest Grouse Harvest

County	Harvest	Hunters	Days	Hrv/Days
ADAMS	0	0	0	0
CHELAN	3,374	1,423	7,078	0.48
DOUGLAS	0	261	435	0
GRANT	0	0	0	0
OKANOGAN	8,828	2,640	12,492	0.71
REGION 2 TOTAL	**12,202**	**3,662**	**20,005**	**0.61**

Mixed forest habitat in north central Washington provides excellent cover for forest grouse.

REGION 2
Duck Distribution

OKANOGAN

CHELAN

DOUGLAS

GRANT

ADAMS

©Wilderness Adventures Press, Inc.

1999-2000 Duck Harvest

County	Harvest	Hunters	Days	Hrv/Days
ADAMS	15,432	1,601	9,951	1.55
CHELAN	5,199	488	2,406	2.16
DOUGLAS	10,195	1,154	4,349	2.34
GRANT	93,240	7,276	48,687	1.92
OKANOGAN	6,531	789	3,694	1.77
REGION 2 TOTAL	**130,597**	**9,863**	**69,087**	**1.89**

Sprague Lake in central Washington attracts many species of ducks.

REGION 2
Canada Goose Distribution

OKANOGAN

CHELAN

DOUGLAS

GRANT

ADAMS

©Wilderness Adventures Press, Inc.

1999-2000 Goose Harvest

County	Harvest	Hunters	Days	Hrv/Days
2 ADAMS	3,149	1,018	3,369	0.93
CHELAN	537	275	1,043	0.51
DOUGLAS	2,688	820	2,118	1.27
GRANT	10,599	4,013	17,646	0.6
OKANOGAN	1,209	436	1,478	0.82
REGION 2 TOTAL	**18,182**	**5,565**	**25,654**	**0.71**

Pre-season conditioning of your retriever, especially in water, is a necessity for goose hunting.

OTHELLO
and Adams County

Population - 5,415	County Population - 15,900
County Area - 1,894 sq. miles	October Temperature - 49.2°
Annual Precipitation - 7.61"	Acres in CRP - 144,217

Othello, the largest community in Adams County, is a small rural farming town. Essentially a high desert climate, irrigation has allowed farming to thrive. Areas not under irrigation are sagebrush hills and flats with scabland coulees and draws.

UPLAND BIRDS
Pheasant, Dove, Quail, Hungarian Partridge, Chukar

Farming has provided the edges, feed, cover, and habitat so important for pheasants and that's where you'll find them. Some farms are still posted "Feel Free to Hunt" and a polite request can still open many doors. Always ask permission if a field is not posted. Public land access is rather limited with the exception of the Columbia National Wildlife Refuge, part of which lies within Adams County.

WATERFOWL
Ducks and Geese

Grain fields provide a lot of feed for waterfowl, and this is where you will find them in the evenings. Many ponds and lakes of the Columbia National Wildlife Refuge, some of which are open to hunting, allow good decoying on water.

ACCOMMODATIONS
Aladdin Motor Inn, 1020 E. Cedar St. / (509) 488-5671 / 52 rooms / Dining on site & nearby, continental breakfast, non-smoking rooms / Dogs allowed / Senior discounts / $
Cabana Motel, 665 E. Windsor St. / (509) 488-2605 / 60 units / Dining on site & nearby, non-smoking rooms, senior discounts, and full RV hookups / $$
Cimarron Motel, 1450 E. Main St. / (509) 488-6612 / 20 rooms. Non-smoking rooms / Dogs allowed / Senior discounts / $

CAMPGROUNDS AND RV PARKS
Sportsmans RV Park, 370 Reynolds Rd. / (509) 488-3424 / Dogs allowed, tent sites, full RV hookups and dump station, showers / $

RESTAURANTS
Davey's Steakhouse, 640 E. Main St. / (509) 488-3252 / Open for breakfast, lunch, and dinner, seven days per week, standard American cuisine.

Casa Mexicana, 1224 E. Main St. / (509) 488-6163 / Mexican favorites, reasonably priced for lunch and dinner.

Pizza Factory, 103 S. 1st St. / (509) 488-3252 / Excellent pizza with homemade sauces and good people.

Time Out Restaurant, 1025 E. Main St. / (509) 488-2788 / Standard American food, reasonably priced for lunch and dinner

Twin Dragons, 67 S. 1st St. / (509) 488-2704 / Chinese and American food, good atmosphere, decent prices, open for lunch and dinner.

Zavalla's Place, 1796 S. Broadway / (509) 488-7686 / A hole-in-the-wall to look at, but some of the best Mexican food around, for lunch and dinner.

VETERINARIANS

Jack Jelmberg, DVM, Bench & Radar Rd. / (509) 488-9653

SPORTING GOODS

Othello United Drug, 718 E. Main St. / (509) 488-3653
Ace Hardware, 420 E. Main St. / (509) 488-5667
Othello Sporting Goods, 745 E. Hemlock / (509) 488-6249

AUTO REPAIR

D & W Repair, 805 S. Broadway / (509) 488-2422
Ron's Repair, 230 N. Broadway / (509) 488-7667

AIR SERVICE

Othello Municipal Airport, 1651 W. Bench Rd. / (509) 488-2544
No commercial flights.

MEDICAL

Othello Community Hospital, 350 N. 14th / (509) 488-2636

BANKS WITH ATMS

US Bank, 401 E. Main St. / (509) 488-3353

FOR MORE INFORMATION

Greater Othello Area Chamber of Commerce
33 Larch St.
Othello, WA 99344
(509) 488-2683

WENATCHEE
and Chelan County

Population - 24,180	County Population - 59,200
County Area - 2,996 sq. miles	October Average Temperature - 50°
Annual Precipitation – 9"	Acres in CRP - 377

The City of Wenatchee, largest in Chelan County, boasts of being the "Apple Capital of the World." Wenatchee has a bustling population and serves as a trade center for the Wenatchee Valley and North Central Washington State. Located 600 feet above sea level, the Greater Wenatchee Area is surrounded by mountains reaching peak elevations of 8,000 feet.

UPLAND BIRDS
Quail, Dove, Blue Grouse, Chukar, Ruffed Grouse, Turkeys, Pheasant, Hungarian Partridge, Spruce Grouse

River and creek bottoms, brushy draws and canyons along with orchard edges, provide abundant habitat for quail and dove, which show up most frequently in hunter game bags. Mountain ridges and open timber hold mountain grouse and turkeys in this county. Public access is excellent with portions of the Wenatchee National Forest; and the Lake Chelan-Sawtooth, Glacier Peak, and Alpine Lakes wilderness areas.

WATERFOWL
Ducks and Geese

Lakes Wenatchee and Chelan, the Wenatchee and Columbia rivers, plus numerous small creeks, provide season-long waterfowling opportunities.

ACCOMMODATIONS
Holiday Lodge, 610 N. Wenatchee Ave. / (509) 663-8167 / 59 rooms / Dining on site & nearby, non-smoking rooms / Dogs allowed / Senior discounts / $
Orchard Inn, 1401 N. Miller Ave. / (509) 368-4571 / 103 rooms / Dining on site & nearby, non-smoking rooms / Dogs allowed / Senior discounts / $
Best Western Heritage Inn, 1905 N. Wenatchee Ave. / (509) 664-6563 / 65 rooms / Dining on site & nearby, continental breakfast, non-smoking rooms / Dogs allowed / Senior discounts / $$
Doubletree Hotel, 1225 N. Wenatchee Ave. / (509) 663-0711 / 149 rooms / Dining on site & nearby, non-smoking rooms available / Dogs allowed / Senior discounts / $$
Starlite Motel, 1640 N. Miller Ave. / (509) 662-8115 / 34 rooms. Non-smoking rooms / Dogs allowed / Senior discounts / $
Welcome Inn, 232 N. Wenatchee Ave. / (509) 663-7121 / 38 rooms / Dining on site & nearby, non-smoking rooms / Dogs allowed / Senior discounts / $$

Campgrounds and RV Parks

Hill Crest Motel & RV Park, 2921 School St. / (509) 663-5157 / 18 units / Dining on site & nearby, non-smoking rooms / Dogs allowed senior discounts, full RV hookups and RV dump / $

Restaurants

EZ's, 1950 N Wenatchee ave/ (509) 663-1957 / One of the best drive-through burgers you'll find anywhere!

Shari's of Wenatchee, 1516 N. Wenatchee Ave. / (509) 662-7811 / Open 24 hours seven days per week, good home style cooking, reasonably priced.

LaFuente No. 2, 816 S Mission St / (509) 664-1910 / Outstanding traditional mexican food with a friendly staff.

Windmill, 1501 Wenatchee Ave / (509) 665-9529 / World-class steaks in a unique setting.

Visconti's, 1737 N. Wenatchee Ave. / (509) 662-5013 / Fine Italian dining in a pleasant atmosphere with decent prices.

Blondie's Diner, 200 S. Wenatchee Ave. / (509) 663-2977 / Open 5:00 a.m. to 4:00 p.m. Monday through Friday and 7:00 a.m. to 4:00 p.m. Saturday and Sunday.

Wenatchee Roaster & Ale House, 201 N. Wenatchee Ave. / (509) 662-1234 / Hearty meals and microbrews for lunch and dinner.

Veterinarians

Countryside Veterinary Clinic, 405 A Ohme Gardens Rd / (509)663-6542

Appleland Pet Clinic, 600 N. Mission / (509) 663-8508

Sporting Goods

Ag Supply Ace Hardware, 220 Grant Rd. / (509) 884-6647

Big 5 Sporting Goods, 144 Easy Way / (509) 663-1332

Hooked on Toys, 1444 N Wenatchee Ave. / (509) 663-0740

Auto Rental and Repair

Cascade Auto Center, 148 Easy St. / (509) 663-0011

U Save Auto Rental, 908 S. Wenatchee Ave. / (509) 663-0587

Auto Doctor, 14 Spokane St. / (509) 662-5154

Brewer's Automotive, 727 S. Mission St. / (509) 663-2853

Air Service

Pangborn Memorial Airport, 1 Pangborn Rd. / (509) 884-2494
Serviced by Horizon Air.

Medical

Central Washington Hospital, 1300 Fuller St. / (509) 662-1511

For More Information

The Wenatchee Area Chamber of Commerce
P.O. Box 850
Wenatchee, WA 98801
(509) 662-2116

Geese over the Columbia River in Chelan County.

BRIDGEPORT
and Douglas County

Population - 2,100	County Population - 31,400
County Area - 1,840 sq. miles	October Temperature - 49°
Annual Precipitation - 10.4"	Acres in CRP - 182,138

Bridgeport is a small farming community in a very sparsely populated county. The terrain is highland desert with high sagebrush plateaus interspersed with dry-land wheat, and irrigated crops. Services in Bridgeport are limited.

UPLAND BIRDS
Dove, Quail, Chukar, Pheasant, Hungarian Partridge, Ruffed, Blue, and Spruce Grouse

Doves are shot during their migration, coming into and leaving grain fields, quail are found along several creeks and lakes, while chukar are found in the higher sagebrush hills. What pheasant and Huns you find are usually along cultivated fields. Public land is a rarity in this county, but polite requests can still gain access on some farms.

WATERFOWL
Ducks and Geese
The Columbia River and several small creeks and lakes all provide opportunities for waterfowlers to decoy or jump shoot ducks on their southward migration. Nearby grain fields offer plenty of food for migrating birds.

ACCOMMODATIONS
Bridgeport Y Motel, 2300 Columbia Blvd. / (509) 686-2002 / 18 rooms / Dining on site & nearby, non-smoking rooms / Dogs allowed / Senior discounts / $
Stirling Motel, 1717 Foster Creek Ave. / (509) 686-4821 / Dining on site & nearby, kitchenettes / Dogs allowed / $

CAMPGROUNDS AND RV PARKS
Big River RV Park, 1415 Jefferson / (509) 686-2121 / 15 units. Tent sites, full RV hookups, and showers / $
Mariana Park, 700 Fairview / (509) 686-4747 / 18 units. tent sites, senior discounts, boat launch, showers, full RV hookups and dump site / $

RESTAURANTS
Cliffhouse, 2165 Columbia Blvd. / (509) 686-2106 / Open seven days per week 6:00 a.m. to 9:00 p.m. with family style meals.
Steak House, 1011 Foster Ave. / (509) 686-9900 / Open 11:00 a.m. to 10:30 p.m. Tuesday through Saturday for lunch and dinner.

VETERINARIANS
The nearest vet is in Brewster -13 miles
Brewster Veterinary Clinic, 25901 Hwy. 97 / (509) 689-2616

AUTO REPAIR
Bridgeport Auto Repair, 1740 Foster Ave. / (509) 686-2020

AIR SERVICE
Lake Chelan Airport, (Nearest is in Chelan - 16 miles) / 28 Airport Way / (509) 682-5976 / No commercial service.

MEDICAL
Okanogon-Douglas County Hospital (Nearest is in Brewster, 13 miles) / 507 Hospital Way / (509) 689-2517

BANKS WITH ATMS
Washington Trust Bank, 1015 Columbia Ave. / (509) 686-4101

FOR MORE INFORMATION
Bridgeport Chamber of Commerce, c/o: Washington Trust Bank
1015 Columbia Ave.
Bridgeport, WA 98813
(509) 686-4101

MOSES LAKE
and Grant County

Population - 13,700	County Population - 70,500
County Area - 2,777 sq. miles	October Temperature - 51.6°
Annual Precipitation - 7.23"	Acres in CRP - 56,341

Moses Lake and Grant County are located in the heart of the Columbia Basin, a geologically unique area that was created by massive lava flows and bisected by the Columbia River. Damming of the river for irrigation and hydroelectric power generation raised the water table in an otherwise high desert environment, creating literally thousands of surface acres of lakes, ponds, potholes, creeks, and streams. Agriculture is the primary industry in this area.

UPLAND BIRDS
Pheasant, Dove, Quail, Chukar, Hungarian Partridge

Agricultural edges, creeks, and irrigation wasteways all provide excellent upland bird habitat with good hunting for dove and pheasant. The area's basalt coulees and cliffs are home to chukar, and wheat stubble fields are always a good bet for Huns. The county has fairly good public access with several large Department of Wildlife areas and BLM holdings.

WATERFOWL
Ducks and Geese

With grain fields for feeding, and large and small bodies of water for resting and security, ducks and geese are plentiful in this area.

ACCOMMODATIONS

Motel 6, 2822 Wapato Dr. / (509) 766-0250 / 111 rooms / Dining on site & nearby, non-smoking rooms, and dogs allowed / $

Interstate Inn, 2801 W. Broadway / (509) 765-1777 / 30 rooms / Dining on site & nearby, non-smoking rooms / Dogs allowed / Senior discounts / $

IMA El Rancho Motel, 1214 S. Pioneer Way / (509) 765-9173 / 20 rooms / Dining on site & nearby / Dogs allowed, non-smoking rooms, senior discounts / $$

Moses Lake Travelodge, 316 S. Pioneer Way / (509) 765-8631 / 40 rooms / Dining on site & nearby, non-smoking rooms / Dogs allowed / Senior discounts / $$

Shilo Inn, 1819 E. Kittleson / (800) 222-2244 / 100 rooms / Dining on site & nearby, continental breakfast, non-smoking rooms / Dogs allowed / Senior discounts / $$$

Holiday Inn Express, 1735 E. Kittleson / (509) 766-2000 / 75 rooms. Continental breakfast, non-smoking rooms / Dogs allowed / Senior discounts / $$$

CAMPGROUNDS AND RV PARKS

Big Sun Resort, 2300 W. Marina Dr. / (509) 765-8294 / 60 units / Dining on site & nearby / Dogs allowed, tent sites, boat launch, full RV hookups, showers.-$

Mar Don Resort, 8198 Hwy. 262 S.E. Othello, WA 99344 / (800) 416-2736 300 units / Dining on site & nearby / Dogs allowed / Senior discounts, tent sites, boat launch, full RV hookups and dumpsite, showers / $

Willows Trailer Village, 1347 Rd. 'M' S.E. / (509) 765-7531 / 61 units / Dogs allowed / Tent sites, full RV hookups and dump station, showers / $

RESTAURANTS

Dana's Coffee House, 105 W. Third Ave. / (509) 766-4227 / Open Monday through Friday for breakfast and lunch, reasonable prices.

Perkins Family Restaurant and Bakery, W. Broadway by I-90 / (509) 765-8462 / Open 24 hours per day 7 days per week, traditional American/steak house fare.

Bassano's Italian Pizzera, 218 W. 3rd St. / (509) 765-9185 / Italian favorites, from lasagna to calzones for lunch and dinner.

Hang Out Restaurant & Lounge, 819 W. 3rd St. / (509) 765-7502 / Open at 6:00 a.m.. for breakfast, with lunch and dinner specials seven days per week.

Elmer's Chinese & American Food, 117 W. 3rd St. / (509) 765-4041 / Lunch and dinner buffets or off the menu seven days per week.

VETERINARIANS

Animal Medical Center, 223 E. Broadway / (509) 765-2120

Moses Lake Veterinary Clinic, 3918 Broadway Ext. / (509) 765-4587

SPORTING GOODS

Rite Aid Pharmacy, 815 N. Stratford Rd. / (509) 765-0362

Tri-State Outfitters, 1224 S. Pioneer Way / (509) 765-9338 / www.t-state.com

AUTO RENTAL AND REPAIR

Practical Rent A Car, 6389 Patton Blvd. N.E. / (509) 762-2488

C & V Auto Sales & Service, 520 S. Pioneer Way / (509) 765-3461

Carton's Auto Repair, 706 E. Penn St. / (509) 764-9707

AIR SERVICE

Grant County Airport, 7810 Andrews St. N.E. / (509) 762-5363 Served by Horizon Air.

MEDICAL

Samaritan Hospital, 801 E. Wheeler Rd. / (509) 765-5606

FOR MORE INFORMATION

Moses Lake Tourism
324 S. Pioneer Way
Moses Lake, WA 98837
(800) 992-6234

OMAK
and Okanogan County

Population - 4,495	County Population - 34,680
County Area - 5,301 sq. miles	October Temperature - 56°
Annual Precipitation - 17.37"	Acres in CRP - 1,942

Omak is Okanogan County's largest town. Located on the floor of the Okanogan River Valley, its economy is based on timber and agriculture. The area is relatively dry and sunny with sage-covered foothills rimmed by mountainous pine forests.

UPLAND BIRDS
Blue and Ruffed Grouse, Quail, Dove, Pheasant, Turkeys, Spruce Grouse, Chukar, Hungarian Partridge

Timbered hills and valleys allow excellent forest grouse and turkey hunting with access through the Okanogan National Forest, Pasayten and Lakechelan-Sawtooth National Wilderness, the Loomis State Forest, and portions of the Colville Indian Reservation. Fruit orchards and other crops provide edge cover for pheasant and quail. Okanogan County is the state's top producer of both blue and spruce grouse.

WATERFOWL
Ducks and Geese

Okanogan County boasts over 100 lakes plus many miles of rivers and streams for waterfowl hunting. Getting to know a local farmer may also allow you the chance to decoy birds in a grain field.

ACCOMMODATIONS

Leisure Village Motel, 630 Okoma Dr. / (509) 826-4442 / 33 rooms / Dining on site & nearby, continental breakfast, non-smoking rooms / Dogs allowed / Senior discounts / $-$$$

Motel Nicholas, 527 E. Grape Ave. / (509) 826-4611 / Dining on site & nearby, non-smoking rooms / Dogs allowed / Senior discounts / $

Royal Motel, 514 E. Riverside Dr. / (509) 826-5715 / 10 rooms. Non-smoking rooms / Dogs allowed / $-$$

Stampede Motel, 215 W. 4th St. / (800) 639-1161 / 14 rooms / Dining on site & nearby / Dogs allowed / $-$$

Thriftlodge Motel, 122 N. Main St. / (800) 578-7878 / 59 rooms / Dining on site & nearby, non-smoking rooms / Dogs allowed / $-$$

CAMPGROUNDS AND RV PARKS

Carl Percut Memorial RV Park, Eastside Park / (509) 826-1170 / Dogs allowed, tent sites, full RV hook-ups and dump station, showers / $

Log Cabin Trailer Court, 509 Okoma Dr. / (509) 826-4462 / 4 units / Full RV hook-ups / $

RESTAURANTS

The Breadline Café, 102 Ash St. / (509) 826-5836 / Open Sunday and Monday for breakfast and lunch, Tuesday through Saturday for breakfast lunch and dinner. Excellent home style food.

Leonel's, 5 N. Main St. / (509) 826-3380 / Open Monday through Thursday 11:00 a.m. - 9:00 p.m., Friday and Saturday 11:00 a.m.. - 10:00 p.m., closed Sunday. Featuring: Italian, Mexican, French, and American cuisine, something for everyone.

Our Place Café, 19 E. Apple / (509) 826-4811 / Open seven days per week for breakfast, lunch, and dinner. Good prices, and wonderful omelets.

Tequila's Mexican Restaurant, 635 Okoma Dr. / (509) 826- 5417 / Open seven days per week for lunch and dinner, excellent Mexican food and good prices.

VETERINARIANS

Alpine Veterinary Clinic, 741 Riverside Dr. / (509) 826-5882

SPORTING GOODS

Wal-Mart, 900 Engh Rd. / (509) 826-6002

AUTO REPAIR

Auto Doctor, 130 N. Main St. / (509) 826-5004

Joe's Auto Repair, 204 N. Main St. / (509) 826-1919

AIR SERVICE

Omak City Airport, 202 Omak Airport Rd. #A / (509) 826-6270

MEDICAL

Mid-Valley Hospital, 810 Valley Way / (509) 826-1760

FOR MORE INFORMATION

Omak Visitor Information Center
401 Omak Ave.
Omak, WA 98841
(800) 225-6625

Okanogan County with its confier forests provides some of the top grouse hunting in the state.

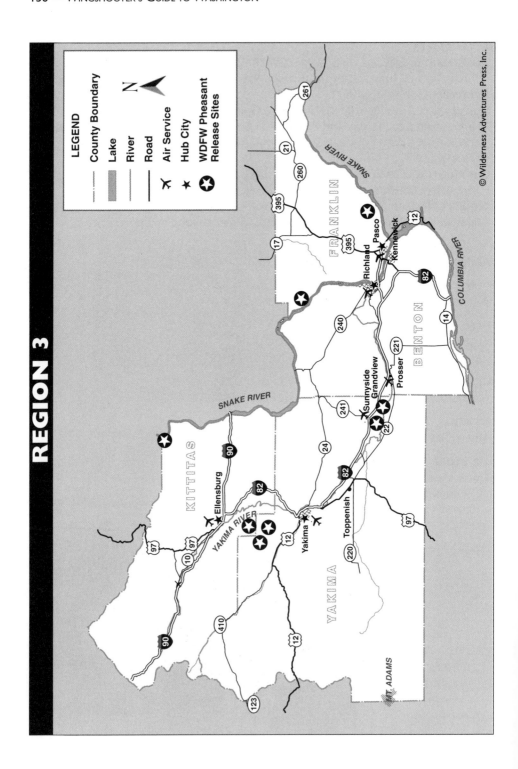

REGION 3

LEGEND
County Boundary
Lake
River
Road
Air Service
Hub City
WDFW Pheasant
Release Sites

N

© Wilderness Adventures Press, Inc.

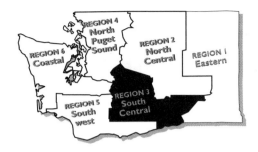

REGION 3
South Central Washington

This region hosts a diversity of broad life zones and habitats from mountain peaks to desert. From the west, the region originates in the high Cascade mountains where more than 100 inches of rain fall annually, supporting tall forests, alpine meadows and glaciers. The "rain shadow" effect created by the Cascades results in progressively drier conditions eastward until the forests eventually yield to arid shrubsteppe. Rainfall in portions of the region can be as little as 5 inches a year.

The Yakima River and the Hanford Reach of the Columbia River are among the region's more striking water resources.

This region offers more than 400,000 acres of department owned land, all of which is open for public recreation. The department has also secured hunter access to an additional 180,000 acres of private land. These lands offer good to excellent hunting prospects for upland birds, and waterfowl, especially along the Columbia, Yakima and Snake river drainages.

Although Region 3 has a higher population density than Regions 1 and 2, the area is still primarily agricultural. Pheasants, quail and huns are plentiful where CRP lands meet cultivated fields.

Fall in the Yakima River Canyon in Kittitas County.

REGION 3
Ring-necked Pheasant Distribution

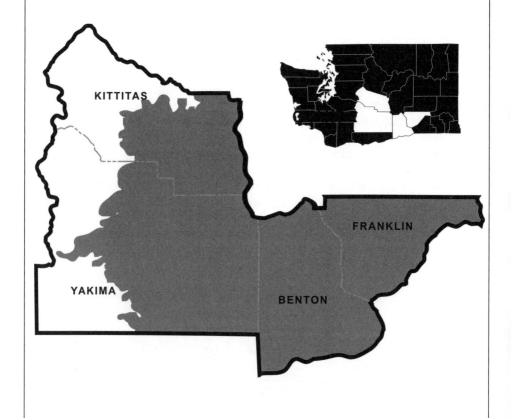

KITTITAS

FRANKLIN

YAKIMA

BENTON

©Wilderness Adventures Press, Inc.

1999-2000 Pheasant Harvest Information

County	Harvest	Hunters	Days	Hrv/Day
BENTON	3,750	1,763	10,270	0.37
FRANKLIN	9,526	2,778	16,377	0.58
KITTITAS	984	670	2,150	0.46
YAKIMA	11,401	4,576	24,470	0.47
REGION 3 TOTAL	**25,661**	**8,956**	53,267	0.48

A Brittany and its young master on a pheasant track in south-central Washington.

REGION 3
Valley Quail Distribution

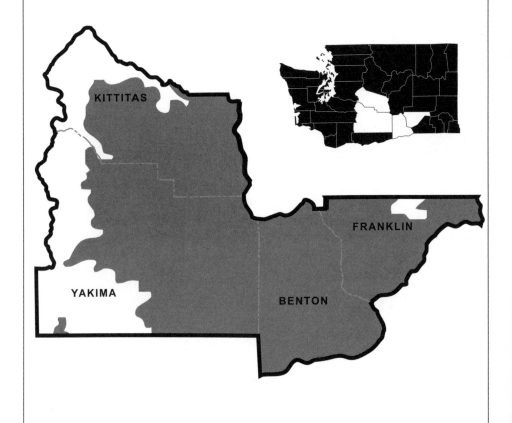

1999-2000 Quail Harvest Information

County	Harvest	Hunters	Days	Hrv/Day
BENTON	4,560	885	3,823	1.19
FRANKLIN	5,685	1,086	5,297	1.07
KITTITAS	1,940	625	1,369	1.42
YAKIMA	23,324	2,697	16,364	1.43
REGION 3 TOTAL	**35,509**	**4,878**	**26,853**	**1.32**

Dense rabbitbrush and sagebrush flats are productive places to find valley quail.

REGION 3
Chukar Partridge Distribution

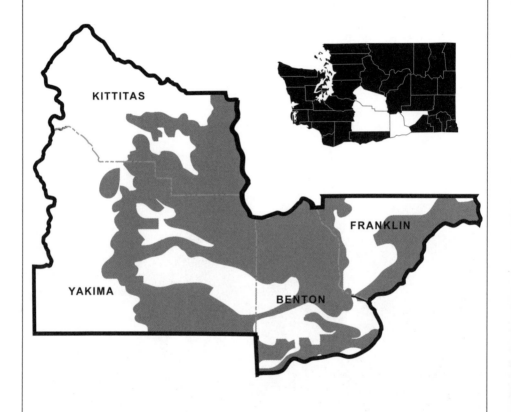

KITTITAS

FRANKLIN

YAKIMA

BENTON

1999-2000 Chukar Harvest Information

County	Harvest	Hunters	Days	Hrv/Day
BENTON	798	403	1,747	0.46
FRANKLIN	55	206	493	0.11
KITTITAS	2,098	730	2,611	0.8
YAKIMA	2,563	1,209	4,598	0.56
REGION 3 TOTAL	**5,514**	**2,132**	**9,449**	**0.58**

A staunch point on a snowy, late season day. Could it be a chukar?

REGION 3
Hungarian (Gray) Partridge
Distribution

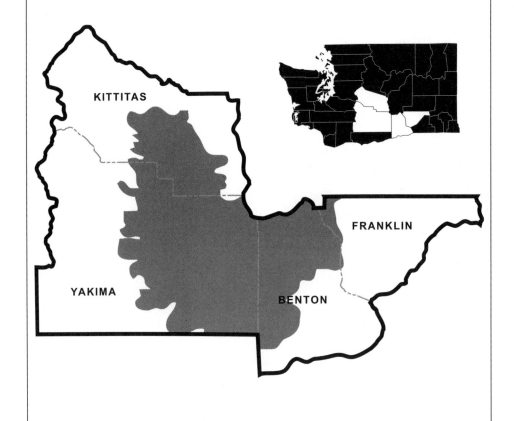

KITTITAS

FRANKLIN

YAKIMA

BENTON

©Wilderness Adventures Press, Inc.

1999-2000 Hungarian Partridge Harvest information

County	Harvest	Hunters	Days	Hrv/Day
BENTON	445	393	1,656	0.27
FRANKLIN	74	247	823	0.09
KITTITAS	371	449	2,047	0.18
YAKIMA	742	521	2,381	0.31
REGION 3 TOTAL	**1,632**	**1,144**	**6,907**	**0.24**

Wheat stubble and huns just go together.

REGION 3
Forest Grouse Distribution

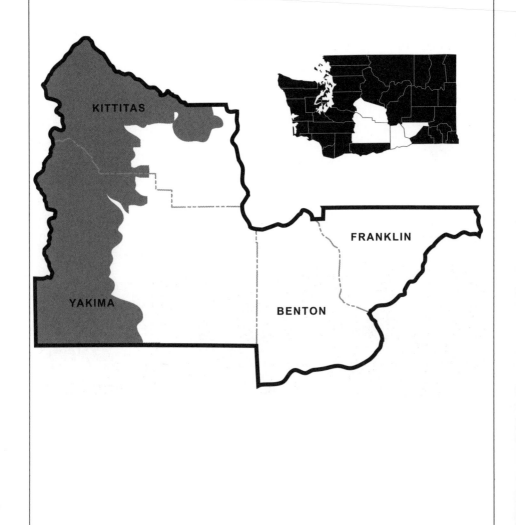

KITTITAS

FRANKLIN

YAKIMA

BENTON

©Wilderness Adventures Press, Inc.

1999-2000 Forest Grouse Harvest Information

County	Harvest	Hunters	Days	Hrv/Day
BENTON	0	0	0	0
FRANKLIN	0	0	0	0
KITTITAS	2,380	1,318	6,268	0.38
YAKIMA	2,311	1,709	6,989	0.33
REGION 3 TOTAL	**4,691**	**2,693**	**13,257**	**0.35**

Any moist areas of ground are good bets for ruffed grouse.

REGION 3
Duck Distribution

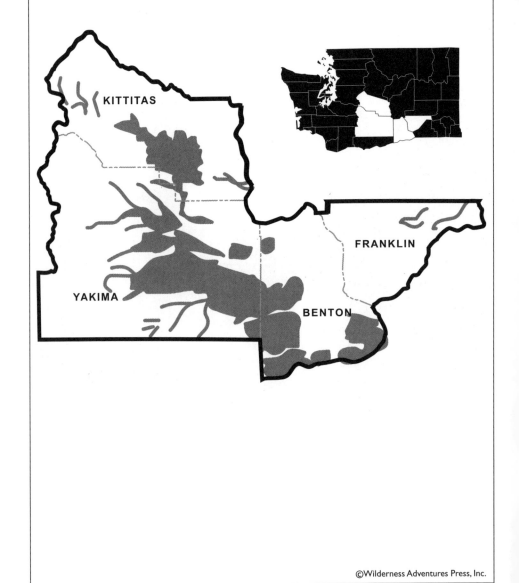

©Wilderness Adventures Press, Inc.

1999-2000 Duck Harvest Information

County	Harvest	Hunters	Days	Hrv/Day
BENTON	24,906	1,519	9,467	2.63
FRANKLIN	30,753	1,892	11,776	2.61
KITTITAS	4,607	675	2,773	1.66
YAKIMA	34,916	2,520	17,069	2.05
REGION 3 TOTAL	**95,182**	**6,038**	**41,085**	**2.32**

Broken coulees often have small ponds that hold ducks for jump-shooting.

REGION 3
Canada Goose Distribution

KITTITAS

FRANKLIN

BENTON

YAKIMA

1999-2000 Goose Harvest Information

County	Harvest	Hunter	Days	Hrv/Day
BENTON	3,878	1,007	3,651	1.06
FRANKLIN	5,760	1,184	4,110	1.4
KITTITAS	1,132	269	1,232	0.92
YAKIMA	1,805	1,249	5,397	0.33
REGION 3 TOTAL	**12,575**	**3,224**	**14390**	**0.87**

Bob Ferris and Pudelpointer friend wait for some geese.

RICHLAND
and Benton County

Population - 36,860	County Population - 120,635
County Area - 1,722 sq. miles	October Temperature - 53.5°
Annual Precipitation - 7.38"	Acres in CRP - 42,888

The city of Richland is part of the Tri-Cities/Mid-Columbia metro area made up of the cities of Pasco, Kennewick, and Richland. This area is the confluence of three major rivers, the Columbia, Snake, and Yakima. Benton County is largely agricultural with a quickly growing wine producing industry.

UPLAND BIRDS
Pheasant, Quail, Dove, Chukar, Hungarian Partridge
The varied farm crops and the edges they produce provide good cover for abundant pheasant and quail, while the rocky scabrock hills hold chukar and Huns. While the majority of land is privately owned there are several large BLM access areas, and access from farmers can sometimes still be gained.

WATERFOWL
Ducks and Geese
With three rivers, many ponds and lakes, plus numerous grain fields, Benton County provides the most productive duck hunting in eastern Washington.

ACCOMMODATIONS
Bali Hi Motel, 1201 George Washington Way / (509) 943-3101 / 44 rooms / Dining on site & nearby, non-smoking rooms / Dogs allowed / $

Vagabond Inn, 515 George Washington Way / (509) 946-6117 / 41 rooms / Dining on site & nearby, continental breakfast, non-smoking rooms / Dogs allowed / Senior discounts / $$

Shilo Inn, 50 Comstock St. / (800) 222-2244 / 150 rooms / Dining on site & nearby, full breakfast, non-smoking rooms / Dogs allowed / Senior discounts / $$

Doubletree Inn - Hanford House, 802 George Washington Way / (509) 946-7611 150 rooms / Dining on site & nearby, non-smoking rooms / Dogs allowed / Senior discounts / $$$

Best Western Tower Inn & Conference Center, 1515 George Washington Way / (509) 946-4121 / 195 rooms / Dining onsite & nearby, non-smoking rooms / Dogs allowed / Senior discounts / $$$

CAMPGROUNDS AND RV PARKS
Desert Gold Motel & RV Park, 611 Columbia Dr. S.E. / (509) 627-1000 / 28 units / Dining on site & nearby / Dogs allowed / $

RESTAURANTS

Denny's, 1301-A George Washington Way / (509) 946-3441 / Open 24 hours per day seven days a week, decent food, fair prices.

Emerald of Siam, 1314 Jadwin Ave. / (509) 946-9328 / Authentic Thai cuisine, good prices, good food, open Monday through Saturday 5:00 a.m. to 9:00 p.m. for dinner and lunch Monday through Friday 11:30 a.m. to 2:00 p.m.

Montrose's Italian Restaurant, 1026 Lee Blvd. / (509) 946-4525 / Excellent Italian cuisine in an antique railroad dining car. Open for lunch and dinner Monday through Saturday.

O'Callahan's Restaurant & Lounge, 50 Comstock / (509) 946-9006 / Good food, nice variety, open 6:00 a.m. to 9:00 p.m. seven days per week.

The Edgewater, 802 George Washington Way / (509) 946-7611 / Serving breakfast, lunch, and dinner seven days per week open at 6:00 a.m.

Baron's Beef & Brew, 1034 Lee Blvd. / (509) 946-5500 / Open for lunch and dinner at 11:00 a.m. seven days per week serving gourmet sandwiches fish, salads, and chicken plus Northwest wines and microbrews.

VETERINARIANS

Animal Medical center PS, 1530 Jadwin Ave. / (509) 943-5671
Desert Vet Clinic Inc. PS, 42 Goethals Dr. / (509) 946-4138

SPORTING GOODS

Rite Aid Pharmacy, 1743 George Washington Way / (509) 946-6128

AUTO RENTAL & REPAIR

Budget Car And Truck Rental, 500 Wellsian Way / (509) 946-5144
Tri-Cities Battery and Auto Repair Inc., 601 George Washington Way / (509) 946-2500
Cronk Automotive, 90-B Wellsian Way / (509) 946-5050

AIR SERVICE

Tri-Cities Airport, 3601 N. 20th Ave. / (509) 547-6352
Serviced by United Express Airlines, (509) 547-1136

MEDICAL

Kadlec Medical Center, 888 Swift Blvd. / (509) 946-4611

BANKS WITH ATMs

Pacific One Bank, 3801 Van Giesen / (509) 735-0807
Seafirst Bank, 1007 Knight / (509) 736-1722

FOR MORE INFORMATION

Richland Chamber of Commerce
515 Lee Blvd.
Richland, WA 99352
(509) 946-1651

PASCO
and Franklin County

Population - 26,090	County Population - 44,400
County Area - 1,253 sq. miles	October Temperature - 53.5°
Annual Precipitation - 7.38"	Acres in CRP - 73,878

Pasco is the county seat of Franklin County and part of the Tri-Cities/Mid-Columbia region. It is located near the confluence of three major Washington river systems: the Columbia, Snake, and Yakima Rivers. Franklin County is largely agricultural with fairly even distributions of dryland and irrigated grounds.

UPLAND BIRDS
Pheasant, Dove, Quail, Hungarian Partridge, Chukar

Agricultural, stream, lake, and pond edges are all good bets for pheasant and quail and for pass-shooting doves. Huns and chukar are found along wheat stubble edges and rocky draws and hills, though they are found in only fair numbers. There is some BLM land access, however most of the county is private.

WATERFOWL
Ducks and Geese

With the three major rivers, numerous ponds and lakes, plus grain fields, Franklin County is one of the best places in eastern Washington for duck and goose hunting.

ACCOMMODATIONS

Motel 6, US Hwy. 12/395 at Spokane/Oregon exits / (509) 546-2010
120 rooms. Non-smoking rooms / Dogs allowed / Senior discounts / $

Airport Motel, 2532 N. 4th St. / (509) 545-1460 / 42 rooms / Dining on site & nearby, continental breakfast, non-smoking rooms / Dogs allowed / Senior discounts / $

King City Truck Stop, 2100 E. Hillsboro / (509) 547-8511 / 36 rooms. Non-smoking rooms / Dogs allowed / Senior discounts / $$

Starlite Motel, 2634 N. 4th St. / (800) 786-8854 / 18 rooms / Dining on site & nearby, non-smoking rooms / Dogs allowed / Senior discounts / $$

Sage 'N Sun Motel, 1232 S. 10th Ave. / (800) 391-9188 / 32 rooms / Dining on site & nearby, non-smoking rooms / Dogs allowed / Senior discounts / $$

Doubletree Hotel, 2525 N. 20th Ave. / (509) 547-0701 / 279 rooms / Dining on site & nearby, non-smoking rooms / Dogs allowed / Senior discounts / $$$

CAMPGROUNDS AND RV PARKS

Arrowhead Campground and RV Park, 3120 Commercial Ave. / (509) 545-8206 / Tent sites, showers, full RV hookups and dump / $

Greentree RV Park, 2200 N. 4th St. / (509) 547-6220 / 40 units / Dining on site & nearby / Dogs allowed, showers, full RV hookups / $

RESTAURANTS

Grizzly Bar, 2525 N. 20th St. / (509) 547-0701 / Open seven days per week for lunch and dinner with burgers, salads, and pizza, plus a nice selection of microbrews.

The Hut, 1205 S. 10th St. / (509) 547-7081 / A family restaurant serving breakfast, lunch, and dinner, seven days per week.

Lil's Pardners Family Restaurant & Espresso, 1320 N. 20th St. / (509) 547-6446 / Family style dining with homemade everything for breakfast, lunch and dinner, seven days per week.

Coffee Garden, 2525 N. 20th St. / (509) 547-0701 / Open at 6:00 a.m. seven days per week for breakfast, lunch, and dinner. Good food, reasonably priced.

Russo's Ristorante, 2525 N. 20th St. / 9509) 547-0701 / Fine Italian dining Monday through Saturday starting at 5:30 p.m.

VETERINARIANS

Coleman Veterinary Clinic, PS, 621 W. Clark / (509) 545-4931
Animal Hospital of Pasco, 3012 Road 92 / (509) 545-9949

SPORTING GOODS

Critter's Outdoor World, Broadmoor Park Outlet Mall / (509) 543-9663
Phil's Sporting Goods Inc., 3806 W. Court St. / (509) 547-9084
Big 5 Sporting Goods, 812 West Vineyard Dr., Kennewick / (509) 586-3739

AUTO RENTAL AND REPAIR

Avis Rent A Car, 3601 N. 20th Ave. / (509) 547-6971
Haler's Rentals, 609 W. Lewis St. / (509) 547-4721
Bernard's Shell Service, 807 W. Lewis St. / (509) 547-7101
C & D Auto, 123 1st St. / (509) 547-3940

AIR SERVICE

Tri-Cities Airport, 3601 N. 20th Ave. / (509) 547-6352
Served by United Express Airlines - (509) 547-1136

MEDICAL

Our Lady of Lourdes Health Center, 520 N. 4th St. / (509) 547-7704

BANKS WITH ATMs

US Bank of Washington, 215 N. 10th St. / (509) 545-9391
Pacific One Bank, 1115 W. Clark / (509) 547-3356

FOR MORE INFORMATION

Pasco Chamber of Commerce
(509) 547-9755

ELLENSBURG
and Kittatas County

Population - 13,600	County Population - 31,500
County Area - 2,317 sq. miles	October Temperature - 45°
Annual Precipitation - 8.92"	Acres in CRP - 3,233

Ellensburg, home of the Central Washington University campus, is located in the foothills of the Cascade Mountains. Its terrain varies from snow capped mountain peaks to river valley farmlands. Farming and ranching are the primary industries for the county. Ellensburg is conveniently located on Interstate 90, the primary freeway running east to west through the state.

UPLAND BIRDS
Quail, Chukar, Ruffed and Blue Grouse, Turkey, Pheasant, Dove, Hungarian Partridge, and Spruce Grouse

Agricultural edges, plus river, creek, and wetland bottoms, provide good hunting for quail and pheasant. Sagebrush hills hold good numbers of chukar and the timbered foothills and mountains provide turkey and grouse action. The county is fairly evenly divided between public and private land holdings. BLM and Wenatchee National Forest lands are easily accessed and some farmers will allow hunting with a polite request.

WATERFOWL
Ducks and Geese

While not located on any major flyway, the rivers, creeks and farm ponds of Kittitas County provide some jump shooting and decoying opportunities for the waterfowler.

ACCOMMODATIONS
Harold's Motel, 601 N. Water / (509) 925-4141 / 60 rooms / Dining on site & nearby, non-smoking rooms / Dogs allowed / Senior discounts. / $
Waites Motel, 601 N. Water / (509) 962-9801 / 60 rooms / Dining on site & nearby, non-smoking rooms / Dogs allowed / $
Best Western Ellensburg Inn, 1700 Canyon Rd. / (509) 925-9801 / 105 rooms / Dining on site & nearby, non-smoking rooms / Dogs allowed / Senior discounts / $$
Nites Inn Motel, 1200 S. Ruby / (509) 962-9600 / 32 rooms / Dining on site & nearby, continental breakfast, non-smoking rooms / Dogs allowed / Senior discounts / $$

Thunderbird Motel, 403 W. 8th Ave. / (800) 843-3492 / 72 rooms / Dining on site & nearby, non-smoking rooms / Dogs allowed / $$

Comfort Inn - Ellensburg, 1722 Canyon Rd. / (509) 925-7037 / 52 rooms / Dining on site & nearby, continental breakfast / Dogs allowed / $$$

CAMPGROUNDS AND RV PARKS

Ellensburg KOA, 32 Thorp Hwy. St. / (509) 925-9319 / Dogs allowed, tent sites, boat launch, showers full RV hook-ups and dump / $

Yakima River RV Park, 791 Ringer Loop / (509) 925-4734 / 36 units / Dining onsite & nearby / Dogs allowed / $

RESTAURANTS

Broadway / Flying J Travel Plaza, 2300 Canyon Rd. / (509) 925-6161 / Truck stop food, large portions, reasonably priced, open 24 hours 7 days per week.

Appleseed Inn, 1713 Canyon Rd. / (509) 925-5809 / Family restaurant, open 7 days per week, for breakfast, lunch, and dinner.

Casa de Blanca, 1318 S. Canyon Rd. / (509) 925-1693 / Mexican food for lunch and dinner.

China Inn, 116 W. 3rd St. / (509) 925-4140 / Good Chinese favorites for lunch and dinner, reasonably priced.

Copper Kettle, 210 W. 8th St. / (509) 925-5644 / Family style restaurant for breakfast lunch and dinner.

Geovanni's on Pearl, 402 N. Pearl / (509) 962-2260 / Fine Italian food for lunch and dinner.

Rolling hills along the Yakima River in Kittitas County.

Veterinarians
Ellensburg Animal Hospital, 1800 Vantage Hwy. / (509) 925-2833
Martin Animal Clinic, 106 W. 4th St. / (509) 925-9418

Sporting Goods
Howell Refrigeration Bullets Gun Shop & Antiques, 313 North Main St. / (509) 925-1109
, 608 E. Mountain View Ave. / (509) 925-6971
Rite Aid Pharmacy, 700 S. Main St. / (509) 925-4334

Auto Rental and Repair
Budget Rent-A-Car, 7th & Pearl / (509) 925-1455
Alyssa's Automotive, 500 S. Main St. / (509) 962-8484
Brass Monkey, 2111 N. Walnut / (509) 925-5678

Air Service
Bowers Field Airport, 1101 Bowers Rd. / (509) 962-7850
No Commercial Service.

Medical
Kittitas Valley Community Hospital, Chestnut & Manitoba / (509) 962-9841

Banks with ATMs
US Bank, 500 N. Pearl St. / (509) 962-7451
Kittitas Valley Bank, 101 W. 8th Ave. / (509) 925-3000

For More Information
Chamber of Commerce
436 N. Sprague St.
Ellensburg, WA 98926

YAKIMA
and Yakima County

Population - 63,510	County Population - 207, 600
County Area - 4,296 sq. miles	October Temperature - 49.9°
Annual Precipitation - 7.97"	Acres in CRP - 34,135

Yakima is the county seat and largest city in Yakima County. It extends from the foothills of the Cascade Mountains through the Yakima River Valley and encompasses the Yakima Indian Reservation. The Yakima Valley is one of the richest agricultural areas in the country and has earned the nickname of "the world's fruit basket."

UPLAND BIRDS
Quail, Dove, Pheasant, Chukar, Turkeys,
Ruffed and Blue Grouse, Hungarian Partridge

The heavily irrigated farmland that makes up the majority of Yakima County provides excellent edge habitat for quail and pheasant. Turkeys and mountain grouse are abundant in the timbered foothills of the Cascade Mountains and chukar and Huns live on the un-timbered hills. Public land access is fair with the Wenatchee National Forest, some BLM land and portions of the Yakima Indian Reservation you best bets.

WATERFOWL
Ducks and Geese

The Yakima River, along with its many seep ponds, lakes, and backwater sloughs, plus the abundant grain fields, attract many ducks and geese. There are many opportunities to both decoy and jump shoot waterfowl.

ACCOMMODATIONS
Bali Hai Motel, 710 N. 1st St. / (509) 452-7178 / 28 rooms / Dining on site & nearby, non-smoking rooms / Dogs allowed / Senior discounts / $
Red Carpet Motor Inn, 1608 Fruitvale Blvd. / (509) 457-1131 / 29 rooms / Dining on site & nearby, non-smoking rooms / Dogs allowed / Senior discounts / $
Days Inn, 2408 Rudkin Rd. / (800) 348-9701 / 118 rooms / Dining on site & nearby, continental breakfast, non-smoking rooms / Dogs allowed / Senior discounts / $$
Red Lion Inn, 818 N. 1st St. / (509) 453-0391 / 58 rooms / Dining on site & nearby, continental breakfast, non-smoking rooms / Dogs allowed / Senior discounts / $$

Cavanaugh's at Yakima Center, 607 E. Yakima Ave. / (509) 248-5900 / 153 rooms / Dining on site & nearby, full breakfast, non-smoking rooms / Dogs allowed / Senior discounts / $$$

Doubletree Hotel - Yakima Valley, 1507 N. 1st St. / (509) 248-7850 / 208 Rooms / Dining on site & nearby, non-smoking rooms / Dogs allowed / Senior discounts / $$$

Campgrounds and RV Parks

Circle H RV Ranch, 1107 S 18 St / ((509) 457-3683

Trailer Inns, 1610 N. 1st St. / (509) 452-9561 / Dogs allowed, tent sites, full RV hookups, showers / $

Yakima KOA, 1500 Keys Rd. / (509) 248-5882 / Dogs allowed, tent sites, showers, full RV hookups and dump / $

Twelve West Resort RV Campground, 37590 US Highway 12, Naches / ((509) 672-2460

Restaurants

Las Margarits, 1430 N. 16th Ave. / (509) 575-1553 / Excellent Mexican food for lunch and dinner open 11:00 a.m. to 10:00 p.m. Sunday and Monday, Tuesday through Saturday 11:00 a.m. to 11:30 p.m..

Black Angus, 501 N. 1st St. / (509) 248-4540 / Good old-fashioned steak house open for lunch and dinner seven days per week, decent prices.

DB's Family Restaurant, 2710 W. Nob Hill Blvd. / (509) 248-2129 / Family style meals for breakfast, lunch, and dinner. Seven days per week 6:00 a.m. to 10:00 p.m.

Gearjammer Truck Plaza, 2310 Rudkin Rd. / (509) 248-9640 / Truck stop stick-to-your-ribs meals seven days per week 24 hours per day. Good prices.

Red Lobster, 905 N. 1st St. / (509) 575-3640 / Good seafood, good prices, and nice people, seven days per week for lunch and dinner.

Trattoria Russo, 315 E. Yakima Ave. / (509) 577-0360 / Excellent Italian food with a nice atmosphere for lunch and dinner Tuesday through Friday, dinner only on Saturday.

Veterinarians

South First Street Veterinary Clinic, 401 S. 1st St. / (509) 248-0084

Airport West Animal Clinic, 5804 W. Washington Ave. / (509) 966-8460

Sporting Goods

Wal-Mart, 1600 E. Chestnut Ave. / (509) 248-3448

K-Mart, 2304 E. Nob Hill Blvd. / (509) 248-1990

High Country Hunting, (509) 965-5620

Wildlands Sports, 102 S. 1st St. / (509) 457-1390

Bi-Mart, 1207 North 40th Avenue / (509) 457-1650

Bi-Mart, 309 South 5th Ave. / (509) 457-5175

Big 5 Sporting Goods, W. Nob Hill Blvd. / (509) 453-6040

Chinook Sporting Goods, 901 S 1st St / (509) 452-8205

AUTO RENTAL AND REPAIR

Avis Rent A Car, 2300 W. Washington Way / (509) 452-1555
Enterprise Rent-A-Car, 312 W. Nob Hill Blvd. / (509) 248-2170
C. & J. Car Clinic, 1602 S. 36th Ave. / (509) 248-7412
Christie's Garage, 5812 Summitview / (509) 966-1090

AIR SERVICE

Yakima Air Terminal, 2400 W. Washington Ave. / (509) 575-6149
Serviced by United Express, 2300 W. Washington Ave. / (509) 457-2494

MEDICAL

Providence Medical Center, 110 S. 9th Ave. / (509) 575-5000

FOR MORE INFORMATION

Greater Yakima Chamber of Commerce
P.O. Box 1490
Yakima, WA 98907
(509) 248-2021

Storm front moving across central Washington.

REGION 4

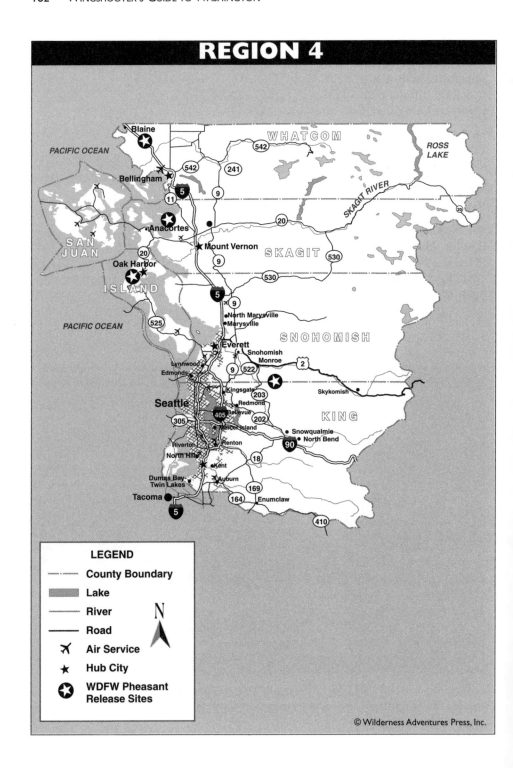

LEGEND

〰〰 County Boundary
▨ Lake
〰 River
— Road
✕ Air Service
★ Hub City
✪ WDFW Pheasant Release Sites

N

© Wilderness Adventures Press, Inc.

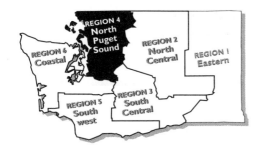

REGION 4
North Puget Sound

This region covers the northern Puget Sound portion of the state from King County to the Canadian border.

The terrain ranges from the alpine forests of the Cascade mountains in the east to the beautiful San Juan islands and Puget Sound to the west. The northern Puget Sound area is the most populated in the state. Upland bird hunting is sparse, although there is fair pheasant hunting on the WDFW pheasant release sites. Duck and goose hunting can be excellent on the national refuges and the three wildlife areas owned and operated by the Washington Department of Fish and Wildlife.

The leaves turn early in the high alpine areas of Washington's northern country.

REGION 4
Ring-necked Pheasant Distribution

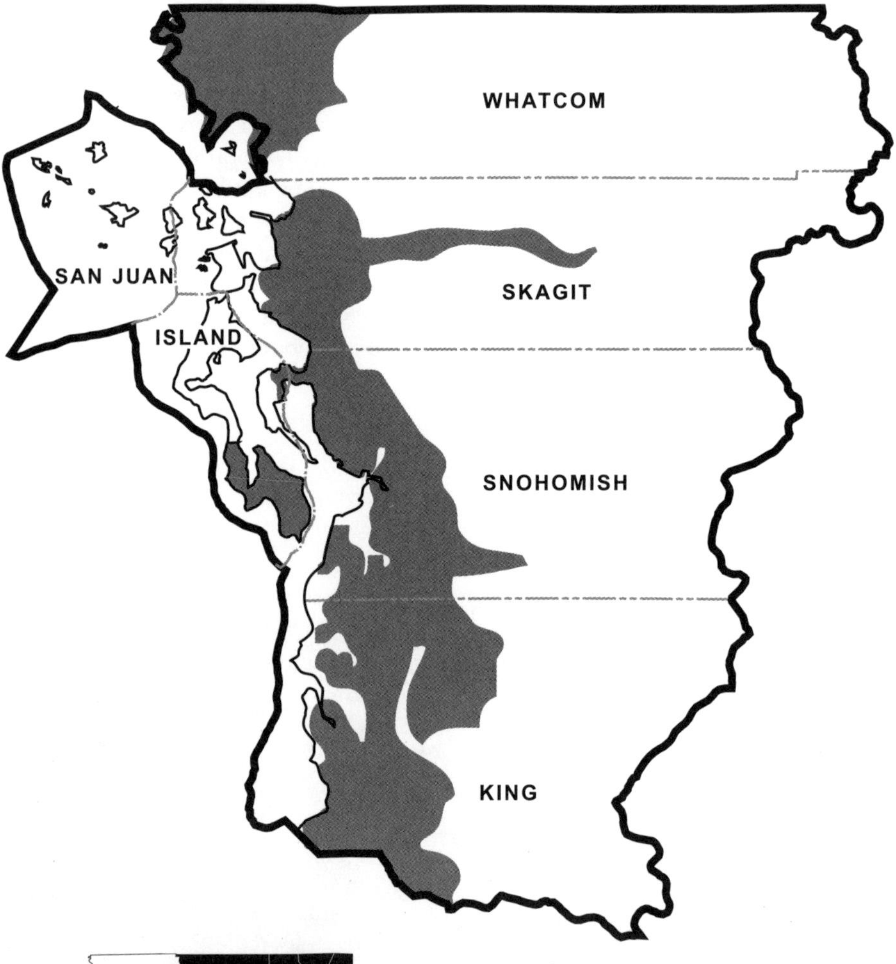

WHATCOM

SAN JUAN

SKAGIT

ISLAND

SNOHOMISH

KING

1999-2000 Pheasant Harvest Information

County	Harvest	Hunters	Days	Hrv/Day
ISLAND	2,284	367	2,394	0.95
KING	3,138	935	5,841	0.54
SAN JUAN	92	106	287	0.32
SKAGIT	1,671	565	2,018	0.83
SNOHOMISH	2,413	669	3,242	0.74
WHATCOM	2,209	602	3,557	0.62
REGION 4 TOTAL	**11,807**	**2,580**	**17,339**	**0.68**

Pheasant or quail — who knows?

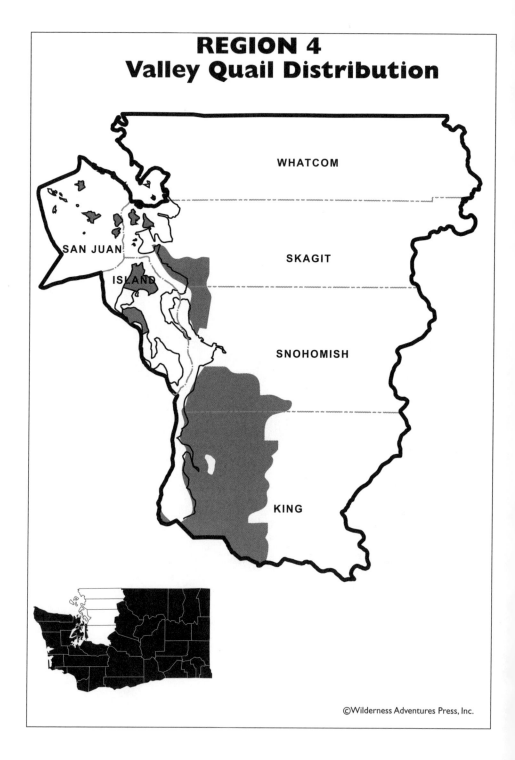

REGION 4
Valley Quail Distribution

WHATCOM

SAN JUAN

SKAGIT

ISLAND

SNOHOMISH

KING

©Wilderness Adventures Press, Inc.

1999-2000 Valley Quail Harvest Information

County	Harvest	Hunters	Days	Hrv/Day
ISLAND	19	146	93	0.2
KING	873	157	765	1.14
SAN JUAN	0	0	0	0
SKAGIT	0	0	0	0
SNOHOMISH	0	0	0	0
WHATCOM	0	0	0	0
REGION 4 TOTAL	**892**	**154**	**858**	**1.04**

Some valley quail are born without the characteristic top-knot.

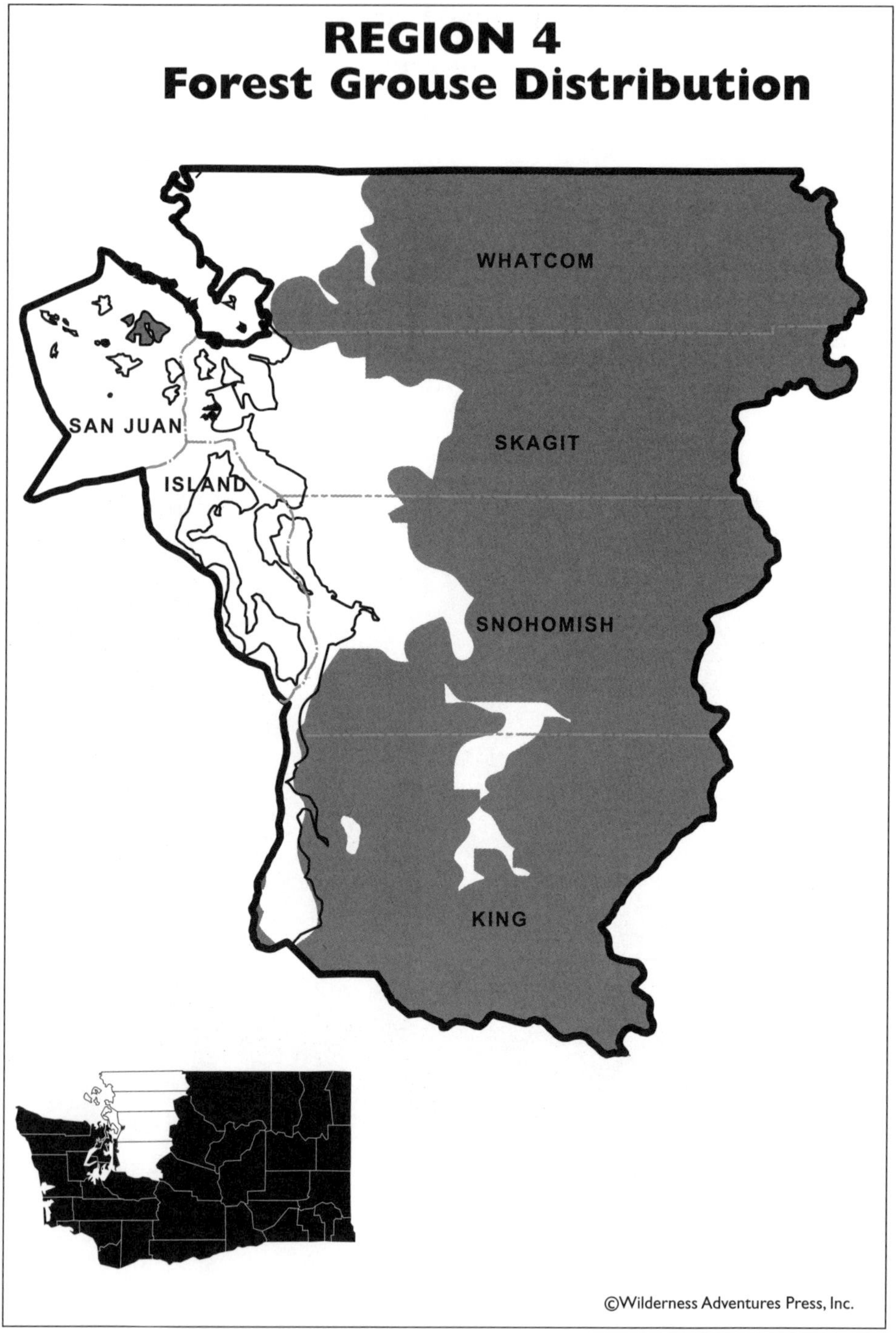

REGION 4
Forest Grouse Distribution
WHATCOM
SAN JUAN
SKAGIT
ISLAND
SNOHOMISH
KING
©Wilderness Adventures Press, Inc.

1999-2000 Forest Grouse Harvest Information

County	Harvest	Hunters	Days	Hrv/Day
ISLAND	0	0	0	0
KING	1109	748	3963	0.28
SAN JUAN	0	0	0	0
SKAGIT	392	621	2861	0.14
SNOHOMISH	1155	813	3929	0.29
WHATCOM	392	554	2260	0.17
REGION 4 TOTAL	**3048**	**1966**	**13013**	**0.23**

Thick forest cover — where ruffed and spruce grouse can be found.

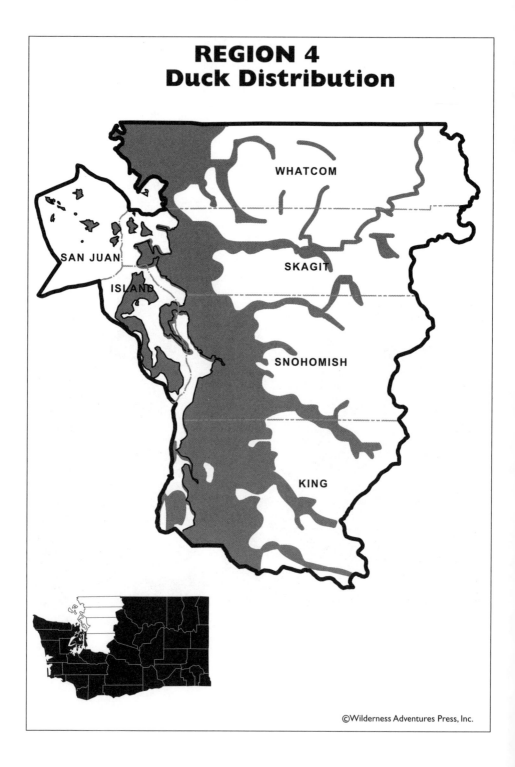

REGION 4
Duck Distribution

WHATCOM

SAN JUAN

SKAGIT

ISLAND

SNOHOMISH

KING

©Wilderness Adventures Press, Inc.

1999-2000 Duck Harvest Information

County	Harvest	Hunters	Days	Hrv/Day
ISLAND	8,696	902	7,595	1.14
KING	6,069	1,045	4,566	1.33
SAN JUAN	2,090	179	1,396	1.5
SKAGIT	36,674	2,827	22,177	1.65
SNOHOMISH	26,959	2,182	15,896	1.7
WHATCOM	19,910	1,312	9,261	2.15
REGION 4 TOTAL	**100,398**	**6,866**	**60,891**	**1.65**

Blinds with natural cover are ideal for early season waterfowling.

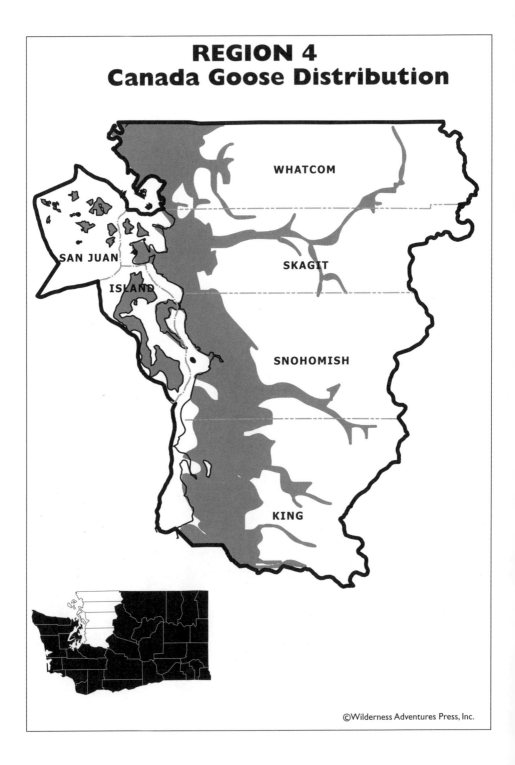

REGION 4
Canada Goose Distribution

WHATCOM

SAN JUAN

ISLAND

SKAGIT

SNOHOMISH

KING

1999-2000 Goose Harvest Information

County	Harvest	Hunters	Days	Hrv/Day
ISLAND	422	209	1,053	0.4
KING	172	319	1,432	0.12
SAN JUAN	0	105	400	0
SKAGIT	1,747	692	3,614	0.48
SNOHOMISH	1,689	753	3,342	0.51
WHATCOM	921	580	2,985	0.31
REGION 4 TOTAL	4,951	2,057	12,826	0.39

Geese flying along the Skagit River valley.

OAK HARBOR
and Island County

Population - 20,190	County Population - 77,900
County Area - 209.8 sq. miles	October Temperature - 52.7°
Annual Precipitation - 31.52"	Acres in CRP - 0

Oak Harbor is the largest city in Island County. It is located in northern Puget Sound, in the northwest corner of the state. Rural in character, much of the land remains blanketed by forests and dense underbrush. Much of the land is privately owned but some public hunting does exist.

UPLAND BIRDS
Pheasant, Quail, Ruffed Grouse

Unfortunately, Island County cannot be recommended as a primary destination for hunting. Fewer than fifty quail and grouse are shot each year, and what pheasant are killed are taken at the Naval Air Station, Arnold Farm, Ebby's Prairie, and Useless Bay WDFG release sites, where pen -raised birds are turned loose to provide hunting opportunities in the county.

WATERFOWL
Ducks and Geese

Being made up of several islands, the county provides many opportunities for sea going ducks and a few puddle ducks. Small ponds and lakes, as well as public seashore, are good bets.

ACCOMMODATIONS
Acorn Motor Inn, 31530 SR 20 / (360) 675-6646 / 34 rooms. Continental breakfast / Dogs allowed / $$
Best Western Harbor Plaza, 33175 SR Hwy. 20 / (360) 679-4567 / 80 rooms / Dining on site & nearby, continental breakfast, non-smoking rooms / Dogs allowed / Senior discounts / $$$
Queen Ann Motel, 1204 W. Pioneer Way / (360) 675-2209 / 23 rooms. Non-smoking rooms / Dogs allowed / Senior discounts / $$$

CAMPGROUNDS AND RV PARKS
North Whidbey RV Park, 565 W. Cornet Bay Rd. / (800) 438-6978 / 110 units / Dining on site & nearby dogs allowed / Senior discounts, tent sites, full RV hook-ups, showers / $

RESTAURANTS

China Harbor Restaurant & Lounge, 630 S.E. Pioneer Way / (360) 679-1557 / Cantonese and Szechwan cuisine for lunch and dinner daily, reasonable prices.

For Pete's Sake, 930 S.E. Pioneer Way #101 / (360) 675-0132 / Steak and seafood plus breakfast served daily.

Island Grill, 5052 N. SR 20 / (360) 679-3194 / Breakfast, lunch, and dinner served seaside.

Kasteel Franssen, 33575 SR 20 / (360) 675-0724 / Trendy (and pricey) European cuisine and seafood for dinner.

VETERINARIANS

Animal Hospital on Midway, 250 N.E. Midway Blvd. / (360) 240-8888

Vets Animal Hospital, 615 S.E. 11th Ave. / (360) 675-4425

SPORTING GOODS

K-Mart, 32165 SR 20 / (360) 679-5545

AUTO RENTAL AND REPAIRS

Budget Rent-A-Car, 75 S.E. Pioneer Way / (360) 675-2000

Enterprise Rent-A-Car, 980 S.E. Pioneer Way / (360) 675-6052

American Car Care Center, 726 N.E. Midway Blvd. / (360) 679-2292

Chiefs Affordable Auto Repair, 35619 SR 20 / (360) 679-6546

AIR SERVICE

Harbor Airlines, 1140 N. Monroe Landing Rd. / (800) 359-3220

MEDICAL - NEAREST

Whidbey General Hospital, 101 Main St. N. Coupeville / (360)678-5151

BANKS WITH ATMs

InterWest Bank, 901 N.E. Midway Blvd. / (360) 675-0792

FOR MORE INFORMATION

Greater Oak Harbor Chamber of Commerce
32630 SR 20
Oak Harbor, WA 98277
(360) 675-3535

KENT
and King County

Population - 70,110	County Population - 1,646,200
County Area - 2,126 sq. miles	October Temperature - 52.5°
Annual Precipitation - 44.66"	Acres in CRP - 0

Kent, although far from the largest city in King County, is centrally located along the Interstate 5 corridor. Midway between the cities of Seattle and Tacoma, it is only minutes from Sea-Tac International Airport, the largest airport in Washington. Although the western part of the county is highly urbanized, eastern King County extends into the Cascade Mountains and the Snoqualmie National Forest. King County cannot be highly recommended as a primary hunting destination. However, it provides all the big city amenities, including professional sporting events, theater, shopping, and five star dining.

UPLAND BIRDS
Pheasant, Ruffed, and Blue Grouse

The pheasant hunting opportunities that do exist are on two WDFW release sites. Mountain grouse are fairly abundant in the Snoqualmie National Forest and access here is good, although the high human population density can make getting away from the crowds a challenge.

WATERFOWL
Ducks and Geese

Waterfowl hunting is limited to a few rivers and ponds located in the eastern part of the county. These are accessible on Snoqualmie National Forest land.

ACCOMMODATIONS
Golden Kent Motel, 22203 84th Ave. S. / (253) 872-8372 / 22 rooms / Dining on site & nearby / Dogs allowed / $$

Howard Johnson, 1233 N. Central / (253) 852-7224 / 85 rooms / Dining on site & nearby, continental breakfast, non-smoking rooms / Dogs allowed / Senior discounts / $$-$$$

Seaview Motel, 25218 Pacific Hwy. S. / (253) 839-5929 / 17 rooms / Dining on site & nearby / Dogs allowed / $

CAMPGROUNDS AND RV PARKS
Seattle/Tacoma KOA, 5801 S. 212th St. / (800) 562-1892 / 140 units. Tent sites, showers full RV hook-ups and dump / $

Willow Vista Estates, 21740 84th Ave. S. / (253) 872-8264 / 52 units / Full RV hook-ups and dump, showers / $

RESTAURANTS

Shari's Restaurant, 24525 Russell Rd. / (253) 859-5774 / Open 24 hours, seven days per week, family style with reasonable prices.

Gambardell's, 1313 W. Meeker St. #138 / (253) 859-4681 / Fine Italian food for lunch and dinner.

Cave Man Kitchen, 807 W. Valley Hwy. / (253) 854-1210 / Hearty barbecue, large portions, good atmosphere, a lot of fun.

Azteca Restaurant & Lounge, 25633 102nd Place S.E. / (253) 852-0210 / Very good Mexican food for lunch and dinner, decent prices.

Hung's Chinese Restaurant, 24437 Russell Road, Suite 120 / (253) 854-8907. Chinese favorites for lunch and dinner, reasonably priced.

VETERINARIANS

Covington Veterinary Hospital, 17414 S.E. 272nd St. / (253) 631-8616

Animal Clinic of Kent, 23613 104th Ave. S.E. / (253) 859-1520

SPORTING GOODS

K Mart, 24800 W. Valley Hwy. / (253) 852-9071

Rite Aid Pharmacy, 24044 104th Ave. S.E. / (253) 852-6180

Big 5 Sporting Goods, 24204 104th Ave. SE. / (253) 852-2524

G.I. Joe's - Issaquah, 1185 NW Gilman Blvd / (425) 961-2000

AUTO RENTAL & REPAIR

Budget Rent A Car, 22005 84th Ave. S. / (253) 682-8782

Enterprise Rent A Car, 945 Central Ave. N. #102 / (253) 859-0720

212th Automotive Repair, 7612 S. 212th St. / (253) 395-4434

Al's Auto Repair, 11426 S.E. 244th St. / (253) 854-5254

AIR SERVICE

Sea Tac International Airport, 2580 S. 156th St. / (206) 431-4444 Served by all major airlines.

MEDICAL

Valley Medical Center, 400 S. 43rd St. Renton / (206) 575-4716

BANK'S WITH ATMS

US Bank, 10231 S.E. 240th St. / (253) 854-2034

Seafirst Bank, 25638 104th S.E. / (253) 358-2685

FOR MORE INFORMATION

Kent Chamber of Commerce
524 W. Meeker St, Suite 1
Kent, WA 98032
(253) 854-1770

MOUNT VERNON
and Skagit County

Population - 23,000	County Population - 96,000
County Area - 1,735 sq. miles	October Temperature - 51.8°
Annual Precipitation - 54.25"	Acres in CRP - 0

Mount Vernon, the seat of Skagit County, is located in the heart of the Skagit River Valley. It is a progressive metropolitan crossroad located halfway between Seattle and Vancouver, British Columbia. With part of the Mt. Baker-Snoqualmie National Forest located in the eastern part of the county, there is much public access for hunting.

UPLAND BIRDS
Ruffed Grouse, Pheasant, Blue Grouse

Mt. Baker-Snoqualmie National Forest lands provide very good grouse hunting and easy access. As is typical, blue grouse are found on high ridges while ruffed grouse are found along brushy creeks, second growth, and aspen groves. Pheasants are hunted on the Skagit Wildlife Area, where pen-raised birds are released at regular intervals as part of the Western Washington Pheasant Release Program.

WATERFOWL
Ducks and Geese

Rivers, creeks, lakes and seashore all provide opportunity for waterfowl hunting, but do be careful. Much of the county is private property so check maps for state or federal land access.

ACCOMMODATIONS

West Winds Motel, 2020 Riverside / (360) 424-4224 / 40 rooms / Dining on site & nearby, non-smoking rooms / Dogs allowed / $

Tulip Inn, 2200 Freeway / (360) 428-5969 / 40 rooms / Dining on site & nearby, non-smoking rooms / Dogs allowed / Senior discounts / $

Best Western College Way Inn, 300 W. College Way / (800) 793-4024 /66 rooms / Dining on site & nearby, continental breakfast, non-smoking rooms / Dogs allowed / Senior discounts / $$

Days Inn, 2009 Riverside Dr. / (360) 424-4141 / 67 rooms / Dining on site & nearby, non-smoking rooms / Dogs allowed / $$

Comfort Inn, 1910 Freeway Dr. / (360) 428-7020 / 68 rooms / Dining on site & nearby, continental breakfast, non-smoking rooms / Dogs allowed / Senior discounts / $$

Best Western Cottontree Inn, 2300 Market St. / (800) 662-6886 / 121 rooms / Dining on site & nearby, continental breakfast, non-smoking rooms / Dogs allowed / Senior discounts / $$$

CAMPGROUNDS AND RV PARKS
Big Lake Resort, 1785 W. Big Lake Blvd. / (360) 422-5755 / 34 units / Dogs allowed, tent sites, boat launch, showers full RV hook-ups and dump / $
Riverbend RV Park, 305 W. Stewart Rd. / (360) 428-4044

RESTAURANTS
Calico Cupboard, 121-B Freeway Dr. / (360) 336-3107 / Country breakfasts and lunches served daily, with dinner Thursday through Saturday.
Cranberry Tree, 2030 Freeway Dr. / (360) 424-7755 / Serving breakfast, lunch and dinner, seven days per week - seafood, steak, and pasta.
Dragon Inn, 225 Riverside Lane / (360) 424-3722 / Chinese favorites for lunch and dinner, seven days per week
Mexico Café, 1320 Memorial Hwy. / (360) 424-1977 / Open seven days per week, serving lunch and dinner, good food and good prices.
The Valley Café, 1302 Avon-Allen Rd. / (360) 416-6892 / Family style breakfast, lunch, and dinner, seven days per week.

VETERINARIANS
Parker Way Veterinary Clinic, 1515 Parker Way / (360) 424-7387
Highland Animal Clinic, 110 N. 15th St. / (360) 428-8600

SPORTING GOODS
Rite Aid Pharmacy, 242 E. College Way / (360) 424-7981

AUTO RENTAL AND REPAIR
Enterprise Rent A Car, 2222 Riverside Dr. #601 / (360) 757-6477
Xtra Car Inc., 1901 Freeway Dr. / (360) 428-2888
Avey's Auto Service, 1513 Bennett Rd. / (360) 424-5410
Integrity Auto Repair, 1522 Riverside Dr. / (360) 424-0560

AIR SERVICE
Skagit Regional Airport, 1180 Higgins Airport Way, Burlington, WA / (360) 757-0011
No scheduled commercial airline service, charters available.

MEDICAL
Skagit Valley Hospital, 1415 E. Kincaid St. / (360) 424-4111

BANKS WITH ATMs
Seafirst Bank, 320 W. Kincaid St / (360) 336-8100
US Bank, 419 S. 2nd St. / (360) 336-9646

FOR MORE INFORMATION
Mount Vernon Chamber of Commerce
P.O. Box 1007
Mount Vernon, WA 98273
(360) 428-8547

A grey day on a high alpine lake in Snohomish County.

EVERETT
and Snohomish County

Population - 85,000	County Population - 551,200
County Area - 2,100 sq. miles	October Temperature- 51.5°
Annual Precipitation - 40.46"	Acres in CRP - 0

Everett, the Snohomish County seat, is situated on Puget Sound and offers visitors a wide range of experiences: big city nightlife and cultural attractions within an hour's drive of national forest land and wilderness areas. Located along the I-5 corridor, the highly urbanized area is escaped by driving east toward the Cascade Mountains.

UPLAND BIRDS
Ruffed Grouse, Pheasant, Blue Grouse

In Snohomish County, ruffed grouse is king of the upland birds. There are thousands of acres of Mt. Baker-Snoqualmie National Forest land open for hunting in the eastern portion of the county in the cascade foothills. Virtually 100% of the pheasant are taken at WDFW Western Washington Pheasant Release Sites. There are two in the County - Smith Farms and Crescent Lake.

WATERFOWL
Ducks and Geese

There are numerous lakes, streams, and estuaries open for public waterfowling. Some have blinds available on either a first come, first served basis or by reservation.

ACCOMMODATIONS

Motel 5 - Everett South, I-5 at Exit 189 / (425) 347-2060 / 119 rooms / Dining on site & nearby, non-smoking rooms / Dogs allowed / Senior discounts / $

Royal Motor Inn, 952 N. Broadway / (425) 259-5177 / 35 rooms / Dining on site & nearby, non-smoking rooms / Dogs allowed / Senior discounts / $

Everett/Broadway Travelodge, 3030 Broadway / (425) 259-6141 / 29 rooms / Dining on site & nearby, non-smoking rooms / Dogs allowed / Senior discounts / $$

Everett Travelodge, 9602 19th Ave. S.E. / (425) 337-9090 / 116 rooms / Dining on site & nearby, non-smoking rooms / Dogs allowed / $$

Holiday Inn Hotel & Conference Center, 101 128th St. S.E. / (425) 337-2900 / 249 rooms / Dining on site & nearby, non-smoking rooms / Dogs allowed / Senior discounts / $$

CAMPGROUNDS AND RV PARKS

Silver Lake RV Park, 11621 W. Silver Lake Rd. / (425) 334-9666 / 28 units / Tent sites, boat launch, showers, full RV hook-ups and dump / $

Lakeside RV Park, 12321 Hwy. 99 S. / (800) 468-7275 / Tent sites, full RV hook-ups and dump / $

RESTAURANTS

Denny's, 2903 Pacific Ave. / (425) 259-5031 / Open 24 hours, seven days per week with predictable food and good prices.

Olive Garden Italian Restaurant, 1321 Everett Mall Way / (425) 347-9857/Italian favorites for lunch and dinner, seven days per week, decent prices.

Anthony's Homeport, 1726 W. Marine View Dr. / (425) 252-3333 / Excellent fresh seafood for lunch and dinner, seven days per week. A little on the expensive side, but if you like really good seafood, its worth it.

41st St. Bar and Grill, 1510 41st St. / (425)259-3838 / Open for breakfast lunch and dinner, seven days per week. Good seafood, steaks, salad and gourmet hamburgers.

Outback Steakhouse, 10121 Evergreen Way / (425) 513-2181 / Open daily for lunch and dinner good food with a good atmosphere.

VETERINARIANS

Broadway Animal Hospital, 2132 Broadway / (425) 252-8266

All Animal & Bird Hospital, 9004 Vernon Rd. / (425) 334-8171

SPORTING GOODS

Big 5 Sporting Goods, 1201 S.E. Everett Mall Way / (425) 353-9100

Rite Aid Pharmacy, 1001 N. Broadway / (425) 258-1131

G.I. Joe's - Lynwood, 19310 60th Ave W. / (425) 712-9200

Auto Rental and Repair
Budget Rent A Car, 12415 Hwy. 99 / (425) 355-8349
Enterprise Rent A Car, 7705 Evergreen Way #G-7 / (425) 355-4279
AJ's Auto Repair, 2110 25th St. / (425) 258-2400
Benson Auto Clinic, 3019 Rucker Ave. / (425) 258-2154

Air Service
Snohomish County Airport, 3220 100th St. S.W. #A / (425) 353-2110
No commercial service, but charters are available for connection to larger airports.

Medical
Providence General Medical Center, 1321 Colby Ave. / (425) 261-2000

Banks with ATMs
Cascade Bank, 2828 Colby Ave. / (425) 339-5500
US Bank, 2000 W. Marine View Dr. / (425) 304-4110

For More Information
The Everett Area Chamber of Commerce
& Convention & Visitor Bureau
1710 W. Marine View Dr.
Everett, WA 98201
(425) 252-5181

*On the west side of the Cascades, the brush is actually this
thick— a great retriever is a necessity.*

BELLINGHAM
and Whatcom County

Population - 61,240	County Population - 157,500
County Area - 2,126 sq. miles	October Temperature - 49.9°
Annual Precipitation - 52.7"	Acres in CRP - 0

Bellingham, the county seat of Whatcom County, is located in the northwestern corner of Washington. Though heavily urbanized along the I-5 corridor, the eastern portion of the county contains beautiful national forest and wilderness areas.

UPLAND BIRDS
Pheasant, Ruffed and Blue Grouse, Quail
The majority of pheasant and quail hunting occurs on three WDFW Western Washington Pheasant Release sites - Lake Terrell, Arco, and Intalco. Grouse are found in the Cascade Mountains with easy national forest and wilderness area access.

WATERFOWL
Ducks and Geese
Bellingham Bay, lakes, streams, and estuaries provide the waterfowl hunter with opportunities for many varieties of ducks and geese.

ACCOMMODATIONS
Aloha Motel, 315 N. Samish Way / (360) 733-4900 / 28 rooms / Dining on site & nearby, continental breakfast, non-smoking rooms / Dogs allowed / Senior discounts / $

Hotel Bellweather, One Bellweather Way / (360) 647-7002 / Dining on site / Full-service, 68-room luxury hotel with the charm of a European inn. 360 degree views and waterfront rooms in a quaint cove on the bay / Dogs allowed with fee / $$$

Cascade Inn, 208 N. Samish Way / (360) 733-2520 / 44 rooms / Dining on site & nearby, non-smoking rooms / Dogs allowed / Senior discounts / $

Days Inn - Bellingham, 125 E. Kellogg Rd. / (360) 671-6200 / 70 rooms / Dining on site & nearby, continental breakfast, non-smoking rooms / Dogs allowed / Senior discounts / $$

Quality Inn Baron Suites, 100 E. Kellogg Rd. / (360)647-8000 / 86 rooms / Dining on site & nearby, continental breakfast, non-smoking rooms / Dogs allowed / Senior discounts / $$

Best Western Heritage Inn, 714 Lakeway Dr. / (888) 671-1011 / 132 rooms / Dining on site & nearby / Dogs allowed / Non-smoking rooms, senior discounts / $$$

CAMPGROUNDS AND RV PARKS

Crest Haven RV Park, 2500 Samish / (800) 215-7879 / Dogs allowed / Senior discounts, boat launch, showers, full RV hook-ups / $

Sudden Valley Campground, 2311 Lake Louise Rd. / (360) 734-6430 / 100 units / Dining on site & nearby / Dogs allowed, tent sites, boat launch, showers, full RV hook-ups and dump / $

Bellingham RV Park, 3939 Bennett Dr. / (360) 752-1224

Larabee State Park, 245 Chuckanut Dr / (360) 676-2093

RESTAURANTS

Denny's, 13600 Byron St. / (360) 676-0553 / Open seven days per week, 24 hours per day, predictable food and decent prices.

Archer Ale House, 1212 10th St. / In the historic Fairhaven District / renovated English pub cellar featuring a large microbrew selection and great pub food, such as beer-battered fried oysters, hearty soups, brats and pizza.

Austin Creek Restaurant, 2145 Lake Whatcom Blvd. / (360) 734-6430 / Lunch and dinner served seven days per week featuring steaks, seafood, chicken and pasta.

Harborside Bistro, One Bellweather Way in the Hotel Bellweather / Savory NW contemporary cuisine with fresh, local seafood and large wine list / Waterfront dining / Open daily /

Old Town Café, 316 W. Holly St. / (360) 671-4431 / Open daily for breakfast lunch and dinner with home style cooking. Breakfast served all day long.

Dos Padres Fine Mexican Food, 1111 Harris Ave. / (360) 733-9900 / Mexican favorites for lunch and dinner seven days per week.

House of Orient, 209 W. Holly St. / (360) 738-4009 / Thai food for lunch and dinner, seven days a week, good prices.

VETERINARIANS

Fairhaven Vet Hospital, 2330 Old Fairhaven Pkwy. / (360) 671-3903

Bellingham Animal Hospital, 720 Virginia St. / (360) 734-0720

SPORTING GOODS

Big 5 Sporting Goods, 1 Bellis Fair Pkwy. #202 / (360) 734-7802

Rite Aid Pharmacy, 1524 Birchwood Ave. / (360) 647-2175

AUTO RENTAL AND REPAIR

A & A Auto Rental Inc., 4575 Guide Meridian / (360) 734-7262

Avis Rent A Car, 4255 Mitchell Way / (360) 676-8840

76 Car Care Center, 801 Ohio St. / (360) 733-1880

Autotech, 106 E. Axton Rd. / (360) 398-9197

AIR SERVICE

Bellingham International Airport, 4255 Mitchell Way #2 / (360) 671-5674

Several connecting flights to and from Sea-Tac International Airport are available, call for current connections.

MEDICAL
St. Joseph Hospital, 809 E. chestnut St. / (360) 734-5400

BANKS WITH ATMS
Key Bank, 101 E. Holly St. / (360) 676-6317
Seafirst Bank, 1275 E. Sunset Dr. / (360) 647-0305

FOR MORE INFORMATION
The Bellingham/Whatcom County
Convention & Visitors Bureau
904 Potter St.
Bellingham, WA 98226
(360) 671-3990

*In this region, hunting along old logging roads and skidder trails are
usually your best bets for forest grouse.*

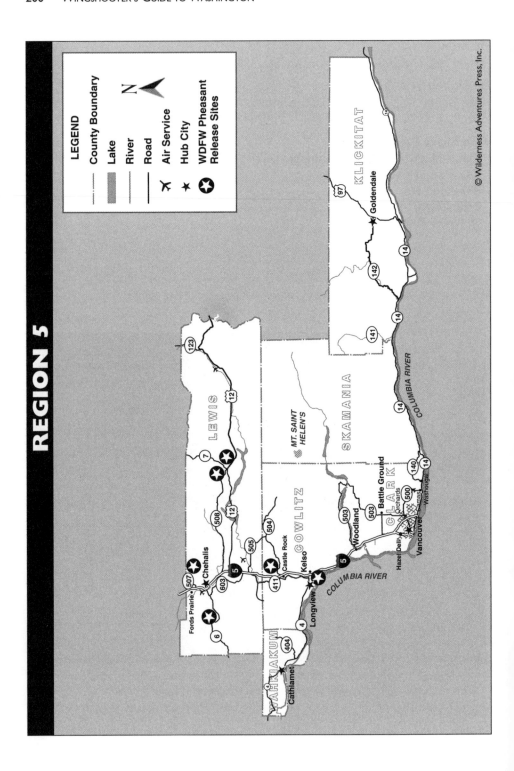

REGION 5

LEGEND
County Boundary
Lake
River
Road
Air Service
Hub City
WDFW Pheasant Release Sites

© Wilderness Adventures Press, Inc.

REGION 5
Southwest Washington

Southwestern Washington is predominantly wet and densely forest. Hunting on national forest land can be productive for all species of forest grouse while waterfowling can be strong on the southern edge along the Columbia River adjacent ponds.

This region offers many resources including a large elk population, many fine steelhead streams and one of the only wild fall Chinook salmon runs in the state.

This southwest corner contains the state's only active volcano, Mount Saint Helens. Also located here are the only active sandhill crane nests and the last western pond turtles in the state.

Washington has thousands of public forested mountain acres.

REGION 5
Ring-necked Pheasant Distribution

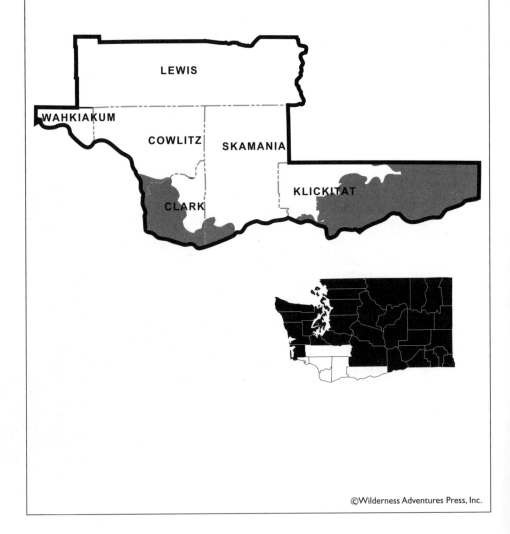

LEWIS

WAHKIAKUM

COWLITZ

SKAMANIA

CLARK

KLICKITAT

©Wilderness Adventures Press, Inc.

1999-2000 Pheasant Harvest Information

County	Harvest	Hunters	Days	Hrv/Day
CLARK	2,358	617	4,301	.55
COWLITZ	705	251	1,306	0.54
KLICKITAT	798	492	1,497	0.53
LEWIS	482	328	1,522	0.32
SKAMANIA	0	0	0	0
WAHKIAKUM	0	0	0	0
REGION 5 TOTAL	4,343	1,421	8,626	0.5

Pheasants can usually be flushed from cattail swamps and sloughs.

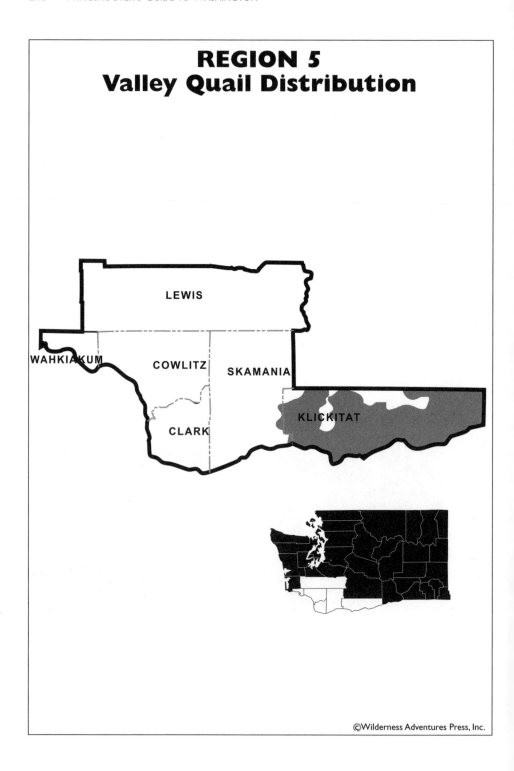

REGION 5
Valley Quail Distribution

©Wilderness Adventures Press, Inc.

1999-2000 Quail Harvest Information

County	Harvest	Hunters	Days	Hrv/Day
CLARK	0	0	0	0
COWLITZ	0	0	0	0
KLICKITAT	2,367	542	1,527	1.55
LEWIS	0	0	0	0
SKAMANIA	38	154	919	0.04
WAHKIAKUM	0	0	0	0
REGION 5 TOTAL	**2,405**	**565**	**2,446**	**0.98**

A covey of valley quail, pinned near sagebrush.

REGION 5
Chukar Partridge Distribution

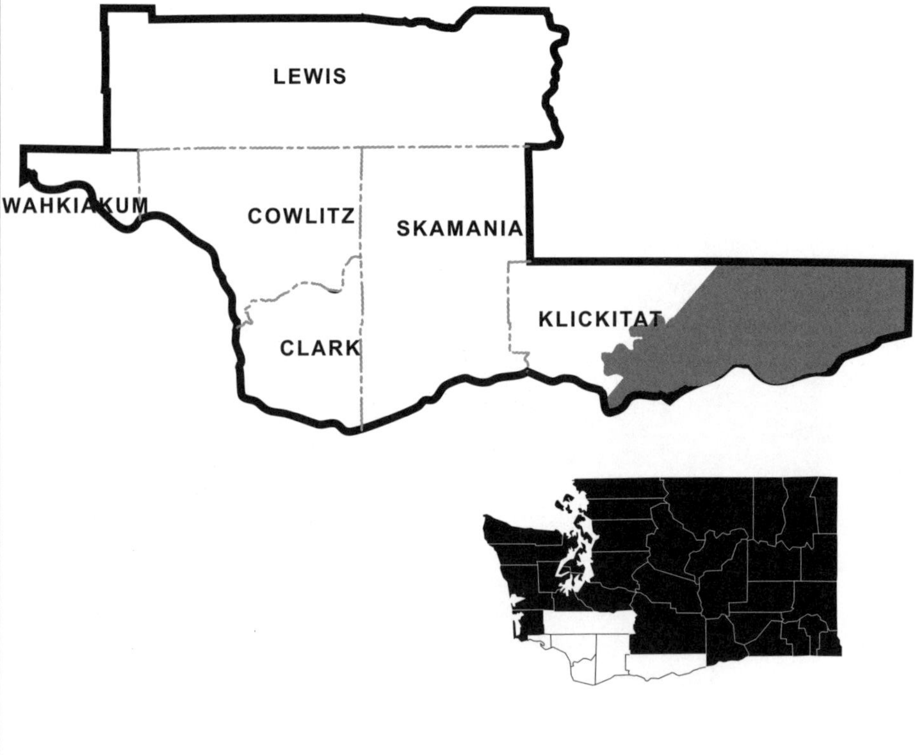

LEWIS

WAHKIAKUM

COWLITZ

SKAMANIA

CLARK

KLICKITAT

©Wilderness Adventures Press, Inc.

1999-2000 Chukar Harvest Information

Count	Harvest	Hunters	Days	Hrv/Day
CLARK	0	0	0	0
COWLITZ	0	0	0	0
KLICKITAT	1,875	669	1,257	1.49
LEWIS	0	0	0	0
SKAMANIA	0	0	0	0
WAHKIAKUM	0	0	0	0
REGION 5 TOTAL	**1,875**	**669**	**1,257**	**1.49**

Jeff Funke and his German wirehair hunting chukar.

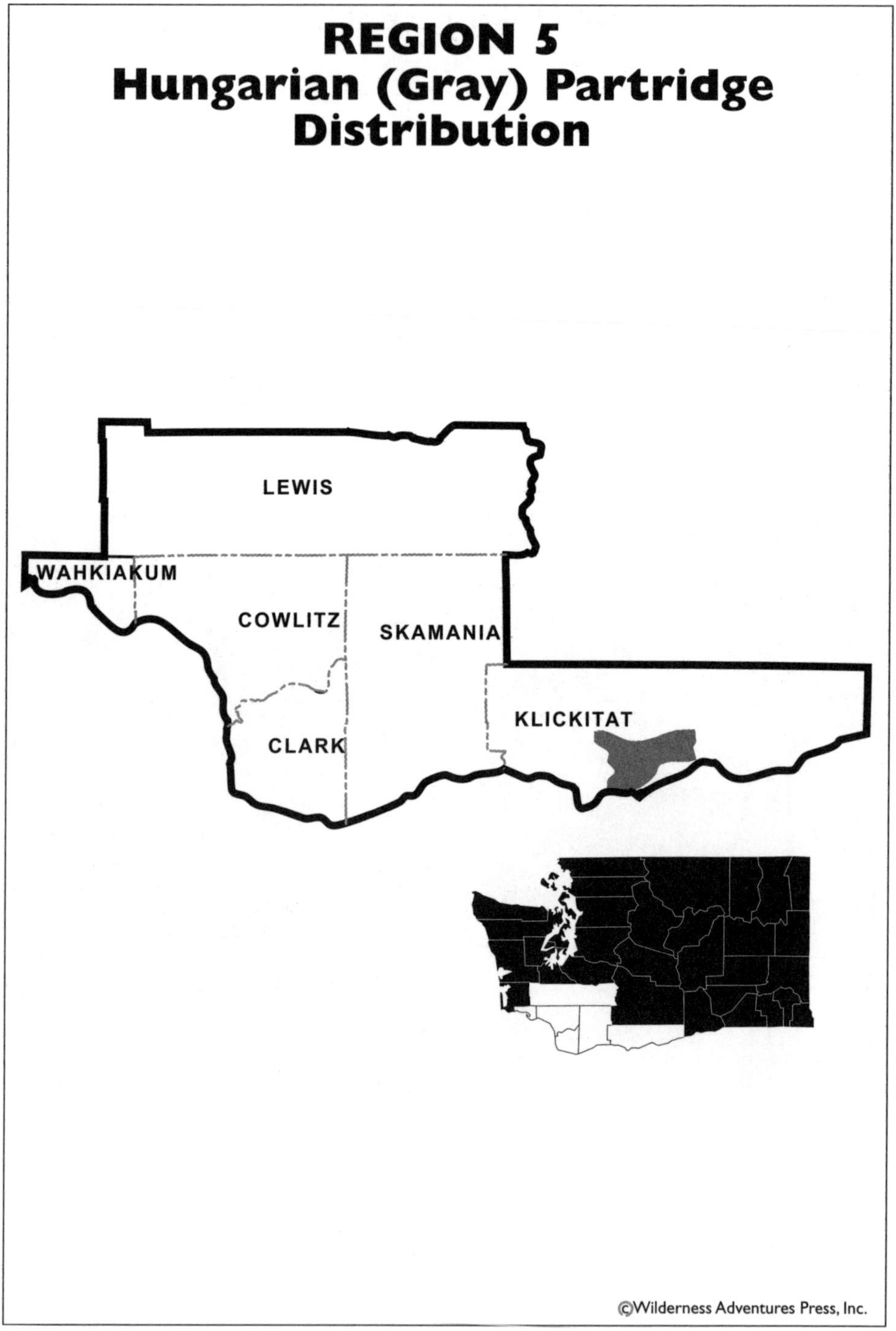

REGION 5
Hungarian (Gray) Partridge
Distribution
LEWIS
WAHKIAKUM
COWLITZ
SKAMANIA
CLARK
KLICKITAT
©Wilderness Adventures Press, Inc.

1999-2000 Hungarian Partridge Harvest Information

County	Harvest	Hunters	Days	Hrv/Day
CLARK	0	0	0	0
COWLITZ	0	0	0	0
KLICKITAT	1,113	442	1,112	1
LEWIS	0	0	0	0
SKAMANIA	0	0	0	0
WAHKIAKUM	0	0	0	0
REGION 5 TOTAL	**1,113**	**442**	**1,112**	**1**

Hungarian partridge.

REGION 5
Forest Grouse Distribution

©Wilderness Adventures Press, Inc.

1999-2000 Forest Grouse Harvest Information

County	Harvest	Hunters	Days	Hrv/Day
CLARK	439	450	1,849	0.24
COWLITZ	2,495	1,244	9,560	0.26
KLICKITAT	1,502	841	3,761	0.4
LEWIS	2,703	1,785	13,136	0.21
SKAMANIA	1,687	1,060	7,586	0.22
WAHKIAKUM	92	274	2,514	0.04
REGION 5 TOTAL	**8,918**	**3,988**	**38,406**	**0.23**

Excellent forest grouse habitat.

REGION 5
Duck Distribution

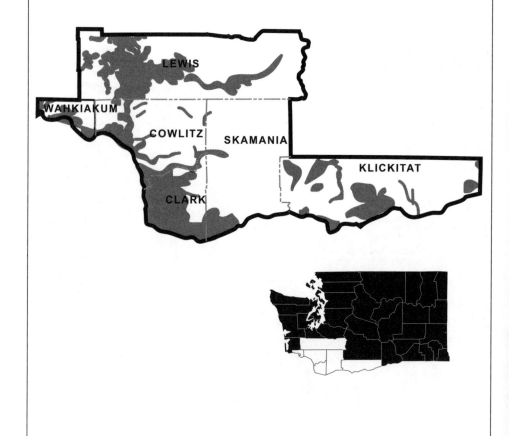

1999-2000 Duck Harvest Information

County	Harvest	Hunters	Days	Hrv/Day
CLARK	15,302	1,338	11,219	1.36
COWLITZ	3,922	684	3,813	1.0
KLICKITAT	1,424	293	1,170	1.22
LEWIS	6,124	695	3,445	1.78
SKAMANIA	1,313	246	1,930	0.68
WAHKIAKUM	2,460	293	1,096	2.24
REGION 5 TOTAL	**30,545**	**2,895**	**22,673**	**1.35**

Broken coulees often have small ponds that hold ducks for jump-shooting.

REGION 5
Goose Distribution

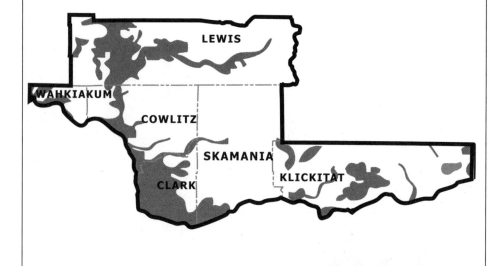

1999-2000 Goose Harvest Information

County	Harvest	Hunters	Days	Hrv/Day
CLARK	3,206	764	4,227	0.76
COWLITZ	1,824	383	1,923	0.95
KLICKITAT	518	235	776	0.67
LEWIS	1,881	583	1,914	0.98
SKAMANIA	38	132	756	0.05
WAHKIAKUM	172	256	484	0.36
REGION 5 TOTAL	**7,639**	**1,671**	**10,080**	**0.76**

In for a landing.

VANCOUVER
and Clark County

Population - 59,225	County Population - 280,000
County Area - 632 sq. miles	October Temperature - 51.7°
Annual Precipitation - 50.01"	Acres in CRP - 0

Vancouver is the county seat of Clark County; it is located on the Columbia River just 100 miles east of the Pacific Ocean. Originally settled in the early 1800s as a Hudson's Bay Company trading post, the area is moderately urbanized, with the eastern part of the county the least developed.

UPLAND BIRDS
Pheasant, Ruffed and Blue Grouse

The majority of pheasant harvested in Clark County are done so at the Shillapoo and Vancouver Lake WDFW Western Washington Pheasant Release sites. Mountain grouse are found in the Cascade Mountain foothills and the woods of the Gifford Pinchot National Forest with fair to good success.

WATERFOWL
Ducks and Geese

Waterfowl are hunted on the many lakes and streams found in Clark County and especially along the Columbia River. Clark County sits right in the middle of the Pacific Flyway.

ACCOMMODATIONS

Best Western Ferryman's Inn, 7901 N.E. 6th Ave. / (360) 574-2151 / Dining on site & nearby, continental breakfast, non-smoking rooms / Dogs allowed / Senior discounts / $

Best Inn and Suites I-5, 7001 NE Highway 99 / (360) 696-0516 / Dining nearby exercise room, swimming pool, continental breakfast / Dogs allowed / Senior discount

Best Inn and Suites Cascade Park, 221 NE Chkalov Dr / (360) 256-7044 / Dining nearby, exercise room, swimming pool, continental breakfast / Dogs allowed / Senior discount

Extended Stay America, 300 NE 115th Ave / (360) 604-8530 / Full kitchen with utensils, dataports, laundry facilities. Weekly rates available. / $$

Vancouver Lodge, 601 Broadway / (360) 693-3668 / 45 rooms / Dining on site & nearby, non-smoking rooms / Dogs allowed / Senior discounts / $

Quality Inn, 7001 N.E. Hwy. 99 / (360) 696-0516 / 72 rooms / Dining on site & nearby, continental breakfast, non-smoking rooms / Dogs allowed / Senior discounts / $$

Shilo Inn - Hazel Dell, 3206 Hwy. 99 / (800) 222-2244 / 65 rooms / Dining on site & nearby, continental breakfast, non-smoking rooms / Dogs allowed / Senior discounts / $$

Shilo Inn - Vancouver, 401 E. 13th St. / (800) 222-2244 / 118 rooms / Dining on site & nearby, continental breakfast, non-smoking rooms / Dogs allowed / Senior discounts / $$$

Doubletree Hotel at the Quay, 100 Columbia St. / (360) 694-8341 / 160 rooms / Dining on site & nearby, non-smoking rooms / Dogs allowed / Senior discounts / $$$

CAMPGROUNDS AND RV PARKS

99 RV Park, 1913 Leichner Rd. / (360) 573-0351 / Showers, full RV hook-ups / $

Sam's Good RV Park, 8510 N.E. Hwy. 99 / (360) 573-9781 / 66 units / Dining on site & nearby, showers, full RV hook-ups / $

Vancouver RV Park, 7603 NE 13th Avenue / (877-756-2972) / 95 sites / Concrete pads

RESTAURANTS

Kettle of Fish, 900 Pacific St / (604) 682-6853 / One of Vancouver's finest fresh seafood restaurants with trees growing right up through the floor, wine cellar featuring Old and New World wines, knowledgeable servers / Open for lunch Mon.-Fri 11:30 a.m.- 2:00 p.m., Daily for dinner at 5:30 p.m.

Denny's, 400 E Mill Plain Blvd. / (360) 696-4917 / Open 24 hours per day, seven days per week, decent food and prices.

The Blind Onion, 2900-B E. Mill Plain Blvd. / (360) 750-7400 / Gourmet pizzas, sandwiches, and salads served in a pub atmosphere. Open daily for lunch and dinner.

Boleto at Ecco II Pane Bakery, 2563 West Broadway / (604) 739-1314 / A classic Italian bistro featuring the finest breads in the city with Old World favorites, fine local wines

Buster's Texas Style Barbecue, 1118 N.E. 78th St. / (360) 546-2439 / Open daily for lunch and dinner with hearty meat lovers favorites.

Chevy's Mexican Restaurant, 4315 N.E. Thurston Way / (360) 256-6922 / Excellent Mexican favorites served daily for lunch and dinner.

Elmer's Steak and Pancake House, 11310 E. Mill Plain Blvd. / (360) 256-0808 / Family style restaurant serving breakfast, lunch, and dinner daily.

The Holland Restaurant, 1708 Main St. / (360) 694-7842 / Open daily for breakfast, lunch, and dinner for American cuisine.

VETERINARIANS

East Mill Plain Animal Hospital, 9705 E. Mill Plain Blvd. / (360) 892-0032

Animal Medicine, 3417 N.E. 78th St. / (360) 573-8838

SPORTING GOODS

Big 5 Sporting Goods, 8700 N.E. Vancouver Mall Dr. / (360) 604-7179

G.I. Joe's Inc., 13215 SE Mill Plain Blvd. / (360) 253-2725

Bi-Mart, 11912 NE 4th Plain Road / (360) 944-5432

Bi-Mart, 2601 Falk Road / (360) 695-6333

Classic Firearms and Hunting Supplies. 14300 NE 20th Ave D102-212 / (360) 546-3104 / (800) 404-1902

AUTO RENTAL AND REPAIR
Auto Rent Cars-Trucks-Vans, 2500 E. 33rd St. / (360) 695-5125
Budget Rent A Car, 8800 N.E. Vancouver Mall Dr. / (360) 574-5331
Andy's Auto Center, 4702 E. Fourth Plain Blvd. / (360) 695-4300
B & L Car Care, 11408 N.E. Rosewood Ave. #E / (360) 896-0901

AIR SERVICE
Pearson Field, E. Reserve St. & 5th St. / (360) 696-8191
No commercial service, however all major carriers are served less than ten miles away.
Portland International Airport, 7000 N.E. Airport Way / (503) 460-4234

MEDICAL
Urgent Care Clinic, 3212 Main St. / (360) 696-5232

BANKS WITH ATMS
Seafirst Bank, 3308 N.E. Auto Mall Dr. / (360) 696-5511
US Bank, 11505 N.E. Fourth Plain Rd. # B / (360) 892-5401

FOR MORE INFORMATION
Vancouver Chamber of Commerce
404 E 15th St., Suite 11
Vancouver, WA 98663
(360) 693-1313

Vancouver Lake in southern Washington.

LONGVIEW
and Cowlitz County

Population - 33,650	County Population - 90,800
County Area - 1,146 sq. miles	October Temperature - 53.2°
Annual Precipitation - 46.14"	Acres in CRP - 0

Longview, the county seat of Cowlitz County, is located on the Columbia River in the I-5 corridor. As with all of western Washington, it is highly urbanized within 20 miles of the interstate. Farther out, however, the foothills of the Cascade Mountains are timbered and lush with undergrowth. Part of the Mount Saint Helens National Volcanic Monument lies within the eastern portion of the county

UPLAND BIRDS
Ruffed and Blue Grouse, Turkeys, Pheasant

The majority of mountain grouse and turkeys are taken in the eastern part of Cowlitz County in the timbered foothills of the Cascade Mountains. There is much private property, including private timber holdings that sometimes allow public hunting. This may vary from year to year. Pheasant are primarily found at two Western Washington Pheasant Release sites operated by the WDFW.

WATERFOWL
Ducks and Geese

Many miles of small rivers and streams, as well as several lakes and the Columbia River, provide good waterfowling in the center of the Pacific Flyway.

ACCOMMODATIONS

Budget Inn - Longview, 1808 Hemlock St. / (360) 423-5816 / 32 rooms / Dining on site & nearby, continental breakfast, non-smoking rooms / Dogs allowed / Senior discounts / $

Town Chalet Motor Hotel, 1822 Washington Way / (360) 423-2020 / 24 rooms / Dining on site & nearby, non-smoking rooms / Dogs allowed / Senior discounts / $

Town House Motel, 744 Washington Way / (360) 423-7200 / 28 rooms / Dining on site & nearby, non-smoking rooms / Dogs allowed / Senior discounts / $

Hudson Manor Motel, 1616 Hudson / (360) 425-1100 / 25 rooms / Dining on site & nearby, non-smoking rooms / Dogs allowed / Senior discounts / $

Holiday Inn Express - Longview, 723 7th Ave. / (360) 414-1000 / 50 rooms / Dining on site & nearby, continental breakfast, non-smoking rooms / Dogs allowed / Senior discounts / $$

Rutherglen Mansion, 420 Rutherglen Rd. / (360)425-5816 / Located near Mt. Solo on a scenic 50-acre homesite / Seven bedrooms with private bath and fireplaces / Rates include full breakfast. $$$ / Dining on site includes contemporary Northwest cuisine / Open for dinner 5:00 - 9:00 p.m. Tuesday through Saturday

Campgrounds and RV Parks
Oaks RV & Trailer Park, 636 California Way / (360) 425-2708 / 150 sites / Dining on site & nearby / Dogs allowed, showers, full RV hook-ups, senior discounts / $

Restaurants
Omelettes & More, 3120 Washington Way / (360) 425-9260 / Serving breakfast and lunch till 2:00 p.m. seven days per week.

Bruno's Pizza, 1108 Washington Way / (360) 425-5520 / Excellent pizza and salad bar for lunch and dinner seven days per week.

Denny's Restaurant, 920 Washington Way / (360) 577-8290 / Open 24 hours, seven days per week, predictable food and decent prices.

Cap'n Yoby's, 2944 Ocean Beach Hwy. / (360) 636-3950 / Good seafood for lunch and dinner.

Casa Azteca, 1124 Washington Way / (360) 636-3031 / Mexican favorites, good prices for lunch and dinner seven days per week.

Chinese Garden Restaurant, 1071 15th Ave. / (360) 423-1510 / Oriental food, for lunch and dinner daily.

Veterinarians
Cowlitz Animal Clinic, 763-Commerce Ave. / (360) 425-6440

Ocean Beach Veterinary Clinic, 4011 Ocean Beach Hwy. / (360) 425-0850

Sporting Goods
Rite Aid Pharmacy, 3 Triangle Shopping Center / (360) 423-4700

Wal-Mart, 3715 Ocean Beach Hwy. / (360) 414-9656

Bob's Sporting Goods, 1111 Hudson / (360) 425-3870

Auto Rental and Repair
Enterprise Rent A Car, 1339 Washington Way # 1 / (360) 423-9999

Auto Shop, 1105 Florida St. / (360) 577-0665

Bell's Auto Service, 438 Oregon Way / (360) 636-4433

Air Service
Kelso-Longview Airport, 2222 S Pacific Ave. Kelso, WA / (360) 425-3688

At 4.7 miles from Longview, this is the nearest airport although there is no commercial service.

Medical
St. John's Medical Center, 1614 E. Kessler Blvd. / (360) 423-1530

BANKS WITH ATMS

Seafirst Bank, 1515 Commerce Ave. / (360) 577-2617
US Bank, 2266 30th Ave. / (360) 577-3230

FOR MORE INFORMATION

Longview Area Chamber of Commerce
1563 Olympia Way
Longview, WA 98632
(360) 423-8400

Klickitat County is characterized by mountainous forests and mixed agriculture.

GOLDENDALE
and Klickitat County

Population - 3,520	County Population - 19,000
County Area - 1,872.5 sq. miles	October Temperature - 48.4°
Annual Precipitation - 16.63"	Acres in CRP - 37,443

Goldendale is the county seat in Klickitat County. It is located on the eastern, dry side of the Cascade Mountains, the area is highly varied in both topography and climate. The eastern portion of the county is dominated by the Horse Heaven Hills plateau, which forms a gently rolling plain that slopes southward toward the Columbia River. Mt. Adams and Oregon's Mt. Hood dominate the western horizon along with the Cascade Mountains. There is a good mixture of both private farmland public land. The Gifford Pinchot National Forest located within the county.

UPLAND BIRDS
Quail, Dove, Chukar, Ruffed Grouse, Turkeys, Pheasant, Hungarian Partridge, Blue Grouse

Quail, dove, and pheasant are hunted primarily in the eastern part of the county, which has most of the agricultural edges these birds need to thrive. Huns and chukar are mostly found along the Columbia River Breaks with the rocky cliffs and hills these species prefer. The grouse, of course, are found in the timbered hills of the northern and western part of the county. This area is one of the top wild turkey producers in the state with the birds found in the central and western part of the county.

WATERFOWL
Ducks and Geese

Klickitat County is not noted for its waterfowling, although a number of ducks and geese are killed each year. Most of these birds are taken along the Columbia or Klickitat Rivers, or on scattered small ponds and lakes.

ACCOMMODATIONS
Barchris Motel, 128 N. Academy / (888) 713-6197 / 9 rooms / Dining on site & nearby, non-smoking rooms / Dogs allowed / $
Ponderosa Motel, 775 E. Broadway / (509) 773-5842 / 28 rooms / Dining on site & nearby, non-smoking rooms / Dogs allowed / $

CAMPGROUNDS AND RV PARKS
Sunset RV Park, 821 Simcoe Dr. / (509) 773-3111 / 33 sites. Tent sites, full RV hook-ups and dump, showers / Dogs allowed / $
Pine Springs Resort, 2471 Hwy. / 97 Satus Pass / (509) 773-4434 / 3 sites / Dining on site & nearby, full breakfast, tent sites, full RV hook-ups / $$

RESTAURANTS

Ayuia Restaurant, 630 E. Simcoe Dr. / (509) 773-7188 / Mexican favorites for lunch and dinner, open daily.

Subway, 1100 E. Broadway / (509) 773-3377 / Deli style sandwiches for breakfast, lunch and dinner, seven days per week.

Gee's Family Restaurant, 118 E. Main St. / (509) 773-6999 / Chinese food for lunch and dinner, Monday through Saturday.

Main Street Café, 120 W. Main St. / (509) 773-6919 / Americana café food for breakfast, lunch, and dinner, Monday through Saturday

Simcoe Café & Dessert Room, 123 W. Main St. / (509) 773-9970 / Breakfast and lunch served Monday through Friday, plus homemade desserts anytime.

VETERINARIANS

Mid-Columbia Veterinary Clinic, 417 E. Broadway St. / (509) 773-4363

SPORTING GOODS

Home & Sport Shop, 126 W. Main St. / (509) 773-5340

AUTO RENTAL AND REPAIR

Stiff Chevrolet-Pontiac Inc., 108 N. Grant Ave. / (509) 773-3711

A 2 Z Auto Clinic, 700 W. Allyn St. / (509) 773-6661

Broadway Automotive, 870 E. Broadway / (509) 773-4488

AIR SERVICE - NEAREST

Chenowith Airpark, 6200 Chenowith Rd. The Dalles, OR / (541) 298-1085
No commercial service, 30.1 miles from Goldendale

MEDICAL

Klickitat Valley Hospital, 310 S. Roosevelt Ave. / (509) 773-4022

BANKS WITH ATMS

Key Bank, 201 W. Main St. / (509) 773-5733

FOR MORE INFORMATION

Goldendale Chamber of Commerce
P.O. Box 524
Goldendale, WA 98620
(509) 773-3400

CHEHALIS
and Lewis County

Population - 7,035	County Population - 68,300
County Area - 2,452 sq. miles	October Temperature - 53°
Annual Precipitation - 64.83"	Acres in CRP - 0

Lewis County is located in southwest Washington with Chehalis the county seat. Approximately 75 percent of the county is forested and mountainous. Nearly one-third of the county area is designated as national forest, primarily in the eastern portion of the county. The majority of the population and private property lies along the I-5 corridor in the western part of the county.

UPLAND BIRDS
Ruffed and Blue Grouse, Pheasant, Turkeys

Mountain grouse and turkeys are found in the timbered hills and mountains of the central and eastern portion of Lewis County. Much of this land is located in the Gifford Pinchot National Forest and has plenty of public access. Pheasants are almost always exclusively hunted on five WDFW Western Washington Pheasant Release sites located throughout the county.

WATERFOWL
Ducks and Geese

There are no grain fields of significant size located in Lewis County, but fair waterfowling can be had along streams large and small, as well as several lakes with public access.

ACCOMMODATIONS
Relax Inn, 550 S.W. Parkland Dr. / (360) 748-8608 / 29 rooms / Dining on site & nearby, non-smoking rooms / Dogs allowed / Senior discounts -$

Howard Johnson, 122 Interstate Ave. / (360) 748-0101 / 71 rooms / Dining on site & nearby, non-smoking rooms / $$

CAMPGROUNDS AND RV PARKS
Chehalis KOA, 118 US Hwy. 12 / (360) 262-9220 / 50 sites / Full RV hook-ups and dump, tent sites, showers / Dogs allowed / Dining on site & nearby, non-smoking cabins / $

RESTAURANTS
Denny's, 118 Interstate Ave. / (360) 784-6851 / Always open with decent food and prices.

The Golden Boat, 601 N. National / (360) 748-0377 / Chinese and American food for lunch and dinner seven days per week.

Kit Carson, 107 S.W. Interstate Ave. / (360) 740-1084 / Open daily for breakfast, lunch, and dinner, for American steak house favorites.

The Old Brickyard, 1587 N. National Ave. / (360) 740-1032 / Hearty western cuisine for lunch and dinner daily.

Plaza Jalisco, 1340 N.W. Maryland / (360) 748-4298 / Mexican favorites for lunch and dinner open every day.

Paradise Teriyaki, 337 Chelhalis Ave. / (360) 748-7513 / Asian style foods, seven days per week for lunch and dinner.

VETERINARIANS

Chehalis-Centralia Veterinary, 1214 N.W. State Ave. / (360) 748-6622
Darnell Veterinary Hospital, 4177 Jackson Hwy. / (360) 262-3811

SPORTING GOODS

Rite Aid Pharmacy, 811 N.E. Hampe Way / (360) 748-0077
Sunbird Shopping Center, 1757 N. National Ave. / (360) 748-3337

AUTO RENTAL AND REPAIR

Practical Rent A Car, 2100 N. National Ave. / (360) 748-0310
U Save Auto Rental, 2590 N.E. Kresky Ave. / (360) 748-4978
B C & C Service, 1696 Bishop Rd. / (360) 748-7566
Dave's Auto Repair, 736 Cousins Rd. / (360) 748-0653

AIR SERVICE

Chehalis-Centralia Airport, 900 N.W. Airport Way / (360) 748-1230
No commercial service.

MEDICAL

Providence Centralia Hospital, 914 S. Scheuber Rd. / (360) 740-8323

BANKS WITH ATMS

Washington Mutual Bank, 681 S. Market Blvd. / (360) 748-0145
Wells Fargo Bank, 473 N. Market Blvd. / (360) 740-8565

FOR MORE INFORMATION

The Chamber of Commerce
500 NW Chamber of Commerce Way
Chehalis, WA 98532
(800) 525-3323

STEVENSON
and Skamania County

Population - 1,300	County Population - 9,985
County Area - 1,672 sq. miles	October Temperature - 47.9°
Annual Precipitation - 103.5"	Acres in CRP - 0

Stevenson is a small, friendly, rural community oriented toward recreation and tourism. It is a destination town for such activities as windsurfing, mountain biking, and hiking. Due to Skamania County's location on the Columbia River in the middle of the Cascade Mountains, there is much public land access The majority of the county is located within the boundaries of the Gifford Pinchot National Forest.

UPLAND BIRDS
Ruffed and Blue Grouse, Turkeys

The mountain grouse and turkey hunting in Skamania County is all highly accessible on National Forest land. Turkeys and ruffed grouse are found in the lower elevations along drainages, and forest/meadow edges. Blue grouse are usually found on the higher ridgelines.

WATERFOWL
Ducks and Geese

Waterfowl hunting is limited and what birds are taken are usually hunted along the Columbia River, although the Wind and Little White Salmon rivers may be productive at times.

ACCOMMODATIONS
Econo Lodge - Stevenson, 40 N.E. Second St. / (509) 427-5628 / 30 rooms / Dining on site & nearby, continental breakfast, non-smoking rooms, senior discounts / $$

The Timbers, 200 S.W. Cascade / (509) 427-5656 / 8 rooms / Dining on site & nearby / $$$

Skamania Lodge, P.O. Box 189 / (800) 221-7117 / 195 rooms / Dining on site & nearby, non-smoking rooms / $$$

CAMPGROUNDS AND RV PARKS
Lewis & Clark RV Park, MP 37 Hwy. 14 / (509) 427-5982 / 75 sites. Tent sites, boat launch, showers, full RV hook-ups and dump / $

Valley RV Park, 50151 SR 14. / (509) 427-5300 / 4 sites / Full RV hook-ups / $

RESTAURANTS
Main Street Deli, West end of 2nd St. / (509) 427-5653 / Deli sandwiches, pizza, and chicken 24 hours per day, seven days per week

Dee's Kich-INN, 10 N.W. 2nd St. / (509) 427-4670 / Homestyle cooking for breakfast, lunch, and dinner, open daily.

A & J Select, 265 2nd St. / (509) 427-7808 / Soups, salads, and sandwiches from 7:00 a.m. to 7:00 p.m. daily

Little Viking Drive-In, 2nd St. / (509) 427-5653 / Hamburgers and tacos for lunch and dinner daily.

VETERINARIANS
Hood River Alpine Hospital, 300 Frankton Rd. Hood River, OR / (541) 386-6658
Nearest to Stevenson at 25.9 miles.

SPORTING GOODS
Rite Aid Pharmacy, 2049 Cascade Ave. Hood River, OR / (541) 387-2424
Nearest to Stevenson at 26.5 miles.

AUTO REPAIR
General Services, 326 S.W. Hwy. 14 / (509) 427-7888

AIR SERVICE
Chenowith Airpark, 6200 Chenoweth Rd. The Dalles, OR / (541) 298-1085
Nearest to Stevenson, 39.7 miles. No commercial service.

MEDICAL
Mid-Columbia Family Health Center, 875 Rockcreek Dr. S.W. / (509) 427-4212

BANKS WITH ATMS
Riverview Savings Bank, 225 S.W. 2nd St. / (509) 427-5603

FOR MORE INFORMATION
Skamania County Chamber of Commerce
P.O. Box 1037
Stevenson, WA 98648
(800) 989-9178

CATHLAMET
and Wahkiakum County

Population - 545	County Population - 3,900
County Area - 261 sq. miles	October Temperature - 52.8°
Annual Precipitation - 50.01"	Acres in CRP - 0

Cathlamet is Wahkiakum's county seat. A small, highly rural county, most of the terrain is heavily forested, and though almost entirely owned by private timber companies, much public access is allowed. There is good public waterfowling available along the Columbia River, including the Julia Butler Hansen National Wildlife Refuge.

UPLAND BIRDS
Ruffed and Blue Grouse, Turkeys

Nearly all grouse and turkey hunting takes place on private timberlands in Wahkiakum County. While many companies allow unrestricted public access, some require written permission. This seems to change on a regular basis, so check locally before hunting.

WATERFOWL
Ducks and Geese

The Columbia River and the Julia Butler Hansen National Wildlife Refuge both provide good waterfowl hunting opportunities, primarily for ducks.

ACCOMMODATIONS
Nassa Point Motel, 851 E. SR 4 / (888) 763-7438 / 6 rooms / Dining on site & nearby, non-smoking rooms / Dogs allowed / Senior discounts / $
The Gallery Bed & Breakfast, 851 E. State Route 4 / 5 rooms / Dogs allowed / $$
Redfern Farm Bed & Breakfast, 277 Cross Dike Rd. / Four miles from downtown Cathlamet, 2 guest rooms in an eclectic mix of old and new, private bath, full breakfast, outdoor spa, deck and country garden / $$

CAMPGROUNDS AND RV PARKS
Marv's RV Park, 276 E. SR 4 / (360) 795-3453 / 20 sites plus tent sites, full RV hook-ups and dump / $

RESTAURANTS
Mace's Rainbow Inn, 395 Jacobson Rd. / (360) 795-3481 / Open 7:00 a.m. to 8:00 p.m. daily, serving classic American food for breakfast, lunch, and dinner.
Ranch House Restaurant, 380 Una Ave. / (360) 795-8015 / Open daily 5:00 a.m. to 8:00 p.m. for breakfast, lunch and dinner. Family style food.

VETERINARIANS

Ocean Beach Veterinary Clinic, 4011 Ocean Beach Hwy. Longview, WA / (360) 425- 0850. Nearest to Cathlamet - 16.6 miles

SPORTING GOODS

Rite Aid Pharmacy, 3 Triangle Shopping Center, Longview, WA / (360) 423-4700 Nearest to Cathlamet - 16.6 miles

AUTO REPAIR

Larry's Auto Parts, 305 E. SR 4 / (360) 795-3269

AIR SERVICE

Kelso-Longview Airport, 2222 S. Pacific Ave., Kelso, WA (360) 425-3688 Nearest to Cathlamet - 21.1 miles

MEDICAL

Peace Health Medical Group, 335 Una Ave. / (360) 795-3201

BANKS WITH ATMS

Seafirst Bank, 75 Main St. / (360) 795-3281

FOR MORE INFORMATION

Lower Columbia Economic Development Council
P.O. Box 98
Skamokawa, WA 98647
(360) 795-3996

Cathlamet, Washington.

REGION 6

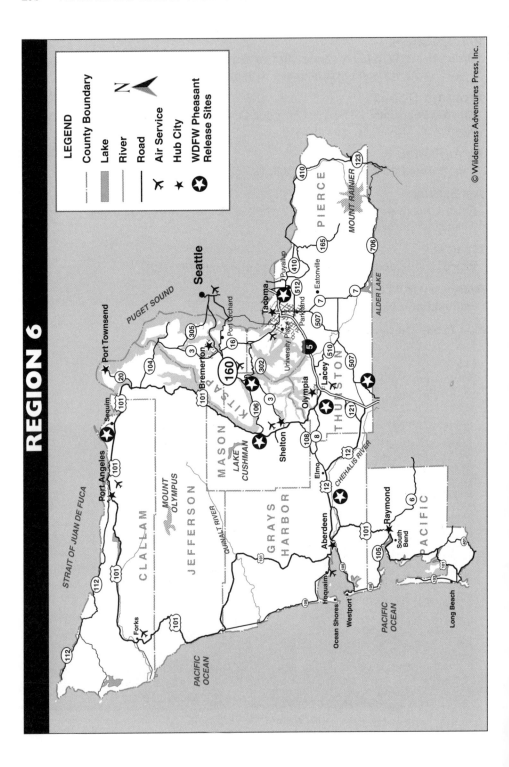

REGION 6
Coastal

The coastal counties from the Long Beach Peninsula in the south to the Strait of Juan de Fuca in the north along with the counties surrounding southern Puget Sound and Hood Canal comprise this region.

The area is rich in fish and wildlife. Unique to this region are Roosevelt elk that make their home on the Olympic Peninsula. The region also includes two major esturine environments, Grays Harbor and Willapa Bay and the most significant remaining natural prairie ecosystems, which hosts unique species of plants and animals. Bowerman Basin, an arm of Grays Harbor, is a world renown bird watching area, particularly during spring and fall shore bird migration. Ocean Shores is Washington's most unique area to watch birds; 290 species have been identified in the area — 70 percent of the species that occur statewide.

The region also includes Olympic National Park and a portion of Mt. Rainier National Park, and the Hood Canal Watershed Project Center. Grouse are the quarry of choice here, especially in the Olympic rain forest. Waterfowl hunting can be strong along estuaries, rivers and inlets.

The waves roll in on Washington's Pacific Coast.

REGION 6
Ring-necked Pheasant Distribution

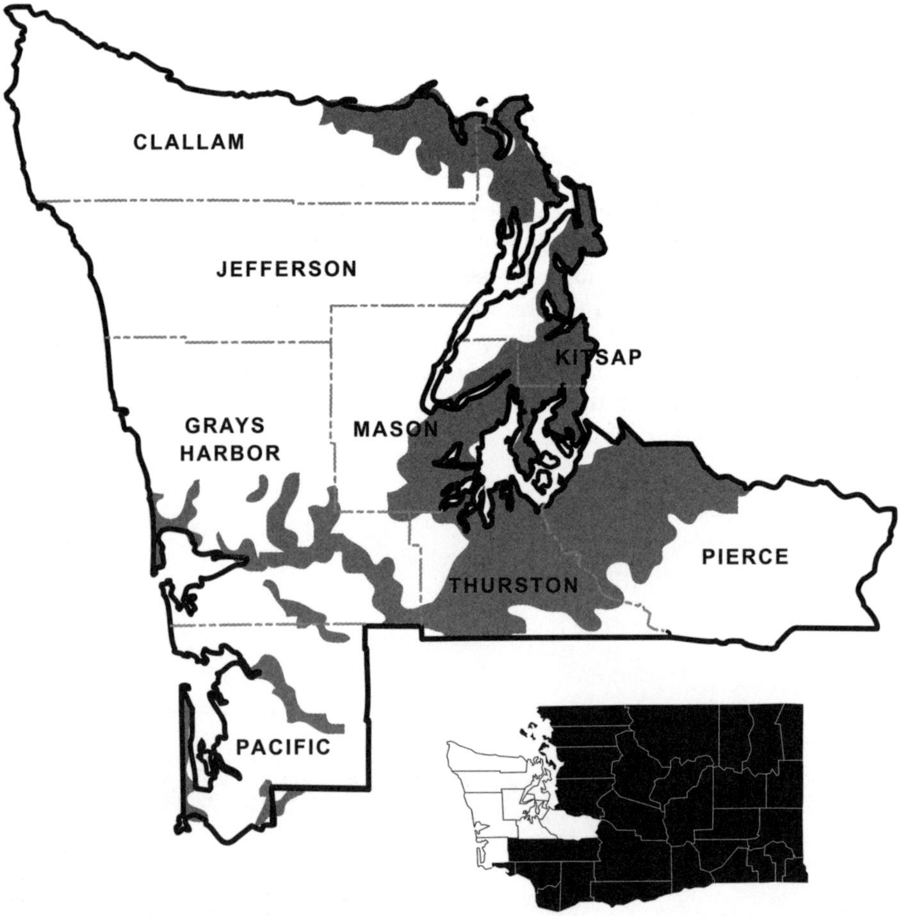

CLALLAM

JEFFERSON

KITSAP

GRAYS HARBOR

MASON

PIERCE

THURSTON

PACIFIC

©Wilderness Adventures Press, Inc.

1999-2000 Pheasant Harvest Information

County	Harvest	Hunters	Days	Hrv/Day
CLALLAM	297	198	1,637	0.18
GRAY'S HARBOR	0	133	178	0
JEFFERSON	0	141	347	0
KITSAP	185	177	1,662	0.11
MASON	1,392	265	2,091	0.67
PACIFIC	519	134	897	0.58
PIERCE	2,302	457	3,019	0.76
THURSTON	3,788	734	6,158	0.62
REGION 6 TOTAL	**8,483**	**1,407**	**15,989**	**0.53**

An early season point.

REGION 6
Mountain Quail Distribution

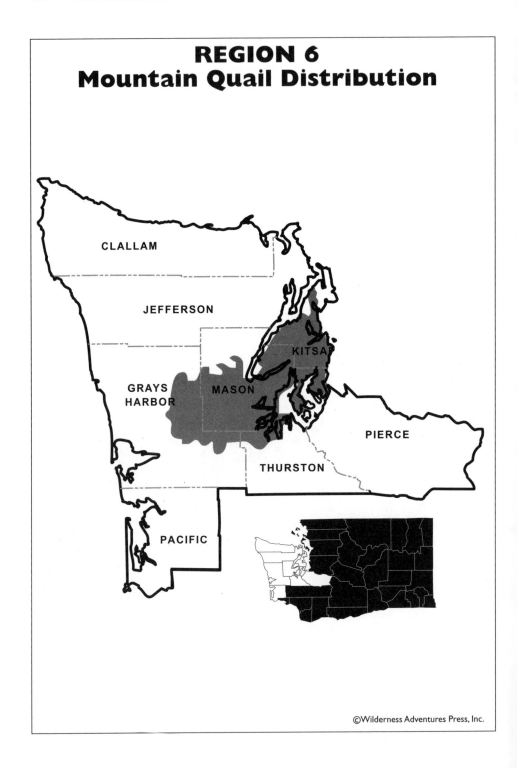

©Wilderness Adventures Press, Inc.

1999-2000 Quail Harvest Information

County	Harvest	Hunters	Days	Hrv/Day
CLALLAM	38	147	149	0.26
GRAY'S HARBOR	0	0	0	0
JEFFERSON	0	0	0	0
KITSAP	0	0	0	0
MASON	58	143	170	0.34
PACIFIC	0	0	0	0
PIERCE	0	106	554	0
THURSTON	19	146	93	0.2
REGION 6 TOTAL	**115**	**235**	**966**	**0.12**

Mountain quail live in thick, brushy areas of mountains, meadows, and along edges of conifer stands.

REGION 6
Forest Grouse Distribution

CLALLAM

JEFFERSON

KITSAP

GRAYS HARBOR

MASON

PIERCE

THURSTON

PACIFIC

©Wilderness Adventures Press, Inc.

1999-2000 Forest Grouse Harvest Information

County	Harvest	Hunters	Days	Hrv/Day
CLALLAM	1,502	593	4,887	0.31
GRAY'S	0	0	0	0
HARBOR	2,241	1,032	8,472	0.26
JEFFERSON	623	556	2,964	0.21
KITSAP	46	284	931	0.05
MASON	1,409	774	6,030	0.23
PACIFIC	1,039	546	3,813	0.27
PIERCE	1,386	916	6,281	0.22
THURSTON	739	751	4,765	0.16
REGION 6 TOTAL	**8,985**	**4,003**	**38,143**	**0.24**

Thick forest covers where ruffed and spruce grouse are likely to be found.

REGION 6
Duck Distribution

1999-2000 Duck Harvest Information

County	Harvest	Hunters	Days	Hrv/Day
CLALLAM	8,104	664	4,100	1.98
GRAY'S HARBOR	13,766	989	6,932	1.99
JEFFERSON	5,218	328	2,537	2.06
KITSAP	1,017	180	1,109	0.92
MASON	1,813	374	1,351	1.34
PACIFIC	8,844	816	4,693	1.88
PIERCE	12,101	1,226	7,966	1.52
THURSTON	8,308	727	3,970	2.09
REGION 6 TOTAL	**59,171**	**4,114**	**32,658**	**1.81**

Coastal beaches and estuaries can provide good hunting for diving ducks.

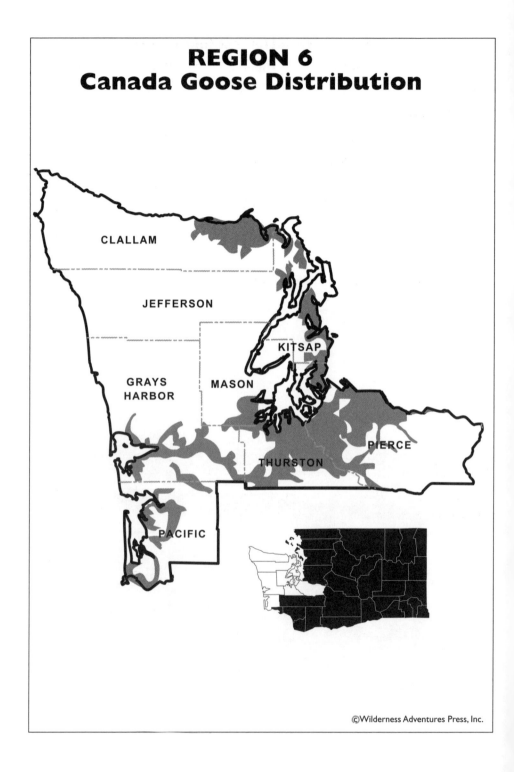

REGION 6
Canada Goose Distribution

CLALLAM

JEFFERSON

KITSAP

MASON

GRAYS
HARBOR

PIERCE

THURSTON

PACIFIC

1999-2000 Goose Harvest Information

County	Harvest	Hunters	Days	Hrv/Day
CLALLAM	902	293	1,502	0.6
GRAY'S HARBOR	614	326	1,613	0.38
JEFFERSON	384	179	1,866	0.21
KITSAP	614	94	664	0.92
MASON	153	183	294	0.52
PACIFIC	307	315	872	0.35
PIERCE	441	493	2,309	0.19
THURSTON	480	336	1,393	0.34
REGION 6 TOTAL	**3,895**	**1,396**	**10,513**	**0.37**

A retriever is a must when goose hunting this region!

PORT ANGELES
and Clallam County

Population - 18,890	County Population - 66,400
County Area - 1,754 sq. miles	October Temperature - 52.5°
Annual Precipitation - 24.61"	Acres in CRP - 0

Port Angeles, the county seat of Clallam County, is located in the northwest corner of Washington on the Olympic Peninsula between the Strait of Juan de Fuca and the Olympic Mountains. The area has a reputation for a mild climate year-round. With much of the Olympic National Forest within county borders, recreational opportunities abound.

UPLAND BIRDS
Ruffed and Blue Grouse, Pheasant

The majority of grouse are taken within the boundaries of the Olympic National Forest. Most pheasant are taken from the Dungeness Recreation Area, a Western Washington Pheasant Release Program site, administered by WDFW.

WATERFOWL
Ducks and Geese

With several lakes and many small to medium streams located on national forest land, waterfowl hunters have good opportunities for floating, decoying, or jump shooting ducks and occasionally geese.

ACCOMMODATIONS
The Pond Motel, 1425 W. Hwy. 101 / (360) 452-8422 / 12 rooms / Dining on site & nearby, non-smoking rooms / Dogs allowed / Senior discounts / $

Travelers Motel, 1133 E. 1st St. / (360) 452-2303 / 11 rooms / Dining on site & nearby, non-smoking rooms / Dogs allowed / $

Log Cabin Resort, 3183 E. Beach Rd. / (360) 928-3325 / 28 rooms / Dining on site & nearby, non-smoking rooms / Dogs allowed / $$

Aggie's Inn, 602 E. Front St. / (360) 457-0471 / 114 rooms / Dining on site & nearby, non-smoking rooms / Dogs allowed / $$

Uptown Inn, 101 E. Laurel / (360) 547-9434 / 35 rooms / Dining on site & nearby, continental breakfast, non-smoking rooms / Dogs allowed / Senior discounts / $$$

Doubletree Hotel Port Angeles, 221 N. Lincoln / (360) 452-9215 / 187 rooms / Dining on site & nearby, non-smoking rooms / Dogs allowed / Senior discounts / $$$

CAMPGROUNDS AND RV PARKS
Lyre River Park, 596 W. Lyre River Rd. / (360) 928-3436 / 90 sites / Dogs allowed, tent sites, boat launch, showers, full RV hook-ups and dump / $

Peabody Creek RV Park, 127 S. Lincoln / (360) 457-7092 / 36 sites / Dining on site & nearby / Dogs allowed, tent sites, showers, full RV hook-ups and dump / $

Conestoga Quarters RV Park, 40 Sieberts Creek Rd. & Hwy. 101 / (360) 452-4637 / 45 sites / Dogs allowed, tent sites, showers, full RV hook-ups and dump / $

RESTAURANTS

Joshua's Restaurant & Lounge, 113 Delguzzi Dr. / (360) 452-6545 / Open daily at 6:00 a.m. for breakfast, lunch, and dinner with homestyle food.

Golden Gate Restaurant, 106 W. Front / (360) 457-6944 / Cantonese and Mandarin Chinese food for lunch and dinner seven days per week.

Bella Italia, 117B E. First St. / (360) 457-5442 / Excellent Italian food served daily for lunch and dinner.

Chestnut Cottage Restaurant, 929 E. Front St. / (360) 452-8344 / American favorites with large portions for breakfast and lunch, seven days per week.

Chihuahua Mexican Restaurant, 408 S. Lincoln St. / (360) 452-8174 / Mexican favorites served daily for lunch and dinner.

Cornerhouse Restaurant, 101 E. Front St. / (360) 452-9692 / Good American style food at reasonable prices, for breakfast, lunch, and dinner served daily.

VETERINARIANS

All Animal Veterinary Hospital, 1811 W. Hwy. 101 / (360) 452-4551

Port Angeles Veterinary Clinic, 829 E. 1st St. / (360) 452-5541

SPORTING GOODS

Rite Aid Pharmacy, 110 Port Angeles Plaza / (360) 457-1106

Wal-Mart, 3500 E. Hwy. 101 / (360) 452-4910

AUTO RENTAL AND REPAIR

Budget Rent A Car, 111 E. Front St. / (360) 452-4774

Evergreen Auto Rental, 808 E. Front St. / (360) 452-8001

AIR SERVICE

Sequim Valley Airport, 468 Dorothy Hunt Ln. Sequim, WA / (360) 683-444 Nearest to Port Angeles, at 11.6 miles, there is no commercial service.

MEDICAL

Olympic Memorial Hospital, 939 Caroline St. / (360) 417-7000

BANKS WITH ATMS

SeaFirst Bank, 134 W. 8th St. / (360) 457-2747

US Bank, 134 E. 7th St. / (360) 457-1184

FOR MORE INFORMATION

Port Angeles Chamber of Commerce
121 E. Railroad
Port Angeles, WA 98362
(360) 452-2363

With much of the Olympic National Forest within county borders, recreational opportunities abound in Region 6.

ABERDEEN
and Grays Harbor County

Population - 16,610	County Population - 67,923
County Area - 1,918 sq. mi.	October Temperature - 52.9°
Annual Precipitation - 106.73"	Acres in CRP - 23

Aberdeen and Grays Harbor County are located in the westernmost part of Washington in the middle of the Olympic National Rainforest. With annual rainfall of over 100 inches, the vegetation is lush and thick. The county is highly rural, with much land being owned by private timber companies.

UPLAND BIRDS
Ruffed and Blue Grouse, Turkeys, Pheasant

Mountain grouse and turkeys are abundant in the lush forests of Grays Harbor County, and while much of the area is private timber holdings, some of the companies allow public hunting, and a portion of the Olympic National Forest lies in northern Grays Harbor County. Pheasants are hunted on the Western Washington Pheasant Release Program site administered by the WDFW.

WATERFOWL
Ducks and Geese

With its many creeks, rivers, and small lakes, plus the Pacific Ocean, waterfowl are quite abundant. Much of this water lies within the borders of the Olympic National Forest, so access is good.

ACCOMMODATIONS

Towne Motel, 7152 W Wishkah St. / (360) 533-2340 / 24 rooms. Non-smoking rooms / Dogs allowed / Senior discounts / $

Flamingo Motel, 1120 E Wishkah / (360) 532-4103 / 20 rooms / Dining on site & nearby, non-smoking rooms / Dogs allowed / Senior discounts / $

Travelure Motel, 623 W Wishkah / (360) 532-3280 / 24 rooms. Non-smoking rooms / Dogs allowed / Senior discounts / $$

Nordic Inn Motel, 1700 S Boone St. / (800) 442-0101 / 66 rooms / Dining on site & nearby, non-smoking rooms / Dogs allowed / Senior discounts / $$

Thunderbird Motel, 410 W Wishkah / (360) 532-3153 / 36 rooms / Dining on site & nearby, non-smoking rooms / Dogs allowed / Senior discounts / $$

Red Lion Inn, 521 W Wishkah St. / (360) 532-5210 / 67 rooms / Dining on site & nearby, continental breakfast, non-smoking rooms / Dogs allowed / Senior discounts / $$$

Campgrounds and RV Parks

Arctic RV Park, 893 US Hwy. 101 / (360) 533-4470
20 sites / Dining on site & nearby / Dogs allowed tent sites, showers, full RV hook-ups and dump, senior discounts / $

Restaurants

Louise's Authentic Mexican, 1915 Simpson Ave. / (360) 533-3104 / Open daily for lunch and dinner for Mexican favorites.

Big Matt's Better Barbecue, 815 E Heron St. / (360) 532-1446 / The "best barbecue on the coast," Big Matt's is open daily for lunch and dinner.

Figaro's Italian Kitchen, 1029 E Wishkah St. / (360) 538-7210 / Excellent Italian food for lunch and dinner, seven days per week.

Denny's, 418 W Heron St. / (360) 533-5922 / Always open with decent, predictable food.

Chinese Village, 2409 Simpson Ave. / (360) 533-1485 / Cantonese and Mandarin favorites for lunch and dinner, daily.

Captains Corner, 701 W Curtis St. / (360) 533-2908 / Excellent, fresh seafood seven days per week for lunch and dinner.

Veterinarians

Olympic Veterinary Service, 2001 Simpson Ave. / (360) 532-9081
Aberdeen Animal Hospital, 1029 E Wishkah St. / (360) 532-9390

Sporting Goods

Rite Aid Pharmacy, 1209 E. Wishkah St. / (360) 533-6125

Auto Repair

Advanced Automotive, 521 E. 1st St. / (360) 538-9786
City Center Service, 115 W Heron St. / (360) 532-9512

Air Service

Bowerman Airport, Airport Way, Hoquiam, WA / (360) 533-6655
Nearest to Aberdeen, 5.4 miles, no commercial service.

Medical

Grays Harbor Community Hospital, 915 Anderson Dr. / (360) 532-8330

Banks with ATMs

Seattle First National Bank, 101 E Market / (360) 532-8040
US Bank, 727 Simpson Ave. / (360) 532-3480

For More Information

The Grays Harbor Chamber of Commerce
506 Duffy St.
Aberdeen, WA 98520
(360) 532-1924

PORT TOWNSEND
and Jefferson County

Population - 8,200	County Population - 25,000
County Area - 1,820 sq. miles	October Temperature - 52.5°
Annual Precipitation - 21.72"	Acres in CRP - 0

Port Townsend is the only incorporated community in all of Jefferson County. It is located in the northeast corner of the Olympic Peninsula, in the "rain shadow" of the Olympic Mountains. Approximately 60 percent of Jefferson County is Olympic National Park, Olympic National Forest, or designated wilderness area. The terrain is heavily forested and mountainous.

UPLAND BIRDS
Ruffed Grouse and Blue Grouse

Grouse are abundant in the forests of Jefferson County. There is no hunting within Olympic National Park. However, the surrounding national forest provides good, although not easy, access to public hunting. The vegetation is extremely thick, this is rain forest with giant ferns and moss growing on everything to prove it.

WATERFOWL
Ducks and Geese

There are many small and medium sized rivers that flow out of the Olympic Mountains and the national park through national forest land, providing good access for those who enjoy jump-shooting for waterfowl.

ACCOMMODATIONS

Valley View Motel, 162 Hwy. 20 / (360) 385-1666 / 6 rooms / Dining on site & nearby, non-smoking rooms / Dogs allowed / $

The Waterstreet Hotel, 635 Water St. / (800) 735-9810 / 16 rooms / Dining on site & nearby, non-smoking rooms / Dogs allowed / Senior discounts / $$

The Palace Hotel, 1004 Water St. / (800) 962-0741 / 15 rooms / Dining on site & nearby, continental breakfast, non-smoking rooms / Dogs allowed / Senior discounts / $$

Port Townsend Inn, 2020 Washington St. / (360) 385-2211 / 33 rooms. Continental breakfast, non-smoking rooms / Dogs allowed / Senior discounts / $$

Aladdin Motor Inn, 2333 Washington St. / (360) 385-3747 / 30 rooms / Dining on site & nearby, non-smoking rooms / Dogs allowed / Senior discounts / $$$

Harborside Inn, 330 Benedict St. / (800) 942-5960 / 63 rooms / Dining on site & nearby, continental breakfast, non-smoking rooms / Dogs allowed / $$$

CAMPGROUNDS AND RV PARKS

Point Hudson Resort & Marina, Point Hudson Harbor / (800) 826-3854 / 60 sites / Dining on site & nearby, non-smoking rooms dogs allowed, boat launch, full RV hook-ups, showers / $

RESTAURANTS

Bayview, 1539 Water St. / (360) 385-1461 / Home style American cuisine served daily for breakfast, lunch, and dinner.

Burrito Depot, 609 Washington St. / (360) 385-5856 / Mexican style food for breakfast, lunch, and dinner, seven days per week.

Lanza's Ristorante, 1020 Lawrence St. / (360) 379-1900 / Italian favorites, served daily for dinner.

Port Townsend Café, 2152 W. Sims Way / (360) 385-7747 / Homestyle meals for breakfast, lunch, and dinner seven days per week.

Silver Palace, 2001 Sims Way / (360) 385-6175 / Chinese cuisine served for lunch and dinner daily.

Silverwater Café, 237 Taylor St. / (360) 385-6448 / Open daily for lunch and dinner for fresh seafood and Northwest favorites.

VETERINARIANS

Pet Townsend Veterinary Service, 274 Otto St. #D / (360) 385-3665

Paradise Bay Veterinary Clinic, 9522 Oak Bay Rd. / (360) 385-7297

SPORTING GOODS

Henery Hardware, 218 W. Sims Way / (360) 385-5900

AUTO RENTAL AND REPAIR

Budget Rent A Car, 518 Logan St. / (360) 385-7766

Auto Works, 2313 3rd St. / (360) 385-5682

Don's Automotive Service, 401 Sherman St. / (360) 385-0110

AIR SERVICE

Jefferson County International Airport, P.O. Box 1180 / (360) 385-0656

Served by Port Townsend Airways, 310 Airport Rd. / (360) 385-6554

MEDICAL

Jefferson General Hospital, 834 Sheridan St. / (360) 385-2200

BANKS WITH ATMS

Seafirst Bank, 734 Water St. / (360) 385-1883

Washington Mutual Bank, 419 Kearney St. / (360) 385-0425

FOR MORE INFORMATION

Port Townsend Chamber of Commerce
2347 E. Sims Way
Port Townsend, WA 98368
(360) 385-2722

BREMERTON
and Kitsap County

Population - 39,610	County Population - 220,600
County Area - 392.7 sq. miles	October Temperature - 51.5°
Annual Precipitation - 52.7"	Acres in CRP - 0

The City of Bremerton and Kitsap County are located on a peninsula within Puget Sound, directly west of the city of Seattle. The county is densely populated with virtually no public lands access. It cannot be recommended as a primary hunting destination. However, the historic Bremerton Naval Shipyards, with its large concentration of mothballed U.S. Navy ships, does make an interesting non-hunting day excursion.

UPLAND BIRDS
Ruffed and Blue Grouse, Pheasant

Fewer than a thousand total upland game birds are bagged in the entire season in Kitsap County. What hunting is available is done on private lands.

WATERFOWL
Ducks and Geese

Even though the county has hundreds of miles of shoreline, again fewer than one thousand combined ducks and geese are taken in Kitsap County.

ACCOMMODATIONS
The Chieftain Motel, 600 National Ave. N. / (360) 479-3111 / 45 rooms / Dining on site & nearby, non-smoking rooms / Dogs allowed / $

The Dunes Motel, 3400 11th St. / (360) 377-0093 / 64 rooms / Dining on site & nearby, non-smoking rooms / Dogs allowed / $$

Midway Inn, 2909 Wheaton Way E. / (360) 479-2909 / 60 rooms / Dining on site & nearby, continental breakfast, non-smoking rooms / Dogs allowed / Senior discounts / $$

Oyster Bay Inn, 4412 Kitsap Way / (360) 377-5510 / 78 rooms / Dining on site & nearby, continental breakfast, non-smoking rooms / Dogs allowed / $$$

Quality Inn - Bremerton, 4303 Kitsap Way / (360) 405-1111 / 103 rooms / Dining on site & nearby, continental breakfast, non-smoking rooms / Dogs allowed / Senior discounts / $$$

CAMPGROUNDS AND RV PARKS
Illahee State Park, 3540 Bahia Vista / (360) 478-6460 / 25 sites / Dogs allowed, tent sites, boat launch, showers, full RV hook-ups / $

Restaurants

Azteca Mexican Restaurant, 5066 State Hwy. 303 NE / (360) 373-9315 / Fine Mexican food served daily for lunch and dinner.

Panda Inn On The Bay, 4188 Kitsap Way / (360) 377-7785 / Mandarin and Szechwan style Chinese cuisine for lunch and dinner seven days per week.

Denny's, 3621 Wheaton Way / (360) 479-4144 / Open daily, 24 hours, with decent predictable food.

Family Pancake House, 3900 Kitsap Way / (360) 479-2422 / American family style food for breakfast, lunch, and dinner, open daily.

Stuart Anderson's Black Angus, 2825 Wheaton Way / (360) 479-5550 / Robust steak house cuisine, open daily for lunch and dinner.

Veterinarians

Wheaton Way Veterinary Clinic, 1220 Sheridan Rd. / (360) 377-0078

Alder Trail Animal Hospital, 5757 State Hwy. 303 NE / (360) 377-3971

Sporting Goods

Rite Aid Pharmacy, 425 Kitsap Way / (360) 479-3395

Auto Rental and Repair

Budget Rent A Car, 2114 6th St. / (360) 479-4500

Enterprise Rent A Car, 280 Wilkes Ave. / (360) 377-1900

Cooper Fuel & Automotive Repair, 3236 Wheaton Way / (360) 377-4100

Air Service

Bremerton National Airport, 8850 State Hwy. 3 SW, Port Orchard, WA / (360) 674-2381 / Nearest to Bremerton, 9.8 miles away, no commercial service.

Medical

Harrison Memorial Hospital, 2520 Cherry Ave. / (360) 792-6505

Banks with ATMS

Seafirst Bank, 1140 Marine Dr. / (360) 479-1511

US Bank, 607 Pacific Ave. / (360) 478-5400

For More Information

Bremerton Area Chamber of Commerce
P.O. Box 229
Bremerton, WA 98337
(360) 479-3579

The moss and ferns in this photo give an indication to the amount of rainfall western Washington receives.

SHELTON
and Mason County

Population - 7,700	County Population - 47,000
County Area - 6188,888 sq. acres	October Temperature - 51°
Annual Precipitation - 88.6"	Acres in CRP - 0

Mason County is located on the southwestern end of Hood Canal and Puget Sound and extends into the Olympic National Forest and Olympic National Park. The terrain is rugged, with mountains and thick forest dominating the topography.

UPLAND BIRDS
Ruffed and Blue Grouse, Turkeys, Pheasant

The forest grouse and turkeys are abundant in heavily forested Mason County. Access is available to public land in the Olympic National Forest and some private timber companies allow public hunting. Pheasant are hunted on the Belfair and Hunter Farms Western Washington Pheasant Release sites administered by the WDFW.

WATERFOWL
Ducks and Geese

Mason County has literally hundreds of small lakes and streams, plus hundreds of miles of saltwater frontage. Much of these wetlands are open to public hunting.

ACCOMMODATIONS
City Center Best Rates Motel, 128 E. Alder / (360) 426-3397 / 13 rooms / Dining on site & nearby, non-smoking rooms / Dogs allowed / Senior discounts / $
Shelton Inn Motel, 628 W. Railroad Ave. / (360) 426-4468 / 30 rooms / Dining on site & nearby, non-smoking rooms / Dogs allowed / Senior discounts / $
Super 8 Motel, 2943 Northview Circle / (360) 426-1654 / 38 rooms / Dining on site & nearby, non-smoking rooms / Dogs allowed / Senior discounts / $$

CAMPGROUNDS AND RV PARKS
The Pines RV Park, 1907 Olympic Hwy. N. / (360) 426-3273 / 16 sites / Dining on site & nearby / Dogs allowed, showers, full RV hook-ups / $
We & U Mobile Home and RV Park, S.E. 261 Craig Rd. / (360) 426-3169 / 22 sites / Dining on site & nearby / Dogs allowed, tent sites, showers, full RV hook-ups / $

RESTAURANTS
Timbers Restaurant, 7th & Railroad. / (360) 426-9171 / Family style American food for breakfast lunch and dinner, seven days per week

Arne's, 1927 Olympic Hwy. N. / (360) 427-4431 / Open daily for family style, home-cooked meals for breakfast, lunch, and dinner.

Burgermaster, 3001 Olympic Hwy. N. / (360) 426-7224 / Burgers and American cuisine for breakfast, lunch, and dinner, seven days per week.

Orient Express, 2517 Olympic Hwy. N. / (360) 427-0560 / Chinese meals for lunch and dinner daily.

El Sarape, 318 W. Railroad / (360) 426-4294 / Mexican favorites for lunch and dinner, seven days per week.

The Grill Restaurant & Lounge, 324 W. Railroad / (360) 426-2186 / Mongolian grill, open daily for lunch and dinner.

VETERINARIANS
Shelton Veterinary Hospital, Inc., 104 E. J St. / (360) 426-2616

SPORTING GOODS
Wal-Mart, 100 E. Wallace Kneeland Blvd. / (360) 427-0500

AUTO RENTAL AND REPAIR
Practical Rent A Car, 1930 Olympic Hwy. N. / (360) 426-5553
Advanced Automotive Service, 2921 N. View Circle / (360) 426-6403
D & L Automotive, 2033 Olympic Hwy. N. / (360) 426-1467

AIR SERVICE
Sanderson Field, 410 W. Business Park Rd. / (360) 426-1151
No commercial service.

MEDICAL
Mason General Hospital, 901 Mountain View Dr. / (360) 426-1611

BANKS WITH ATMS
Key Bank, 410 W. Railroad Ave. / (360) 426-8234
Seafirst Bank, 425 W. Franklin St. / (360) 426-8295

FOR MORE INFORMATION
Shelton-Mason County Chamber of Commerce
P.O. Box 2389
Shelton, WA 98584
(360) 426-8678

RAYMOND
and Pacific County

Population - 2,901	County Population - 18,882
County Area - 908.2 sq. miles	October Temperature - 50.7°
Annual Precipitation - 105.64"	Acres in CRP - 0

Pacific County is located on the southwest coast of Washington. The Columbia River borders the county on the south, with Willapa Harbor on the north. The terrain is heavily timbered, and with over 100 inches of rainfall each year, the undergrowth is very thick.

UPLAND BIRDS
Ruffed and Blue Grouse, Turkeys, Pheasant

Public land access is minimal in Pacific County; however, private timber companies and rural landowners often allow hunting if asked politely. Forest grouse are abundant throughout the county as are turkeys. Pheasants are hunted on the WDFW Western Washington Pheasant Release site at the Raymond Airport.

WATERFOWL
Ducks and Geese

On the many rivers, creeks, lakes, and ponds of Pacific County, ducks are abundant and geese slightly less so. Willapa Bay is also a vast estuary that provides excellent waterfowling.

ACCOMMODATIONS
Mountcastle Motel, 524 3rd St. / (360) 942-5571 / Dining on site & nearby / Dogs allowed / $
Willis Motel, 425 3rd St. / (360) 942-5313 / 2 rooms / Dining on site & nearby / Dogs allowed / Senior discounts / $

CAMPGROUNDS AND RV PARKS
Timberland RV Park, 850 Crescent St. / (800) 563-3325 / 24 sites / Dining on site & nearby / Dogs allowed, tent sites, showers, full RV hook-ups, senior discounts / $

RESTAURANTS
Raymond Café, 216 N. 3rd St. / (360) 942-3408 / Open daily for breakfast, lunch, and dinner, serving American favorites.
The Barge Restaurant, 160 Laurel / (360) 942-5100 / Family style meals for breakfast, lunch, and dinner, seven days per week.
Bridges Inn, 410 N. 3rd St. / (360) 942-5146 / Open Monday through Saturday for lunch and dinner with a full menu from steaks to seafood.

Eastern Garden, 411 N. 3rd St. / (360) 942-2079 / Authentic Chinese cuisine for lunch and dinner daily.

Pizza Loft, Duryea and 3rd. St. / (360) 942-5109 / Pizza, pasta, and sandwiches for lunch and dinner, seven days per week.

VETERINARIANS

Willapa Veterinary Service, 231 Ocean Ave. / (360) 942-2321
Vetter's Veterinary Clinic, 2521 Ocean Ave. / (360) 942-3440

SPORTING GOODS

Dennis Company, 146 5th St. / (360) 942-2427

AUTO REPAIR

Bent Wrench Auto Repair, Hwy. 6 & Oldani Rd. / (360) 942-5511
Downtown Auto Repair, Blake St. & 4th St. / (360) 942-3755

AIR SERVICE

Willapa Harbor Airport, Rt. 2 Box 303 / (360) 942-9954
No commercial Service.

MEDICAL

Willapa Harbor Hospital, 800 Alder St., South Bend, WA / (360) 875-5526
Nearest to Raymond 9.9 miles away.

BANKS WITH ATMS

Seafirst Bank, 314 Duryea St. / (360) 942-3425

FOR MORE INFORMATION

Raymond Chamber of Commerce
300 5th St.
Raymond, WA 98577
(360) 942-5419

TACOMA
and Pierce County

Population - 185,600	County Population - 686,800
County Area - 1,6759 sq. miles	October Temperature - 52.8°
Annual Precipitation - 67.09"	Acres in CRP - 13

Pierce County has two distinct areas, eastern and western. The city of Tacoma, located in the western portion of the county, is a metropolitan community complete with industry and crowding. The eastern portion of Pierce County is highly rural. It includes portions of Snoqualmie National Forest and Mt. Rainier National Park. The rural portions of the county are heavily timbered, and the hills and valleys are lush with vegetation.

UPLAND BIRDS
Ruffed Grouse, Pheasant, and Blue Grouse
The ruffed grouse is king on the west slope of the Cascade Mountains. National forest land provides public access along with some private timber company land. Pheasants are primarily hunted at the Fort Lewis site of the Western Washington Pheasant Release Program administered by the WDFW.

WATERFOWL
Ducks and Geese
Several good-sized lakes and rivers, plus estuaries on Puget Sound, provide good waterfowl action throughout the season.

ACCOMMODATIONS
Motel 6 - Tacoma, I-5 at Exits 128/129 / (253) 473-7100 / 119 rooms / Dining on site & nearby, non-smoking rooms / Dogs allowed / Senior discounts / $
Colonial Motel, 12117 Pacific Hwy. SW / (253) 589-3261 / 34 rooms / Dogs allowed / $
Comfort Inn - Tacoma, 5601 Pacific Hwy. E. / (253) 926-2301 / 40 rooms / Dining on site & nearby, continental breakfast, non-smoking rooms / Dogs allowed / Senior discounts / $$
La Quinta Inn, 1425 E. 27th St. / (253) 383-0146 / 158 rooms / Dining on site & nearby, continental breakfast, non-smoking rooms / Dogs allowed / Senior discounts / $$
Royal Coachman Inn, 5805 Pacific Hwy. E. / (800) 422-3051 / 94 rooms / Dining on site & nearby, non-smoking rooms / Dogs allowed / Senior discounts / $$

Shilo Inn - Tacoma, 7414 S. Hosmer / (800) 222-2244 / 132 rooms / Dining on site & nearby, continental breakfast, non-smoking rooms / Dogs allowed / Senior discounts / $$

Chinaberry Hill Bed & Breakfast, 302 Tacoma Ave. N in the Stadium historic district / (253) 272-1282 / An 1889 grand Victorian inn with fireplaces, private cottages and waterfront views, within walking distance of downtown Tacoma / $$$

CAMPGROUNDS AND RV PARKS

Karwan Village, 2621 84th St. S. / (253) 588-2501 / 7 sites / Full RV hook-ups, showers / $

Dash Point State Park, 5 miles NE of Tacoma / (800) 223-0321 / (800) 452-5687

RESTAURANTS

Denny's, 5924 6th Ave. / (253) 565-6037 / Always open with decent, predictable food and good prices.

Elmer's Pancake & Steakhouse, 7427 S. Hosmer St. / (253) 473-0855 / American cuisine for breakfast, lunch, and dinner daily.

Cucina! Cucina! Italian Café, 4201 S. Steele St. / (253) 475-6000 / Excellent Italian food for lunch and dinner, seven days per week.

Harvester Restaurant, 29 Tacoma Ave. N. / (253) 272-1193 / Family style American food for breakfast, lunch, and dinner, daily.

The Old Spaghetti Factory, 1735 Jefferson Ave. South (253) 383-2214 / Italian cuisine with good food and good fun served in the midst of old world antiques.

La Costa, 928 Pacific Ave. / (253) 272-0300 / Mexican cuisine served daily for lunch and dinner.

The Lobster Shop South, 4015 N. Ruston Way / (253) 759-2165 / Fine seafood, seven days per week for lunch and dinner.

VETERINARIANS

Brookside Veterinary Hospital, 11719 State Route 302 NW / (253) 857-7302

Jones Animal Hospital, Inc., 3322 S. Union Ave. / (253) 383-2616

SPORTING GOODS

Big 5 Sporting Goods, 2505 S 38th St. # F / (253) 474-1747

Gart Sports, 1905 S 72nd St. # B / (253) 572-9900

's - Federal Way , 35020 Federal Way / (253)927-2943

G.I. Joe's - Puyallup, 120 31st Ave SE, Ste 6 / (253) 445-8090

Bulls Eye Shooter Supply, 414 Puyullap Ave.

Sports Authority, 4104 Tacoma Mall / (253) 572-6417

Welcher's Gun Shop, 16400 Pacific Ave / (253) 472-1113

AUTO RENTAL AND REPAIR

Budget Car & Truck Rental of Tacoma, 616 Broadway / (253) 627-7141

Enterprise Rent-A-Car, 455 St. Helens Ave. / (253) 566-6480

Bitterlings Auto & Towing Service, 6801 S. Tacoma Way / (253) 472-0415

Bucky's 48th Street, 4802 Pacific Ave. / (253) 473-3773

AIR SERVICE
Pierce County Sheriff Civil Airport, 930 Tacoma Ave. S. / (253) 798-7250
No Commercial Service

MEDICAL
Puget Sound Hospital, 215 S. 36th St. / (253) 474-0561

BANKS WITH ATMS
Seafirst Bank, 3408 S. 23rd St. / (253) 305-3000
US Bank, 1102 Commerce St. / (253) 594-7300

FOR MORE INFORMATION
Tacoma-Pierce County Chamber of Commerce
950 Pacific Ave., Ste. 300
Tacoma, WA 98402
(253) 627-2175

*Rain forest vegetation in
Olympic National Park.*

OLYMPIA
and Thurston County

Population - 38,650	County Population - 199,700
County Area - 17.69 sq. miles	October Temperature - 49.9°
Annual Precipitation - 64.83"	Acres in CRP - 0

Olympia is Washington's state capital, where residents brag of enjoying a big city, with a small-town atmosphere. Located on Puget Sound, Olympia has easy access to both the Cascade Mountains and the Olympic Peninsula.

UPLAND BIRDS
Pheasant, Ruffed and Blue Grouse, Turkeys

Thurston County is one of the smaller counties in Washington. With a high population density, hunting opportunities are limited. The WDFW does operate the Scatter Creek and Skookumchuck pheasant release sites in the county, which account for most of the pheasant harvest. Forest grouse and turkey hunting is fair on private lands when permission to hunt can be obtained.

WATERFOWL
Ducks and Geese

With several medium sized rivers and their estuaries on Puget Sound, there are good duck hunting opportunities in Thurston County. Smaller creeks and ponds can be good bets for jump-shooting as well.

ACCOMMODATIONS

Shalimar Suites, 5895 Capitol Blvd. / (360) 943-8391 / 29 rooms / Dining on site & nearby, non-smoking rooms / Dogs allowed / $

Holly Motel, 2816 Martin Way / (360) 943-3000 / 37 rooms / Dining on site & nearby, non-smoking rooms / Dogs allowed / $

King Oscar Motel, 8200 Quinault Way N.E. / (888) 254-5464 / 129 rooms / Dining on site & nearby, continental breakfast, non-smoking rooms, senior discounts / $$

Best Western Aladdin Inn, 900 S. Capitol Way / (360) 352-7200 / 99 rooms / Dining on site & nearby, non-smoking rooms, senior discounts / $$

Holiday Inn Select - Olympia, 2300 Evergreen Park Dr. / (360) 943-4000 / 177 rooms / Dining on site & nearby, non-smoking rooms / Dogs allowed / Senior discounts / $$

Tyee Hotel, 500 Tyee Dr. / (800) 386-8933 / 146 rooms / Dining on site & nearby, non-smoking rooms / Dogs allowed / Senior discounts / $$

CAMPGROUNDS AND RV PARKS
Columbus Park, 5700 Black Lake Blvd. S.W. / (800) 848-9460 / 32 units / Dogs
allowed, tent sites, boat launch, showers, full RV hook-ups and dump / $
Olympia Campground, 1441 83rd Ave. S.W. / (360) 352-2551 / 99 units / Dogs
allowed, tent sites, showers, full RV hook-ups and dump / $

RESTAURANTS
Denny's, 1616 Black Lake Blvd. S.W. / (360) 943-6023 / Open 24 hours, 365 days
per year. Decent prices and predictable food.
International House of Pancakes, 3519 Martin Way E. / (360) 459-5649 / Open
daily for breakfast lunch and dinner, breakfast served all day, American cuisine.
Genoa's on the Bay, 1525 Washington St. N.E. / (360) 943-7770 / Excellent seafood
for lunch and dinner, seven days per week.
China Town, 213 4th Ave. E. / (360) 357-7292 / Chinese cuisine served daily for
lunch and dinner.
Louisa Ristorante, 205 Cleveland Ave. S.E. / (360) 352-3732 / Fine Italian cuisine
for lunch and dinner, seven days per week.
El Nopal Mexican Restaurant, 3002 Harrison Ave. N.W. / (360) 352-2755 / Open
daily for lunch and dinner for Mexican favorites.

VETERINARIANS
Vet Smart Care Clinic, 719 Sleater Kinney Rd. S.E. / (360) 459-8242
Chambers Prairie Veterinary, 3100 Yelm Hwy. S.E. / (360) 491-3800

SPORTING GOODS
Big Foot Outdoor, 518 Capitol Way (360) 352-4616
Big 5 Sporting Goods, 909 Cooper Point Rd. S.W. / (360) 786-6529
Rite Aid Pharmacy, 1515 Marvin Rd. N.E. / (360) 456-4900

AUTO RENTAL AND REPAIR
Budget Rent A Car, 720 Legion Way S.E. / (360)943-3852
Enterprise Rent A Car, 2115 Carriage St. S.W. / (360) 956-3714
Aduco Automotive, 5201 Capitol Blvd. S. #185 / (360) 754-1294
B & B Auto Repair, 613 State Ave. N.E. / (360) 754-2374

AIR SERVICE
Olympia Airport, 7643 Old Highway 99 S.E. / (360) 586-6164
No commercial service available at this time.

MEDICAL
Providence St. Peter Hospital, 413 Lilly Rd. N.E. / (360) 491-9480

BANKS WITH ATMS
Seafirst Bank, 1243 Marvin Rd. N.E. / (360) 753-9816
US Bank, 402 Capitol Way S. #15 / (360) 753-9800

FOR MORE INFORMATION

Olympia/Thurston County
Chamber of Commerce
P.O. Box 1427
Olympia, WA 98507-1427
(360) 357-3362

Dense underbrush typical of the habitat where you might find forest grouse in this region.

Hunting on Indian Lands

Washington is home to six reservations representing 26 tribes and encompassing over 2.6 million acres. The cultural diversity represented between the coastal and inland tribes is truly amazing.

Public hunting is allowed on only two of the reservations, and with a few exceptions, the state regulations for seasons and bag limits are followed. A Washington State Small Game Hunting license, in addition to a non-member bird-hunting permit, is required to hunt on both the Yakima and Colville Reservations.

The game and fish departments of both reservations have excellent pamphlets with maps of land open to public hunting, for the asking. Phone numbers and addresses are listed below. See map on page 278.

Yakima Indian Reservation

YAKIMA NATION
Wildlife Resource Management
P.O. Box 151
Toppenish, WA 98948
865-6262 Ext. 6685
Size: 1.1 million acres

Species allowed: Pheasant, Quail, Chukar, Hungarian Partridge, Ruffed Grouse, Dove, Ducks and Geese.

The Yakima Indian Reservation is located in the south-central part of the state, south of I-82. Located in the Yakima Valley and bordering the Yakima River, hunting is an accepted and popular recreation. Much of the reservation is under agricultural lease and pheasant and quail hunting are excellent. The Yakima River, with its many sloughs, ponds, and wetlands, provides very good waterfowling, and the reservation has provided several management areas with enhanced duck and goose hunting opportunities. There are currently 10,000 acres open to public hunting.

See Yakima for a listing of accommodations.

YAKIMA NATION HUNTING PERMIT VENDORS

Inter-Valley Hardware, Toppenish / (509) 865-4525
Ox-Bow Motor Inn, Toppenish / (509) 865-5800
Yakima Nation RV Park, Toppenish / (509) 865-2000
Johnson's True Value Hardware, Wapato / (509) 877-2334
Kile's Corner, Wapato / (509) 877-4632
Ace Hardware Store, Sunnyside / (509) 837-6401
Bi-Mart 5th Avenue, Yakima / (509) 457-5175
Chinook Sporting Goods, Yakima / (509) 452-8205
RiteAid Drugs, Yakima / (509) 965-2033

Colville Indian Reservation

FISH AND GAME DEPARTMENT
Colville Confederated Tribes
P.O. Box 150 Nespelem, WA 99155
(509) 634-8845
Size: 1.6 million acres

Species available: Pheasants, Chukar, Hungarian Partridge, Valley Quail, Mourning Dove, ducks, Geese and Snipe

The Colville Reservation is located in north-central Washington, east of the Cascade Mountains. The topography varies from high desert sage to rolling timbered hills. The area itself is lightly populated and the reservation currently has 440,000 acres open to public hunting in three distinct regions within the reservation boundaries.

Upland hunting is excellent, with pheasants, quail and dove found primarily along agricultural edges. Chukar and Huns are best hunted in the coulees and adjacent cheatgrass covered hills. Duck and goose hunters will find very good hunting along the many rivers and pothole lakes within the reservation borders.

See Omak for a listing of accommodations. Contact the Colville Reservation Game and Fish Department listed above for a current list of tribal permit vendors.

Washington tribal lands are mapped on pages 278 and 279.

The rolling sagebrush of this area can be home to chukar, hun, valley quail or pheasant.

National Wildlife Refuges

Washington has 23 national refuges providing protection to 177,679 acres of essential wildlife habitat. Eight of these refuges allow public hunting; however, each refuge may set its own seasons and regulations. These areas have excellent duck and goose hunting and most have good upland hunting as well. Hunting pressure is directly related to proximity to large population centers, although virtually all have very light usage during mid-week.

Both federal and state duck stamps are required in addition to a state hunting license. Each refuge that allows hunting is covered below. Please call or write individual refuges to request maps and confirm current hunting seasons/regulations. See map on page 278.

WDFW REGION 1
UMATILLA NATIONAL WILDLIFE REFUGE — 16,300 acres
c/o Mid-Columbia River Complex
P.O. Box 700
Umatilla, OR 97882-0700
(541) 922-3232, fax: (541) 922-4117

Umatilla National Wildlife Refuge located in southeastern Washington, includes 20 miles of the Columbia River and upland habitat on both the Oregon and Washington sides of the river. Established in 1969, the refuge provides waterfowl habitat that was lost when the John Day Dam flooded the old Columbia River channel.

The refuge covers different land and water areas, which include everything from dense vegetation and uneven terrain to deep water and thick mud. Hunters should be cautious while using the refuge hunting areas.

Hunting for ducks, geese, pheasant, and quail is permitted in designated areas of the refuge. All state and federal hunting regulations are in effect.

WDFW REGION 1
LITTLE PEND OREILLE NATIONAL WILDLIFE REFUGE — 39,999 acres
1310 Bear Creek Rd.
Colville, WA 99114-9713
(509) 684-8384, fax: (509) 684-8381

Little Pend Oreille Refuge located in the northeastern portion of the state, takes its name from the river that flows through its northern portion. It was established in 1939, making it one of the nation's earliest refuges. The area contains two mountain ranges, numerous glacial valleys, and many streams, rivers, bogs, marshes, and lakes both large and small.

Hunting is permitted on the refuge for ducks, geese, pheasant, quail, blue and ruffed grouse during Washington's hunting season. All state and federal regulations apply.

WDFW REGION 1
MCNARY NATIONAL WILDLIFE REFUGE — 3,631 acres
c/o Mid-Columbia River Complex
P.O. Box 700
Umatilla, OR 97882-0700
(541) 922-3232, fax: (541) 922-4117
    The McNary National Wildlife Refuge is located in southeastern Washington, adjacent to the Umatilla National Wildlife Refuge. McNary consists of three divisions: McNary, Strawberry Island, and Hanford Islands. The McNary and Strawberry Island divisions are located near the confluence of the Snake and Columbia rivers; The Hanford Islands Division is located 15 miles upstream on the Columbia River near Richland, Washington.
    Public hunting is permitted only on Wednesdays, Saturdays, Sundays, and two holidays (Thanksgiving, and Christmas) during the Washington hunting season. Upland bird hunting (pheasant only) is permitted only from noon until the end of state shooting hours.
    Ducks and geese may be hunted during normal federally set hunting hours.

WDFW REGION 2
COLUMBIA NATIONAL WILDLIFE REFUGE — 29, 597 acres
P.O. Box Drawer F
735 E. Main St.
Othello, WA 99344-0227
488-2668, fax: (509) 488-0705
    Columbia National Wildlife Refuge is in the middle of Washington's famous Channeled Scablands, in the south-central portion of the state. The refuge is a scenic mixture of rugged cliffs, canyons, lakes, and arid sagebrush grasslands. The favorable mixture of lakes and surrounding irrigated croplands, combined with generally mild winters and protection provided by the refuge, attracts large numbers of migrating waterfowl and upland birds.
    The refuge offers hunting opportunities for ducks geese, quail, pheasant, and chukar during the Washington hunting season for migratory waterfowl. These areas are posted with signs. Entry into all other areas of the refuge (outside public hunting areas) is prohibited from October 1 until March 1.

WDFW REGION 3
TOPPENISH NATIONAL WILDLIFE REFUGE — 1,979 acres
c/o Mid-Columbia River Complex
P.O. Box 700
Umatilla, OR 97882-0700
922-3232, fax: (541) 922-4117
    The Toppenish National Wildlife Refuge, located in the lower Yakima Valley in south-central Washington, consists of the Lower Toppenish Unit and several

scattered tracts located along Toppenish Creek and the Yakima River. The refuge consists of brushy creek bottoms, wetlands, croplands, and sagebrush uplands.

Hunting for ducks, geese, pheasant, and quail is permitted on 650 acres of the refuge in accordance with state and federal laws. The refuge is open for hunting daily from 5:00 a.m. to 1½ hours after sunset during the state waterfowl hunting season. Entry prior to 5:00 a.m. is prohibited. Entry is permitted only from designated parking area.

WDFW REGION 5
CONBOY LAKE NATIONAL WILDLIFE REFUGE — 5,814 acres
Box 5
Glenwood, WA 98619-0005
(509) 364-3410, fax: (509) 364-3667

Conboy Lake Refuge is nestled at the base of Mt. Adams in south-central Washington. It is a large seasonal marsh on a land of dense pine and fir forests. For centuries, swans, geese, ducks, and sandhill cranes have used this mountain oasis for nesting, and for resting and feeding during spring and fall migrations.

Hunting for ducks and geese is permitted on approximately half of the refuge lands. All state and federal regulations are in effect.

WDFW REGION 5
RIDGEFIELD NATIONAL WILDLIFE REFUGE — 5,218 acres
P.O. Box 457
Ridgefield, WA 98642-0457
(360) 887-4106, fax: (360) 887-4109

Ridgefield National Wildlife Refuge, located on the Columbia River floodplain in southwestern Washington, provides vital migration and wintering habitat for birds migrating through the region west of the Cascade Mountains. The mild, rainy winter climate, combined with wetlands along the Columbia River, creates ideal resting and feeding areas for migrating waterfowl.

Hunting is permitted on approximately 760 acres of the refuge for ducks and geese only. All applicable state and federal regulations are in effect, plus several special conditions specific to this area, including special access permits and user fees. Contact the refuge directly for a copy of their specific hunting regulations.

WDFW REGION 6
WILLAPA NATIONAL WILDLIFE REFUGE — 14,394 acres
HC 01, P.O. Box 910
Ileac, WA 98624- 9707
(360) 484-3482 fax: (360) 484-3109

The Willapa National Wildlife Refuge, located in the southwestern corner of Washington, is a unique combination of Pacific Coast, salt and fresh water marshes, coniferous forest, dunes, pastures, and wooded uplands with many small lakes, creeks and streams.

Hunting for ducks and geese is permitted only on the Lewis, Riekkola, and Leadbetter Point units of the refuge. Hunter registration is required on all areas prior to entry and all state and federal waterfowl regulations are in effect.

The author and Dutchess in her first year with the results of a preserve hunt, using a bow and arrow.

Access Guide to Federal and State Lands

Approximately 40 percent of Washington's total land area is owned by the public and managed by state and federal agencies. The rules and regulations for public land use are complex. Plan your hunt with accurate maps and make sure that you understand the regulations. There is a listing of all state and federal agencies at the end of this section. We strongly urge you to get the regulation guides and maps. All you need to access and hunt state lands is a Washington hunting license. See map on page 278.

U.S. Department of the Interior Fish Wildlife, and Parks

The FWP manages 238,429 acres of national wildlife refuges and waterfowl production areas in Washington, and over 800,000 acres of wildlife areas. See the section entitled National Wildlife Refuges for a listing of those refuges which allow public hunting.

Bureau of Land Management

The BLM manages some 370,000 acres of federal lands in Washington. Most of this land is in eastern Washington. There is excellent hunting on BLM lands, especially for chukar, Huns, and pheasant. However, access to many of the acres of BLM can be difficult. We suggest that you obtain the BLM section maps for the areas that you plan to hunt. These maps are available from DNR SE Region, 713 E. Bowers Rd., Ellensburg, WA 98926. The phone number is (509) 925-8510.

Orders may be sent with checks made payable to the DNR. Maps are currently $5 each. An index map is available free of charge.

State Lands

Washington has 3.4 million acres of state lands. Many of these acres are managed by and open to public hunting. The WDFW is divided into six management regions. The headquarters for each region is listed below. Maps of the WDFW managed lands for each region may be obtained by contacting these offices.

Washington Department of Fish and Wildlife Offices

OLYMPIA OFFICE - MAIN OFFICE
600 Capitol Way N.
Olympia, WA 98501-1091
((360) 902-2200
TDD (360) 902-2207

EASTERN WASHINGTON - REGION 1 OFFICE
N. 8702 Division St.
Spokane, WA 99218-1199
(509) 456-4082

NORTH CENTRAL WASHINGTON - REGION 2 OFFICE
1550 Alder St. N.W.
Ephrata, WA 98823-9699
(509) 754-4624

SOUTH CENTRAL WASHINGTON - REGION 3 OFFICE
1701 S. 24th Ave.
Yakima, WA 98902-5720
(509) 575-2740

NORTH PUGET SOUND WASHINGTON - REGION 4 OFFICE
16018 Mill Creek Blvd.
Mill Creek, WA 98012-1296

SOUTHWEST WASHINGTON - REGION 5 OFFICE
2108 Grand Blvd.
Vancouver, WA 98661
(360) 696-6211

COASTAL WASHINGTON - REGION 6 OFFICE
48 Devonshire Rd.
Montesano, WA 98563-9618
(360) 249-4628

National Forest Headquarters

Seven national forests are located totally or partially within Washington. A total of over 9 million acres are available for public use. Listed below are the offices of each forest. Maps may be purchased from these offices, which include information on land ownership, roads, trails, lakes, streams, and campgrounds.

COLVILLE NATIONAL FOREST
765 S. Main St.
Colville, WA 99114
(509) 684-7000

GIFFORD PINCHOT NATIONAL FOREST
10600 N.E. 51st Circle
Vancouver, WA 98682
(360) 891-5000

MOUNT BAKER - SNOQUALMIE NATIONAL FOREST
21905 64th Ave. W.
Mountlake Terrace, WA 98043
(206) 442-0170

OKANOGAN NATIONAL FOREST
1240 S. 2nd Ave.
Okanogan, WA 98840
(509) 826-3275

OLYMPIC NATIONAL FOREST
1835 Black Lake Blvd. S.W.
Olympia, WA 98512-5623
(360) 956-2400

UMATILLA NATIONAL FOREST / WALLA WALLA RANGER DISTRICT
1415 W. Rose St.
Walla Walla, WA 99362
(509) 522-6290

WENATCHEE NATIONAL FOREST
215 Melody Lane
Wenatachee, WA 98801
(509) 662-4335

Washington state is home to seven national forests.

Access to Private Land

The state of Washington has strict laws prohibiting trespassing on private land and owners are not required to post their land. If land is posted "Hunting with written permission only," the written permission slip must be in your possession while on that property. Please ask politely for permission to hunt private property, and if denied, be gracious and thank the landowner anyway.

Landowners in Washington have the option of putting their land into the Conservation Reserve Program (CRP) which encourages farmers to plant long-term resource-conserving covers to improve soil, water and enhance wildlife resources. In return, they receive annual rental payments from the federal government and cost-share assistance. Land in CRP is still private and permission must be obtained before hunting as with all private lands.

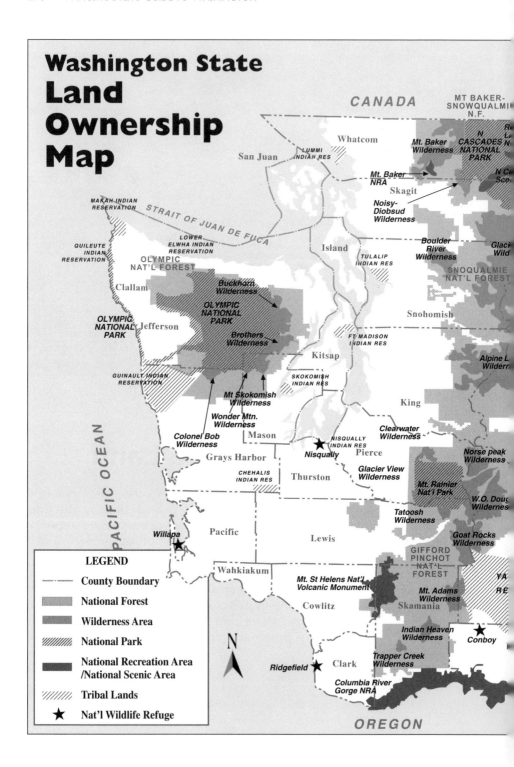

Washington State Land Ownership Map

CANADA

MT BAKER-SNOWQUALMIE N.F.

Whatcom

San Juan

LUMMI INDIAN RES

Mt. Baker Wilderness

N CASCADES NATIONAL PARK

Re L N

Mt. Baker NRA

Skagit

N Ca Sce

Noisy-Diobsud Wilderness

MAKAH INDIAN RESERVATION

STRAIT OF JUAN DE FUCA

Island

TULALIP INDIAN RES

Boulder River Wilderness

Glaci Wild

QUILEUTE INDIAN RESERVATION

LOWER ELWHA INDIAN RESERVATION

OLYMPIC NAT'L FOREST

SNOQUALMIE NAT'L FOREST

Clallam

Buckhorn Wilderness

OLYMPIC NATIONAL PARK

Snohomish

OLYMPIC NATIONAL PARK

Jefferson

Brothers Wilderness

FT MADISON INDIAN RES

Kitsap

Alpine L Wildern

GUINAULT INDIAN RESERVATION

SKOKOMISH INDIAN RES

King

Mt Skokomish Wilderness

Wonder Mtn. Wilderness

Colonel Bob Wilderness

Mason

Clearwater Wilderness

Norse peak Wilderness

Grays Harbor

CHEHALIS INDIAN RES

NISQUALLY INDIAN RES

Nisqually

Pierce

Glacier View Wilderness

Mt. Rainier Nat'l Park

W.O. Doug Wildernes

PACIFIC OCEAN

Thurston

Tatoosh Wilderness

Goat Rocks Wilderness

Willapa

Pacific

Lewis

GIFFORD PINCHOT NAT'L FOREST

YA RE

LEGEND

Wahkiakum

Mt. St Helens Nat'l Volcanic Monument

Mt. Adams Wilderness

————— County Boundary

Cowlitz

Skamania

National Forest

Indian Heaven Wilderness

Conboy

Wilderness Area

N

Trapper Creek Wilderness

National Park

Ridgefield

Clark

National Recreation Area /National Scenic Area

Columbia River Gorge NRA

Tribal Lands

★ Nat'l Wildlife Refuge

OREGON

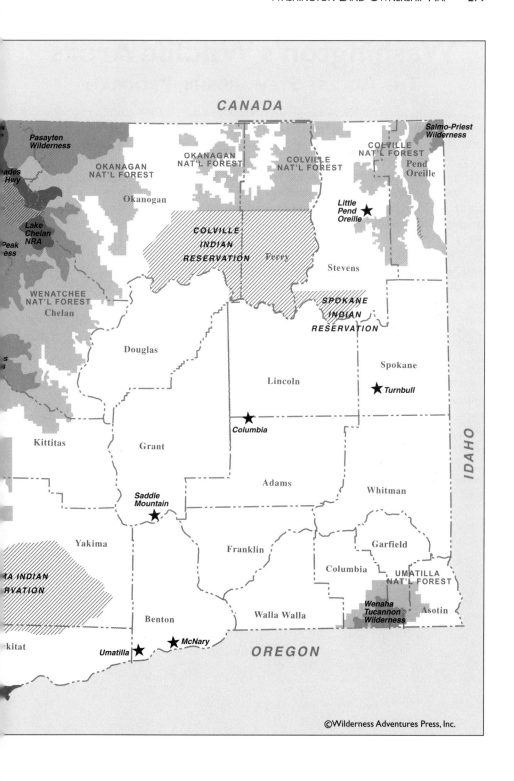

CANADA

Pasayten
Wilderness

Salmo-Priest
Wilderness

ades
Hwy

OKANAGAN
NAT'L FOREST

OKANAGAN
NAT'L FOREST

COLVILLE
NAT'L FOREST

COLVILLE
NAT'L FOREST

Pend
Oreille

Okanogan

Lake
Chelan
NRA

COLVILLE
INDIAN
RESERVATION

Ferry

Little
Pend
Oreille

Peak
ess

WENATCHEE
NAT'L FOREST

Chelan

Stevens

SPOKANE
INDIAN
RESERVATION

Douglas

Spokane

Lincoln

Turnbull

Columbia

Kittitas

Grant

Saddle
Mountain

Adams

Whitman

Yakima

Franklin

Garfield

A INDIAN
RVATION

Columbia

UMATILLA
NAT'L FOREST

Benton

Walla Walla

Wenaha
Tucannon
Wilderness

Asotin

IDAHO

kitat

Umatilla

McNary

OREGON

©Wilderness Adventures Press, Inc.

Washington's Wildlife Areas
THE ACCESS STEWARDSHIP PROGRAM

Washington's Wildlife Areas — over 800,000 acres — are found in every part of the state and were selected as key lands to benefit a particular species or group of animals. For waterfowl, areas are either ancestral migration stopover points or breeding grounds. Estuaries and riparian areas protect threatened and endangered fish species; migratory corridors are key habitat for deer, elk and big horn sheep.

Some of the highest quality habitats for fish and wildlife are protected as Wildlife Areas by the Department of Fish and Wildlife. Scattered across the state, Washington's Wildlife Areas have immense social, economic, and fish and wildlife value.

The Washington Department of Fish and Wildlife maintains 800,000 acres of the best fish and wildlife habitat, and 600 boating and fishing access sites.

Washington is blessed with many beautiful natural features: mountains, forests and prairies, deep lakes and mighty rivers, ancient marine shorelines of sand and stone, and the nation's greatest variety of fish and wildlife species, but the vast majority of WDFW's land is in the mountains and plateaus of eastern Washington, some of which were formerly large ranches.

In 1939, Washington State created its first game refuge, now the Sinlahekin Wildlife Area in northern Okanogan County. Recognizing that deer, elk, waterfowl, upland birds and other wildlife need large stretches of habitat. Running 16 miles north to south, this Wildlife Area protects an entire valley for mule deer, white-tailed deer, bighorn sheep, black bear, pheasant, turkey, quail, chukar, waterfowl, pine squirrel, badger, skunk, porcupine, beaver, swallows and songbirds.

WDFW manages 19 estuaries from Skagit County, around Puget Sound, and out to the coast in Pacific County for waterfowl and salmon habitat. See map on page 280.

For more information, contact:
Elyse Kane, 360-902-2402
e-mail at kaneeak@dfw.wa.gov

State lands open for bird hunting are listed below. Check ahead for current hunting regulations. Write to the Department of Wildlife, 600 North Capitol Way, Olympia, WA 98504; Call (360) 753-5740. Visit the website at: www.wa.gov/wdfw/lands/wildarea/htm

NAME	TOWN	PHONE	ACREAGE	WATERFOWL	PHEASANT	PARTRIDGE	GROUSE	QUAIL	TURKEY
Asotin Creek Wildlife Area	13 mi. SW of Asotin	(509) 456-4082	12,300		X		X		X
Banks Lake Wildlife Area	10 mi. SW of Electric City	(509) 754-4624	44,662	X	X			X	
Big Valley Unit Wildlife Area	5 mi. NW of Winthrop	(509) 754-4624	845				X		
Black River Wildlife Area	1.5 mi. E of Gate	(360) 753-2600	87,040	X					
Chelan Butte Wildlife Area	Chelan Falls	(509) 575-2740	9,424		X		X		
Chesaw Wildlife Area	16 mi. E of Oroville	(509) 754-4624	2,500				X		X
Chief Joseph Wildlife Area	30 mi. S of Asotin	(509) 456-4082	9,176			X	X		X
The Colockum Wildlife Area	16 mi. SE of Wenatchee	(509) 575-2740	92,108			X	X		X
Crab Creek Wildlife Area	2.5 mi. E of Beverly	(509) 754-4624	25,592	X	X			X	
Desert Wildlife Area	16 mi. SW of Moses Lake	(509) 754-4624	27,719	X	X			X	
Dungeness Wildlife Area	6 mi. NW of Sequim	(360) 533-9335	216	X					
Entiat Wildlife Area	Entiat	(509) 575-2740	9,675				X		
Gloyd Seeps Wildlife Area	6.5 mi. N of Moses Lake	(509) 754-4624	10,111	X	X				
I-82 Ponds Wildlife Area	8 mi. N of Toppenish	(509) 575-2740	900	X				X	
John s River Wildlife Area	12 mi. SW of Aberdeen	(360) 533-9335	1,528	X					
Klickitat Wildlife Area	13.5 mi NW of Goldendale,	(360) 696-6211	11,848				X		X
L.T. Murray Wildlife Area	10 mi. W of Ellensburg	(509) 575-2740	106,119		X	X	X		X
Lake Lenore Wildlife Area	7 mi. N of Soap Lake	(509) 754-4624	8,941	X					
Lake Terrell Wildlife Area	4 mi. W of Ferndale	(206) 775-1311	1,320	X					
Leclerc Creek Wildlife Area	1 I mi. N of Cusick	(509) 456-4082	893				X		X
Little Pend Oreille Wildlife Area	10 mi. SE of Colville	(509) 4.56-4082	41,555				X		X
Methow National Wildlife Area	8 mi. N of Twisp	(509) 754-4624	20,437	X		X	X		X
Nisqually Delta Wildlife Area	9.5 mi. NE of Olympia	(360) 753-5700	648	X					
Oak Creek Wildlife Area	18 mi. NW of Yakima	(509) 575-2740	142,400		X	X	X		X
Olympic Wildlife Area	13 mi. N of Aberdeen	(360) 533-9335	5,645	X			X		
Oyhut Wildlife Area	Ocean Shores	(360) 533-9335	682	X					
Potholes Wildlife Area	4.5 mi. SW of Moses Lake	(509) 754-4624	38,588	X	X			X	
Priest Rapids Wildlife Area	3 mi. W of Mattawai	(509) 754-4624	2,500	X				X	
Quilomene Wildlife Area	20 mi. E of Ellensburg	(509) 575-2740	45,143		X	X	X		X
Quincy Wildlife Area	8 mi. SW of Quincy	(509) 754-4624	13,508	X	X			X	
Rattlesnake Slope Wildlife Area	12 mi. NW of Richland	(509) 575-2740	3,662		X			X	
Rocky Ford Creek Wildlife Area	5 mi. E of Ephrata	(509) 754-4624	1,025	X					
Scatter Creek Wildlife Area	18 mi. S of Olympia	(360) 533-9335	1,269		X			X	
Scotch Creek Wildlife Area	10 mi. NW of Omak	(509) 754-4624	9,000		X		X		X
Seep Lakes Wildlife Area	8 mi. SW of Warden	(509) 754-4624	3,054	X					
Sherman Creek Wildlife Area	5.5 mi. W of Kettle Falls	(509) 456-4082	7,508				X		X
Shillapoo-Vancouver Wildlife Area	12 mi. N of Vancouver	(360) 696-6211	432	X					
Sinlahekin Wildlife Area	4 mi. S of Loomis	(509) 754-4624	14,035				X		X
Skagit Wildlife Area	3 mi. N of Stanwood	(206) 775-1311	10,892	X					
Snoqualmie Valley Wildlife Area	Stillwater	(206) 775-1311	1,201	X					
Stratford Wildlife Area	12 mi. E of Soap Lake	(509) 754-4624	6,020	X	X				
Sunnyside Wildlife Area	4 mi. SE of Mabton	(509) 575-2740	7,604	X	X			X	
Swakane Wildlife Area	2 mi. NW of Lincoln Rock	(509) 575-2740	11,199				X		X
Tunk Valley Wildlife Area	2 mi. NE of Omak	(509) 754-4672	1,000				X		X
W.T. Wooten Wildlife Area	13 mi. E. of Dayton	(509) 456-4082	11,185		X		X		X
Wahluke slope Wildlife Area	6 mi. E of Wahluke	(509) 754-4624	57,839	X	X			X	
Wells Wildlife Area	5 mi. N of Bridgeport	(509) 754-4624	7,328	X	X				
Winchester Wasteway Wildlife Area	15 mi. W of Moses Lake	(509) 754-4624	1,919	X					

Washington Department of Wildlife
Wildlife Areas Map

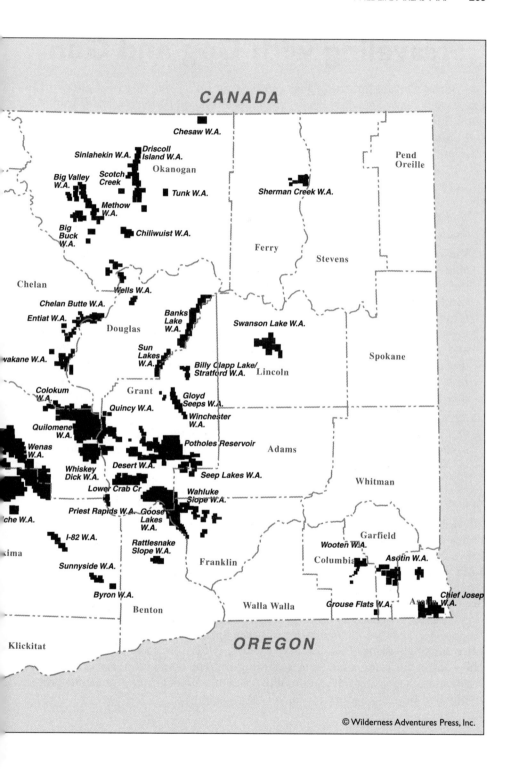

CANADA

Chesaw W.A.

Sinlahekin W.A.
Driscoll Island W.A.
Okanogan

Scotch Creek

Big Valley W.A.

Methow W.A.

Tunk W.A.

Sherman Creek W.A.

Pend Oreille

Big Buck W.A.

Chiliwuist W.A.

Ferry

Stevens

Chelan

Wells W.A.

Chelan Butte W.A.

Entiat W.A.

Douglas

Banks Lake W.A.

Swanson Lake W.A.

Spokane

vakane W.A.

Sun Lakes W.A.

Billy Clapp Lake/ Stratford W.A.

Lincoln

Colokum W.A.

Grant

Gloyd Seeps W.A.

Quincy W.A.

Winchester W.A.

Quilomene W.A.

Potholes Reservoir

Adams

Wenas W.A.

Whiskey Dick W.A.

Desert W.A.

Seep Lakes W.A.

Whitman

Lower Crab Cr

Wahluke Slope W.A.

Priest Rapids W.A.

Goose Lakes W.A.

che W.A.

I-82 W.A.

Rattlesnake Slope W.A.

Franklin

Garfield

Wooten W.A.

Columbia

Asotin W.A.

ima

Sunnyside W.A.

Byron W.A.

Benton

Walla Walla

Grouse Flats W.A.

Asotin W.A.

Chief Josep W.A.

Klickitat

OREGON

© Wilderness Adventures Press, Inc.

Traveling with Dog and Gun

The regulations for taking dogs and firearms on a plane vary from airline to airline. Listed below are some basic guidelines but it will be necessary for you to ask about specific policies when you make your reservation.

Insurance is available for both animals and firearms. Check with your airline for costs and limits.

Dogs

1. Your dog will have to be checked as baggage. Most airlines charge an extra fee per dog (usually around $50).

2. You will need a travel kennel for each dog accompanying you. Kennels are available at most pet supply stores and sometimes at the airport. It is best to familiarize your dog with the kennel 2-3 weeks prior to the trip so that he will be comfortable. Your dog must be able to stand up, turn around, and lie in a comfortable position. There must be absorbent material in the bottom of the kennel (a towel or black-and-white newspaper is acceptable). Two empty dishes for food and water must be accessible from the outside. Also, don't forget to label your dog's kennel with your name, address, phone number, and final destination. It is necessary to attach certification that the animal has been fed and watered within four hours of departure time. Label the kennel with signs stating "Live Animal" and "This Side Up" with letters at least one inch high.

3. You will need a certificate of health from your veterinarian, including proof of rabies vaccination. Tranquilizers are not recommended because high altitude can cause dangerous effects. If you must sedate your dog, be sure to discuss it with your vet first.

4. Federal regulations exist regarding safe temperatures for transport of your dog.

Animals will not be accepted if the temperature is below 10 degrees Fahrenheit at any point in transit. If the temperature at your destination is below 45 degrees Fahrenheit, a certificate of acclimation stating that your dog is used to low temperatures may be necessary. This is available from you vet. Temperatures above 85 degrees Fahrenheit can be dangerous for animals in transit. Many airlines will not accept dogs if the temperature at any transit point is more than 85 degrees.

Temperatures during Washington's bird season vary widely. Early chukar season (September) may see the mercury hitting the upper 90s; December and January can often hit single digits. This also varies widely within the state. It is a good idea to check with the reservation desk regarding current temperatures and make your reservations accordingly. If you run into problems transporting your canine partner, remember these regulations are for your dog's safety.

GUNS AND AMMUNITION

1. Firearms and ammunition must be checked as baggage and declared by the passenger. You will be required to fill out a declaration form stating that you are aware of the federal penalties for traveling with a loaded firearm and that your gun is unloaded.
2. Guns must be packed, unloaded, in a hard-sided crushproof container with a lock, specifically designed for firearm air transport. If you do not already have a case, they are usually available at the airport. Call your airline for details about dimensions. If your gun does not arrive on the baggage carousel you may be required to claim it at a special counter in the baggage claim area.

Ammunition must be left in the manufacturer's original packaging and securely packed in a wood or metal container separate from the firearm. In most cities in Washington a large variety of ammunition is available in sporting good and hardware stores. It might be easier to purchase shells at your destination rather than traveling with them. If you use a rare or special type of ammo, you can pre-ship it through a service like UPS to your final destination.

Hunter Conditioning and Equipment

The state of Washington can provide vastly different weather challenges within the same week, let alone the season. It is very possible to start a morning shooting ducks over decoys in a Pacific Ocean backwater slough in a driving rain storm, then finish the day pounding the hills for chukar in 85 degree shirt sleeve weather. In addition, while the state's Olympic Peninsula is a rainforest, south-central and southeastern Washington is desert country.

A typical hunt for quail, chukar, Huns, or pheasant may begin at first light with early season (September and October) temperatures in the mid 30s, while the mercury may top out near 90 during mid-day. A full day's hunt can easily cover 15 miles. To fully enjoy your hunt, do some homework and get into shape well ahead of the season opener.

CONDITIONING

Begin an aerobic conditioning program three to four months before the season opens. My personal favorite pre-season conditioning program consists of carrying a daypack with 20% of my body weight up and down stadium stairs or hills. Going up really conditions the heart, lungs, and legs, and going down prepares the knees for the downhill part of the hunt, minimizing any post hunt knee pain. It's a good idea to wear the boots you'll be hunting in, too. As a precaution, check with your family physician before beginning any exercise program.

CLOTHING

Layering is the only way to go, think of your clothes a being part of a system. Your base layer - underwear (shorts and shirt) and lightweight liner socks - should all be synthetic, like polypropylene. Synthetic fabrics wick moisture away from your skin, minimizing chafing, blisters, and chilling, should the temperature suddenly drop. Mid layer - long john top and bottom - also synthetic. For an outer layer in warm weather, I'll wear a pair of lightweight nylon or cotton pants and add a pair of brush chaps if I'm in briar and bramble country. In cooler, dry weather, I highly recommend field pants made by Wrangler. These are Wrangler's standard, comfortable denim jean with a facing of cordura nylon. They will turn away almost any thorn. In wet weather, I'm sold on Cabela's Gore-tex jeans. These are waterproof, breathable and very comfortable. In sticker country, I'll throw on brush chaps again. When the temperatures drop enough that the synthetic shirt and long john top are insufficient, I usually add a windproof fleece top. Thus attired, I have spent many days chasing quail or chukar with the mercury resting in the low 20s.

Over my liner socks I wear a pair of mid-weight wool socks. I wear lightweight ankle high hunting boots. Because many times quail are concentrated around ponds and seeps, I also like a Gore-tex (uninsulated) liner.

During early season, sunburn is a real threat, primarily in eastern Washington. Good sun block, a brimmed hat, and possibly a bandana for your neck should be considered mandatory items.

Over the years, I have tried a variety of shell pouches, hunting vests, and coats. Currently my favorite is a vest made in Montana by the Quilomene Company. The model I use is capable of holding two Camelback water reservoirs (over a gallon), two boxes of shells, with room left over for dog boots, lead, lunch, and snacks for the dogs and me and incidentals like shooting glasses, hearing protectors, and a pair of hemostats for removing thorns, cactus spines, or porcupine quills. I consider my lightweight leather shooting gloves essential for keeping my hands protected. I also carry a Swiss army knife, butane lighter, dog whistles, chukar, and quail calls, and a camera.

As a final thought on preparation, don't let opening day be the first shots you've taken with your scattergun since the close of last season. Get out and shoot a few rounds of trap, skeet, or sporting clays. These shooting games help keep your eye sharp and will improve your opening day hit-to-miss ratio.

Hunting birds with a muzzle-loading shotgun increases the challenge.

Conditioning of Hunting Dogs

Your dog will cover three to five times the number of miles you will. Please give him an edge by getting him in shape before the season begins. Your canine companion is an athlete and all athletes need training to stay in top form. If you are going to own a hunting dog, discipline yourself to work with it year-round. If that's not possible, at a minimum begin running him three to four days per week for 30-60 minutes, five to six weeks prior to opening day.

Hard working hunting dogs need to be fed a high quality, high protein food, and they need access to unlimited quantities of cool fresh water. The dog should not be fed within 90 minutes before exercising or 30 minutes following exercise.

In the field, water your dog often, and provide a nutritious snack occasionally throughout the day. Give him rest breaks every few hours. The dog's needs come first. Take care of thorns and burrs immediately. At the end of the day see to your four-legged partner's food, water, and comfort first. And remember, if she/he is anything like my dogs, they have just worked their heart out for you.

Pete, a German wirehaired pointer retrieves a duck.

Equipment Checklist

Clothing

___ polypropylene underwear

___ inner socks

___ wool socks

___ long sleeve canvas/chamois shirt

___ pants\double-faced

___ hunting boots

___ billed hat (orange)

___ bandana

___ shooting gloves

___ shooting glasses

___ ear protectors

___ hunting vest/coat

___ down vest/coat

___ chaps/raingear

___ hip boots/waders for waterfowl hunting

Dog Supplies

___ beeper collar

___ lead

___ dog boots, pad toughener

___ hemostat

___ whistle

___ water bottles

___ *Field Guide to Dog First Aid*

___ dog first aid kit

___ record of dog vaccinations

___ scissors

___ toenail clippers

Hunting Supplies

___ shotgun/shells

___ cleaning kit

___ maps

___ knife

___ fanny pack

___ water bottle

___ camera, film

___ binoculars

___ game shears

___ ice chest

___ license

___ matches

___ axe, shovel

___ sunscreen

___ twine

___ decoys, decoy anchors

___ compass

___ flashlight

___ bird calls

___ spare choke tubes

___ magnifying glass (to read maps)

___ *Field Guide to Upland Birds and Waterfowl*

Preserving Game Birds for Mounting

Exploding into the sky with a cackle and brilliant color, the rooster pheasant flushed and I momentarily lost my mind. Regaining my composure, I pulled the trigger and with the crack of my shotgun, the bird fell. That pheasant was a memory well worth preserving, and it now glides across our living room wall in a graceful, open-winged mount.

When deciding if you should mount a game bird, there are a few things to consider. The bird should be mature and have good plumage — we recommend saving birds that have been shot late in the season, ideally after the first of November. However, this doesn't apply to all game birds. Look for pinfeathers on the head and neck, and check the beak, feet, tail, and wings for shot damage. Since most taxidermists use the bird's skull, a bird that has been head-shot may be too damaged or disfigured to be mountable. All of these factors will affect the quality of a finished mount.

If a downed bird is wounded and in good enough condition to mount, do not ring the neck because it will cause skin damage and hemorrhaging. We feel the best method is to grasp the bird from the back just behind wings and then, with your thumb on one side of the rib cage and your fingers on the other, squeeze firmly. This will kill the bird in a humane and timely manner without causing damage to the feathers.

Keep the birds that you plan to have mounted separate from the others in your bag. Carrying them from the field by the feet saves them from damage and allows some cooling. We do not recommend carrying the bird in your game vest because feathers may become damaged, broken, or bloodstained.

After you've chosen the best bird or birds to mount, stop any bleeding by placing tissue or a cotton ball in the wounds. Wipe off any blood that may have run onto the feathers with a dabbing motion. Try not to push the blood down into the feathers. Also, place a cotton ball in the mouth to catch any body fluids that may potentially leak out onto the feathers.

Although some washing may be necessary before mounting, a taxidermist prefers that the bird be blood and dirt free upon delivery. Gently smooth the feathers into place, tuck the head to the chest, and wrap in clean paper towels. Place the bird head first into a plastic bag and store in a cool, protected place until the bird can be frozen.

Another popular method for preserving a bird is using a nylon stocking or cheesecloth. After caring for the bird, place the bird, with its head tucked, chest first into the nylon or cheesecloth. If you choose this method, remember that the only way to get the bird back out is to cut a hole in front of the chest and head and then push it through. If you pull it out by the feet, there will be feather damage.

Once the bird is securely in the nylon or cheesecloth, put the bird in a plastic bag to prevent dehydration or freezer burn. It is best to freeze the bird as soon as possible, and it can be stored in the freezer until you are able to get it to a taxidermist. Make sure that the bag is labeled with the type of bird, date harvested, as well as your name and license number. Taxidermists are required to have this information while the bird is in their possession.

When possible, take two birds to the taxidermist for determining which bird has the best plumage and is in the best shape for mounting.

With just a little care, you can preserve the memory of your hunt through the art of taxidermy. Bird mounts are easy to care for and will provide you with years of enjoyment.

Tip: To clean a mounted bird, use a cottonball dampened with rubbing alcohol. Start from the head using a sweeping motion in the direction of the feathers and work down the bird. Dust is lifted onto the cottonball, and the alcohol will evaporate. Make sure to change the cottonball regularly because they become soiled quickly.

—John and Laurel Berger
Berger Taxidermy
705 South Church Avenue
Bozeman, MT 59715
586-4244

A mixed bag of grouse.

After the hunt — we all feast!

Field Preparation of Game for the Table

The most important single act in readying wild game for the table is to immediately begin the cooling process. The feathers on game birds act as very efficient insulation, trapping body heat in and increasing the chance that bacteria may taint the meat. Especially in warmer weather, it is very important to gut your birds as soon as possible. Carrying game shears, a knife, and water make this a simple chore. It is also a good idea to have a cooler with ice in your vehicle to continue the cooling process upon returning to your rig.

Personally, I prefer to skin my birds at the end of the day, storing them frozen in vacuum-sealed bags. The meat will keep for many months this way and allows me to enjoy roast pheasant or barbecued quail in the spring or summer.

Information on Hunting and Maps

LICENSES

Washington Department of Fish and Wildlife
Natural Resources Building
License Division - First Floor
1111 Washington St. SE
Olympia, WA 98501
(360) 902-2200

Licenses are also available online:
www.wa.gov/wdfw/lic/formpage.htm

VACATION INFORMATION

Washington State Tourism
1 (800) 544-1800, ext. 800
www.experiencewashington.com

MAPS AND PUBLICATIONS

Several agencies produce maps and publications helpful to the hunter. These agencies, with addresses and phone numbers, are listed under the section entitled: Access Guide to Federal and State Lands.

MAPS ONLINE

www.topozone.com
Lets you create custom USGS topographic maps and download them to your desktop. You can make maps to your specifications at USGS 1:100,000, 1:63,360, 1:25,000, and 1:24,000 scale. Topographic maps for Washington as well as the entire United Statesare available. Just type a place name in the search box and go!

www.mapquest.com
A site with maps, driving directions, a road trip planner, city guides, and yellow and white pages.

Washington Bird Hunting Guides and Outfitters

BEAR PAW OUTFITTERS
Dale Denney
345 Highway 20 E #A, Colville, WA 99114
Phone: (509) 684-6294
E-mail: bearpaw@huntinfo.com
Area hunted: Region 1
Species hunted: Turkeys, grouse, and ducks

BURBANK GOOSE CLUB
Paul Sullivan
370 McNary Ridge Road, Burbank, WA 99323
Phone: (509) 545-8000
E-mail: hunt@burbankgoose.com
Area hunted: Region 1
Species hunted: Geese, ducks, and pheasant

CANYON CREST HUNTING RANCH, INC.
2902 Belsby Road, Cheney, WA 99004
Phone: (888) 235-5211
E-mail: louiseb@ieway.com
Area hunted: Region 1
Species hunted: Quail, pheasant, ducks, and geese

CLINT'S GUIDE SERVICE
(425) 257-4553
Area hunted: Region 4
Species hunted: Ducks

EARLY WINTERS OUTFITTING
Aaron Lee and Judy Burkhart
HCR 74 Box B6, Mazama, WA 98933
Phone: (800) 737-8950
E-mail: horse@methow.com
Area hunted: Region 2
Species hunted: Quail and chukar

FINCH RANCH
(509) 334-0867
E-mail: palouse.net/finchranch
Area hunted: Region 1
Species hunted: Pheasant, quail, chukar, and Huns

MESEBERG BROTHERS DUCK TAXI
8198 Highway 262 SE, Othello, WA 99344
Phone: (509) 346-2651
Area hunted: Region 2
Species hunted: Ducks

NATE JOHNSON HUNT CLUB
(360) 445-6015
Area hunted: Region 4
Species hunted: Ducks and geese

PURE COUNTRY GUIDE SERVICE
Loren & Cyrena Lehman
P.O. Box 804, Kettle Falls, WA 99141
Phone: (509) 738-4270
E-mail: purcountry@theofficenet.com
Area hunted: Region 1
Species hunted: Turkeys, ducks, pheasant, chukar, and quail.

WASHINGTON WATERFOWL GUIDE SERVICE
C. Gross & Sons
P.O. Box 1120, Northbend, WA 98045
Phone: (425) 888-4771
Area hunted: Region 2
Species hunted: Ducks

Sporting Goods Stores by Region

REGION 1

CLARKSTON

Schurman's True Value Hardware,
801 6th St. / (509) 758-6411

Ron's Gun's, 510 3rd St/
(509) 758-0160

Tri-State, 120 Thain Road, Lewiston,
ID / (877) 878 2835
www.t-state.com

DAYTON

Dingle's True Value of Dayton,
179 E. Main St. / (509) 382-2581

REPUBLIC

Republic Appliance, 15 N. Clark Ave. /
(509) 775-3222

Harding Hardware, 85 N Clark /
(509) 775-3368

Republic Sports Shop, 8 Creamery Rd.
/ (509) 775-3040

POMEROY

Meyers Hardware, 796 Main St. /
(509) 843-3721

DAVENPORT

Davenport Building Supply,
801 Morgan St. / (509) 725-7131
The only place in town for licenses
and hunting supplies.

SPOKANE

All American Arms, 3601 East Boone
Ave. / (509 536-3834

Brocks Gunsmithing, 2104 N Division
St. / (509) 328-9788

Classic Guns of Spokane, 9119 E.
Boone Ave. / (509) 926-4867

Ed's Gunatorium, 5323 N. Argonne Rd.
/ (509) 924-3030

Gart Sport, 15118 E. Indiana Ave. /
(509) 891-1500

White Elephant, 12614 E. Sprague,
Ave. / (509) 924-3006

White Elephant, 1730 N. Division St. /
(509) 328-3100

Outdoor Sportsman, 1602 N. Division
St. / (509) 328-1556

Big 5 Sporting Goods, 7501 N. Division
St. / (509) 467-6970

Big 5 Sporting Goods, 5725 E. Sprague
Ave. / (509) 533-9811

Creative Arms, 1200 North Freya Way /
(509) 533-9801

General Store Ace Hardware, 2424 N.
Division St. / (509) 444-8000

Whites Outdoors, 4002 East Ferry Ave.
/ (509) 535-1875

Fred Meyer, E. 525 Francis Ave. /
(509) 489-3750

Fred Meyer, 12120 N. Division /
(509) 465-4400

COLVILLE

Clark's All-Sports, 557 S. Main St. /
(509) 684-5069

Wal-Mart, 10 N. Hwy. 395 /
(509) 684-3209

WALLA WALLA

Bi-Mart, 1649 Plaza Way /
(509) 529-8840

PULLMAN

Rite Aid Pharmacy, 1630 S. Grand Ave.
/ (509) 334-1521

Tri-State, 1104 Pullman Rd., Moscow,
ID. / (208) 882-4555
www.t-state.com

NEWPORT

Pend Oreille Valley Sportsman, 307 N.
State Route 2 / (208) 437-3636

Region 2

Othello

Othello United Drug, 718 E. Main St. / (509) 488-3653

Ace Hardware, 420 E. Main St. / (509) 488-5667

Othello Sporting Goods, 745 E. Hemlock / (509) 488-6249

Wenatchee

Ag Supply Ace Hardware, 220 Grant Rd. / (509) 884-6647

Big 5 Sporting Goods, 144 Easy Way / (509) 663-1332

Hooked on Toys, 1444 N Wenatchee Ave. / (509) 663-0740

Fred Meyer, 11 Grant Road (Corner of Grant Road & State Route 28) / (509) 881-2800

Moses Lake

Rite Aid Pharmacy, 815 N. Stratford Rd. / (509) 765-0362

Tri-State Outfitters, 1224 S. Pioneer Way / (509) 765-9338

Omak

Wal-Mart, 900 Engh Rd. / (509) 826-6002

Region 3

Richland

Rite Aid Pharmacy, 1743 George Washington Way / (509) 946-6128

Fred Meyer, 2811 W. 10th Ave. , Kennewick, WA 99336 / (509) 735-8700

Fred Meyer, 101 Wellsian Way

Pasco

Critter's Outdoor World, Broadmoor Park Outlet Mall / (509) 543-9663

Phil's Sporting Goods Inc., 3806 W. Court St. / (509) 547-9084

Big 5 Sporting Goods, 812 West Vineyard Dr., Kennewick / (509) 586-3739

Ellensburg

Howell Refrigeration, Bullets, Gun Shop and Antiques, 313 N Main / (509) 925-1109

Bi-Mart, 608 E. Mountain View Ave. / (509) 925-6971

Rite Aid Pharmacy, 700 S. Main St. / (509) 925-4334

Yakima

Wal-Mart, 1600 E. Chestnut Ave. / (509) 248-3448

K-Mart, 2304 E. Nob Hill Blvd. / (509) 248-1990

High Country Hunting, (509) 965-5620

Wildlands Sports, 102 S. 1st St. / (509) 457-1390

Bi Mart, 1207 North 40th Avenue / (509) 457-1650

Bi Mart, 309 South 5th Ave. / (509) 457-5175

Big 5 Sporting Goods, W. Nob Hill Blvd. / (509) 453-6040

Fred Meyer, 1206 N. 40th / (509) 576-6800

Region 4

Oak Harbor

K-Mart, 32165 SR 20 / (360) 679-5545

Kent

K-Mart, 24800 W. Valley Hwy. / (253) 852-9071

Rite Aid Pharmacy, 24044 104th Ave. S.E. / (253) 852-6180

Big 5 Sporting Goods, 24204 104th Ave. SE. / (253) 852-2524

G.I. Joes, Issaquah, 1185 NW Gilman
Blvd. / (425)854-5254

Fred Meyer, 16735 SE 272nd /
(253) 639-7400

Fred Meyer, 10201 SE 240th /
(253) 859-5500

Fred Meyer, 25250 Pacific Hwy. S. /
(253) 941-2900

MT VERNON

Rite Aid Pharmacy, 242 E. College Way
/ (360) 424-7981

EVERETT

Big 5 Sporting Goods, 1201 S.E. Everett
Mall Way / (425) 353-9100

Rite Aid Pharmacy, 1001 N. Broadway
/ (425) 258-1131

G.I. Joe's – Lynwood, 19310 60th Ave W.
/ (425) 712-9200

Fred Meyer, 8530 Evergreen Way /
(425) 348-8400

Fred Meyer, 12906 Bothell-Everett
Hwy.

BELLINGHAM

Big 5 Sporting Goods, 1 Bellis Fair
Pkwy. #202 / (360) 734-7802

Rite Aid Pharmacy, 1524 Birchwood
Ave. / (360) 647-2175

Fred Meyer, 800 Lakeway Dr. /
(360) 676-1102

REGION 5

VANCOUVER

Big 5 Sporting Goods, 8700 N.E.
Vancouver Mall Dr. / (360) 604-7179

G.I. Joe's Inc., 13215 SE Mill Plain Blvd.
/ (360) 253-2725

Bi Mart, 11912 NE 4th Plain Road /
(360) 944-5432

Bi Mart, 2601 Falk Road /
(360) 695-6333

**Classic Firearms and Hunting
Supplies,** 14300 NE 20th Ave. D102-
212 / (360) 546-3104 / (800) 404-
1902

Fred Meyer, 16600 SE McGillivray Blvd.
/ (360)260 3300

Fred Meyer, 2201 Grand Blvd. NE /
(360) 694-1536

Fred Meyer, 7700 Highway 99 / (360)
699 8100

Fred Meyer, 11325 SE Mill Plain Blvd.
/ (360)-253-7053

Fred Meyer, 7411 NE 117th Ave. / (360)
896-3500

Fred Meyer, 800 NE Tenney Rd. / (360)
571-2540

LONGVIEW

Rite Aid Pharmacy, 3 Triangle
Shopping Center / (360) 423-4700

Wal-Mart, 3715 Ocean Beach Hwy. /
(360) 414-9656

Bob's Sporting Goods, 1111 Hudson /
(360) 425-3870

GOLDENDALE

Home & Sport Shop, 126 W. Main St. /
(509) 773-5340

CHEHALIS

Rite Aid Pharmacy, 811 N.E. Hampe
Way / (360) 748-0077

Sunbird Shopping Center, 1757 N.
National Ave. / (360) 748-3337

STEVENSON

Rite Aid Pharmacy, 2049 Cascade Ave.
Hood River, OR / (541) 387-2424
Nearest to Stevenson at 26.5 miles.

CATHLAMET

Rite Aid Pharmacy, 3 Triangle
Shopping Center, Longview, WA /
(360) 423-4700
Nearest to Cathlamet - 16.6 miles

REGION 6

PORT ANGELES
Rite Aid Pharmacy, 110 Port Angeles Plaza / (360) 457-1106
Wal-Mart, 3500 E. Hwy. 101 / (360) 452-4910

ABERDEEN
Rite Aid Pharmacy, 1209 E. Wishkah St. / (360) 533-6125

PORT TOWNSEND
Henery Hardware, 218 W. Sims Way / (360) 385-5900

BREMERTON
Rite Aid Pharmacy, 425 Kitsap Way / (360) 479-3395

SHELTON
Wal-Mart, 100 E. Wallace Kneeland Blvd. / (360) 427-0500
Fred Meyer Marketplace, 301 E. Wallace-Kneeland Blvd. / (360) 4272979

RAYMOND
Dennis Company, 146 5th St. / (360) 942-2427

TACOMA
Big 5 Sporting Goods, 2505 S 38th St. # F / (253) 474-1747
Gart Sports, 1905 S 72nd St. # B / (253) 572-9900
Bulls Eye Shooter Supply, 414 Puyallup Ave. / (253) 572-6417
Sports Authority, 4104 Tacoma Mall / (253) 471-0262
Welchers Gunshop, 16400 Pacific Ave. / (253) 472-1113
Fred Meyer, 6901 S. 19th St. / (253) 564-7477
Fred Meyer, 7250 Pacific Ave. / (253) 475-6040

Fred Meyer, 4505 S. 19th / (253) 756-9280

OLYMPIA
Big 5 Sporting Goods, 909 Cooper Point Rd. S.W. / (360) 786-6529
Rite Aid Pharmacy, 1515 Marvin Rd. N.E. / (360) 456-4900
Big Foot Outdoor, 518 Capitol Way S. / (360) 352-4616

FEDERAL WAY
G.I. Joe's, 35020 Federal Way / (253) –27-2943

PUYALLUP
G.I. Joe's, 120 31st Ave SE, Ste 6 / (253) 445-8090

SEATTLE
Ed's Surplus, 5911 196th Street Southwest, Lynnwood / (425) 778-1441
Big 5 Sporting Goods,
4315 University Way Northeast / (206) 547-2445
2500 Southwest Barton Street / (206) 932-2212
125 Southwest 148th Street / (206) 246-2707
1140 North Aurora Village Place / (206) 546-4443
1133 North 205th Street / (206) 546-4443
1101 Northwest Leary Way / (206) 706-7531
Capitol Hill Camping & Surplus, 910 East Pike Street / (206) 325-3566
Gart Sport
17450 Southcenter Parkway / (206) 575-2100
19800 44th Avenue West / (425) 712-0900

Outdoor & More, 510 Westlake Avenue
North / (206) 340-0677
Outdoor Emporium, 420 Pontius
Avenue North / (206) 624-6550
Timid Gun Shop, 14032 Aurora Avenue
North / (206) 365-9984
Warshals Sporting Goods &
Photographic Supply,
1st & Madison / (206) 624-7301
Fred Meyer
915 NW 45th St., / (206) 297-4300

14300 1st Ave. S., (206) 433-6411

417 Broadway East, Box 2 /
(206)-328-6920

100 NW 85th St., (206) 784-9600

13000 Lake City Way NE ,
(206) 440-2400

9620 28th Ave. SW (Roxbury & 28th)
/ (206) 933-5490

Recommended Reading

Washington Atlas & Gazetteer. DeLorme Mapping. Freeport: DeLorme Mapping, 1988.

The Audubon Society Field Guide to North American Birds (Western Region). Miklos D.F. Udvardy. New York: Knopf, 1977.

Hunting Upland Birds. Charles F. Waterman. New York: Winchester Press, 1972

Best Way to Train Your Gun Dog: The Delmar Smith Method. Bill Tarrant. New York: David McKay Company, Inc., 1977

Bill Tarrant's Gun Dog Book: A Treasury of Happy Tails. Bill Tarrant. Honolulu: Sun Trails Publishing, 1980

A Field Guide to Dog First Aid. Randy Acker, D.V.M. and Jim Fergus. Bozeman, MT: Wilderness Adventures Press, 1994.

Field Guide to Upland Birds and Waterfowl. Christopher S. Smith; Belgrade MT Wilderness Adventures Press, 2000

Western Wings: Hunting Upland Birds on the Northern Plains. Ben O. Williams. Bozeman, MT: Wilderness Adventures Press, 1998

The Training and Care of the Versatile Hunting Dog. Sigbot Winterhelt and Edward D. Bailey. Puslinch, Ontario, Canada: The North American Versatile Hunting Dog Association, 1973

Index